Where Does Imagination End and Reality Begin?
Re-Examining the Horror Classic

Where Does Imagination End and Reality Begin?
Re-Examining the Horror Classic

Matthew E Banks © 2022

Where Does Imagination End and Reality Begin?
Re-Examining the Horror Classic

© 2022 By Matthew E Banks

All Rights Reserved.

No portion of this publication may be reproduced, stored, and/or copied electronically (except for academic use as a source), nor transmitted in any form or by any means without the prior written permission of the publisher and/or author.

Published in the United States of America by:

BearManor Media
1317 Edgewater Dr #110
Orlando FL 32804
bearmanormedia.com

Printed in the United States.

All photos used with permission.

Typesetting and layout by DataSmith Solutions

Cover Based on a concept by the author

ISBN — 978-1-62933-864-4

Contents

Introduction and acknowledgements..................1

1: A Catalogue of Satanism, Sadism, Homoerotica, Necrophilia and Murder: The Black Cat — Re-Examining A Horror Classic..............4

2: "Poe, You are Avenged!" Sex, Sadism, a Stuffed Bird and a Two Year Ban The Raven — Re-examing a Horror Classic..................20

3: Rukh's in the Closet: Glowing hands, homosexuality and Radium X The Invisible Ray: Re-Examining a Horror Classic..................44

4: There are Bats in her Belfry, a monster in a closet and the Death of Universal: Dracula's Daughter: Re-Examining a Horror Classic..............66

5: "Princes', Mord, Princes'!" — A Bald Executioner, A Handsome Richard III — The completely Horrid History of Tower of London — Re-Examining a Horror Classic..................114

6: Over the fields and through the Skies, Witches Flying High I Married a Witch: A Re-Examination (with a brief history of witches in film!)..........132

7: A Suicidal Wolf Man and a Cry-baby Monster. What could possibly go wrong? Frankenstein Meets the Wolf Man..................192

8: Where are all the bodies? Karloff and Lugosi's Last haunting collaboration:
The Body Snatcher... 210

9: "Where does imagination end and reality begin?"
Night of the Demon / Casting the Runes — A Comparison............... 228

Where Does Imagination end and Reality Begin?
An Introduction and acknowledgements

Since the beginning of film, horror and the supernatural have been a mainstay. The genre has been consistently prevalent for nearly one hundred and twenty-five years although like many genres it has waxed and waned in terms of its popularity. Through its highs and lows, my love of horror has never diminished; I remember as a young child I was fascinated by (and bought in droves) comedy horror cards, featuring Lon Chaney's The Wolf Man, The Creature from the Black Lagoon and Frankenstein amongst others. In the summer of 1976, my father managed a hotel, and on a Saturday afternoon, he showed a compilation film of Bela Lugosi and I was hooked, and that love has stayed with me ever since. My father also liked to have fun scaring me by (comedically to my adult self, quite the opposite at the time) chasing me around the house wearing a skull mask.

This book has been a labour of love and consists of previously published material, writers' cuts (just think of directors' extended cuts) and previously unpublished material. My article on Universal's *The Black Cat*, was initially published in issue 11 of *We Belong Dead*, which gave me my first front cover. This was followed by *The Raven* in issue 13 of *We Belong Dead*. The third piece in the Karloff / Lugosi cycle, *The Invisible Ray*, was written for *We Belong Dead* but was not published. *Dracula's Daughter* was published by Vicki and Don Smeraldi in Scary Monsters of the Movies magazine. Tower of London was originally published in Eric McNaughton's Son of Unsung

Horrors in a highly edited form. The full writer's cut was published in Scary Monsters presents Castle of Frankenstein 2021 Annual Scary Monsters #120. Likewise, "Where are all the Bodies? Karloff and Lugosi's Last Haunting Collaboration - The Body Snatcher" is a writer's extended cut. "I Married a Witch & a brief history of Witches / Witchcraft in Film 1896 – 1941" was written especially for this book. "Night of the Demon / Casting the Runes: A Comparison," originally published in We Belong Dead's comeback issue, No.9 is not a re-examination like the rest of the book, but a comparison between the film and its literary counterpart. A Suicidal Wolfman and a Cry-Baby Monster. What Could Possibly Go Wrong? Frankenstein Meets the Wolf Man was requested by a publisher, but this sees its first publication.

Over the course of writing this, I have had the help and support of authors, friends and those in the know and I wish to extend my thanks to, and in no particular order: Dr. Gary D. Rhodes, Stephen Jacobs, Chris Workman, Troy Howarth, Carol Estey, Beth Lebowsky, the late Fred Tobias and his wife Lee Tobias, and the late Scott Allen Nollen for their wisdom and insights regarding the movies themselves. My editors and publishers who have had faith in my work: Eric McNaughton, Don and Vicki Smeraldi, and Ben Ohmart of Bear Manor Media who made this project a reality.

A big thank you goes out to my wife, Sam, who hates horror films as much as I love them (and suffered editing this tome.) A special thank you to Stone Wallace whose expertise, advice and knowledge was invaluable in the editing of this book.

This book is dedicated to my wife Sam and my late father, Eddie, without whom …

UNIVERSAL WEEKLY
VOL. 54 NO. 17   APRIL 7, 1934

Coming "The Black Cat"

A Catalogue of Satanism, Sadism, Homoerotica, Necrophilia and Murder: The Black Cat – Re - Examining A Horror Classic

On a Continental train, a young newlywed couple, Peter and Joan Alison (David Manners and Jacqueline Wells), meet and befriend Dr. Vitus Werdegast (Lugosi). They then join him to continue the journey in a motor coach as they are on their way to a holiday resort and he is on his way to visit a former army engineer, Hjalmer Poelzig (Karloff). The coach crashes in the desolate Hungarian countryside and their newfound friend, Dr. Werdegast, takes them to Poelzig's mansion, built over the site of a mined military fort, for shelter. Werdegast is going there in search of his wife and daughter and for revenge against Poelzig' for treachery that cost the lives of ten thousand men and had him condemned to a Russian prison for fifteen years.

Unknown to Werdegast, Poelzig not only married his wife and after her death, his daughter, he is leader of a Satanic Coven and plans to sacrifice Joan in a Black Mass. Poelzig challenges Werdegast to a game of chess for the freedom of the young couple. Poelzig wins the game and the heroine is to be sacrificed. Werdegast, after finding out what happened to his wife and discovering his daughter dead, manages to overpower Poelzig, thus allowing the young couple to escape as he flays Poelzig alive, before blowing the mansion up.

In 1934 someone at Universal studios decided to resurrect the idea of teaming the two "Masters Of Menace" Bela Lugosi and Boris Karloff in a film[1]. An idea that had first circulated in 1932, when both were riding on the success of their respective box office hits *Dracula* and *Frankenstein*. Universal hoped to cash in on their 'Stars' bankability and a number of film concepts were under discussion including *The Invisible Man* and *The Suicide Club*. Neither of these collaborations came to fruition and the idea seemed to have died. By 1934 Lugosi found that his career was virtually over as a leading man at Universal as the studio was concentrating on their 'new' horror star, Karloff. Between 1932 and 1934 Universal had attempted to bring *The Black Cat* to the silver screen and it had already had three different scripts by the time that Ulmer came to the project and by all accounts was going to be a vehicle just for Karloff, who had just scored major hits in *The House of Rothschild (United Artists 1934)* and *The Lost Patrol (RKO Radio 1934)*. As Gregory Mank points out, '*[ ] it's not clear exactly who came up with the idea of adding Bela to The Black Cat.*'[1]

So when the idea was revived it was decided to team the pair up for a film based on two short stories by Edgar Allen Poe - *The Black Cat* and *The Fall Of The House Of Usher*, and in the end it was the former title that formed the film's name over a script by Peter Ruric and the film's director Edgar G. Ulmer. Many years later, in conversation with Peter Bogdanovich, Ulmer recollected how he got the idea for the film and its setting:

---

1. "[ ]when I came to him with the idea of The Black Cat, which would employ Lugosi and Karloff at the same time in the same picture, because each one had been successful, Junior gave me free rein to write a horror picture in the style we had started in Europe with Caligari [1919]. And he gave me my head for the first time. He was a very, very strange producer; he didn't have much education, but had great respect for intelligence and for creative spirit." Ulmer speaking to Peter Bogdanovich in 1970 Speaking to Rick Atkins Carl Laemmle Jr. would say "It was my idea to cast them in the same picture. Both proved to be successful, so why not."

> "That came out many years before I met Gustav Meyrinck, the man who wrote Golem as a novel. Meyrinck was one of these strange Prague Jews, like Kafka, who was much tied in the mystic Talmudic background. We had a lot of discussions and Meyrinck at that time was contemplating a play based upon Doumont, which was a French fortress the German's shelled to pieces during the First World War There were some survivors who didn't come out for years. And the commander was a strange Euripides figure who went crazy three years later when he was brought back to Paris, because he had walked on that mountain of bodies. And I thought it was a great subject that was quite important. And that feeling was in the air in the twenties. I wanted to write a novel really, because I did not believe the literature after the war and during the war, on both sides. In Germany and in England war was very much the heroic thing... I couldn't believe that, Therefore, I took two men who knew each other and who fought their private war during the time that capitalism flourished. I thought it was quite a story stylistically. I had a wonderful cameraman (John Mescall), and producer (Carl Laemmle) let me do the set and everything at the same time. It was very much out of my Bauhaus period."**2**

The film had little to nothing to do with Poe, except for a brief scene illustrating Lugosi's ailurophobia (an intense and irrational fear of cats) and had more plot holes in it than the Titanic. Karloff's Bauhaus-styled house built over a graveyard of thousands that he betrayed and sent to their deaths, with Lugosi muttering, *"I can still sense death in the air"***3** as he's led down to the mausoleum where his wife's corpse is encased in a glass tomb. John Mescall's prowling camerawork, moving through endless corridors and past reminders of the fortress that the house is built upon, the use of a musical score that relies heavily on the classics, all echo the melancholic atmosphere and capture with an almost abstract web of anguish and pain, the essence of Poe.

The film was given a budget of $91,125. For his role Karloff received a flat fee of $7,500 to Lugosi's $1,000 per week for a three-week shoot. This would be the only time the two horror stars shared equal billing and equal screen time. Shooting began on February 28th and was completed on March 28th. It was released in May and became Universal's top grossing film for 1934 with receipts of $236,000 approximately for the USA. With a running time of 65 minutes it was the second longest of the three main Lugosi / Karloff films.

Partly based on Aleister Crowley[2] who was in the news at that time with the publication of Nina Hamnett's biography and his libel suit against her. According to Mank, *"the raving, raping, ripping and rendering of Aleister Crowly fascinated Ulmer,"*[4] so out went Poe's original tale and in came Crowley and his alleged escapades, as well as hints of director Fritz Lang, whom Ulmer knew and admired, but thought him a sadist and the film became a morality tale of betrayal, revenge and retribution.

> *"You say your soul was killed, that you have been dead all these years. And what of me? Did we not both die here in Marmorus 15 years ago? Are we any the less victims of the war than those whose bodies were torn asunder? Are we not both the living dead? And now you come to me, playing at being an avenging angel, childishly thirsting for my blood. We understand each other too well. We know too much of life."*[5]
> [Poelzig to Werdegast after the latter goes to shoot him, but is halted by the appearance of a black cat.]

The implication that the war destroyed their humanity, the acts that they were forced to do corrupted their morality combined with Lugosi's return is like some sort of euthanasia suicide pact, which of course it is. They are both morally dead - in the original cut Lugosi, driven mad by seeing his dead wife, rapes Joan. Karloff had married Lugosi's wife and after her death (or murder!) his daughter, whom he murders after finding her learning the truth that her father is alive from Joan. The two adversaries stalk in and out of secret

---

2. "The headlines of Crowleys' unsavoury activities were current when Ulmer concocted his script." Lennig, P. 161.

passages, down spiral staircases, exchanging portentous pleasantries and challenging each other to a game of chess that will decide the fate of the heroine, thus revealing that Lugosi is a vindictive protagonist. Ulmer, in showing us this depth of character in the central roles, we see two men who are beyond mortal concerns, because one has passed all limits of suffering (Lugosi) and the other has passed all limits of cruelty (Karloff). This is elegantly implied by Karloff: *"The phone is dead. Do you hear that, Vitus? Even the phone is dead..."***6** and reinforced by his costume and movements: black skin tight pyjamas, crew cut with a sinister widow's peak, moving stiffly, rising from his bed as if raised by wires thus implying that he is one of the living dead. In *Cult Movies #3* Danny Peary gives an insightful observation on the two lead actors' performances: *'Karloff's deadpan, tongue in cheek performance is perfectly balanced by Lugosi, whose early dignified manner soon gives way to his singular brand of histrionics...'***7**

In his role of Hjalmar Poelzig, an Austrian architect, Karloff gives one of his better performances, and Lugosi, who was always desperate to lose his typecasting as a villain gives one of his best performances as the dubious hero Dr. Vitus Werdegast. Richard Bojarski states of the lead actors, *"[Lugosi] ...an unforgettable portrait of a tortured individual, ultimately decent, but haunted by the scars of war and living only for vengeance ... [ ] well opposite Karloff's cold corrupt Poelzig."***8**

Arthur Lennig points out that, *"Admittedly Lugosi wanted to get away from being typecast as a villain, but still he was far more suited to the devil cultish than Karloff. The British actor is curiously restrained and does not entirely suggest the sinister ... [ ] Lugosi was far more apt to design such a building, put attractive mummified women in cases, and commander a cult of evil-worshippers."***9** This casting debate would be brought up again in their third and final collaboration under the Laemmles, *The Invisible Ray* (1936). The debate is that Lugosi would have been better suited to the roles of Poelzig and the mad scientist Rukh, rather than that of humanitarian and kindly Dr. Felix Benet in the latter. If the first and third films in this collaboration showed Lugosi could play the "semi-hero', then *The Raven* (1935) showed film audiences that he could dominate as the villain and also gives a glimpse of how he may have portrayed the other two roles differently from Karloff.

Yet let us not be dismissive of Karloff. He perfectly captures the perversity, corruption and evil incarnate that is Poelzig:

> *Dr. Vitus Werdegast: You sold Marmorus to the Russians. You scurried away in the night and left us to die. Is it to be wondered that you should choose this place to build your house? A masterpiece of construction built upon the ruins of the masterpiece of destruction - a masterpiece of murder.*
>
> *[laughs hideously]*
>
> *The murderer of 10,000 men returns to the place of his crime. Those who died were fortunate. I was taken prisoner to Kurgaal. Kurgaal, where the soul is killed, slowly. Fifteen years I've rotted in the darkness... waited. Not to kill you, but to kill your soul - slowly.*[10]

In the opening credits the principal players are shown with brief shots from the film, except Karloff who is shot from behind, thus hiding his face. By doing this, the studio banked on the audience's expectation of how Karloff may be made up. They had seen him as the Frankenstein Monster, as The Mummy, so how would he look in this film? Even his introduction, shot through a gauze of netting, rising up as though one of the un-dead, adds to the audiences' anticipation and his first full frontal appearance is reminiscent of the Frankenstein Monsters' entrance, three years previously, which here revealed to the audience the face of corruption.

Not only is he the betrayer of Werdegast, and brought about the deaths of ten thousand men, he is also step-father and husband to Werdegast's daughter, Karen, thus making him not only his betrayer but son and father-in-law, as well as her murderer. He gets pleasure from his mausoleum of glass-encased embalmed beautiful women, who in turn were raped and sacrificed in his satanic rituals, including Karen's mother! He is lecherous towards Joan so much so that she feels compelled to cover herself up; does everything he can to prevent their leaving, sneaks into the room he thinks Werdegast is sleeping in – either to kill him or seduce him. He gleefully gloats after Werdegast has killed a black cat, and here Karloff's delivery is perfect: *"You must be indulgent of Dr.Werdegast's weakness. He is the unfortunate victim of one of the commoner phobias, but in an extreme form. He has an intense and all-consuming horror... of cats!"* **11**

He later taunts Werdegast over what fate has in store for the young couple:

> *Poelzig: Do you dare play chess with me for her?*
> *Werdegast: Yes. I will even play you chess for her. Provided if I win, they are free to go.*
> *Poelzig: You won't win, Vitus.* **12**

Not before nor since has such a decadent character been brought to life on the screen and the dialogue between both the actors seems to have been set out to deliberately take advantage not only of their accents but of their alleged feud and by doing so extract the maximum effect from their lines. Jacqueline Wells is suitably cast as the swooning heroine, but David Manners is your typical useless hero - being knocked out and locked up after offering only token resistance and in many ways just reiterating his performance from *Dracula* as the useless and dim-witted Harker, and his likewise ineffectual "hero" in *The Mummy*. The *Times* for Monday September 3rd 1934 summed up perfectly the supporting cast: *"[ ] The House of Doom is robbed of excellence only by the presence of two American honeymooners whose loose textured, flat personalities and voices repeatedly shatter the dominating atmosphere of tension."* **13**

David J. Skal in his book *The Monster Show: A Cultural History of Horror* states that: *"Ruric's shooting script apparently also contained some intima-*

tions of homosexuality among minor characters, which were deleted." **14** Rhona J Bernstein states: *"the combination of the social and erotic charges that bind rivalrous men together in narratives, and second, as a description of the manner in which patriarchy excludes women. [ ] Lugosi and Karloff [ ] their rivalry depends on intimate conversations, homoerotic interactions with each other, and the near-seduction of the hero."***15** In an early scene, after Werdegast has killed a black cat, Joan comes in, trance-like and taunts the doctor over his fear of cats, goes to her host and flirtily introduces herself, before going over to her husband and kissing him passionately. Mescal's camera catches this from below Poelzig's sleeve and as they kiss, Poelzig grabs the statue of a naked woman on his desk, and the focus goes between the two. If we are to take Bernstein's view of the film, then it opens up this scene to a totally different interpretation – in that it is not Joan who Poelzig wants, it is her husband! Another remnant of this 'homoerotica' is the bedroom swapping scene, where after swapping rooms, Werdegast asks Peter if he can keep the adjoining door open:

> *As Alison checks that his wife is still asleep:*
>
> *Werdegast: Do you mind if I keep this door open?*
>
> *Alison closes door to wife's room and moves around his. Sits on bed.*
>
> *Alison: I'd sleep in a cold sweat if you didn't. You know...this is a very tricky house. The kind of place where I'd like to have company.* **16**

Whether either actor realised the implication of what was shot or not is open to debate, but the smile that Manners has on his face as he gets undressed for bed, implies that at least he does. Yet it is the end scenes, where Karloff is skinned alive that are visually the most sadomasochistic. Poelzig having been overpowered is hung up on his own embalming rack, like some decadent variation of crucifixion. Lugosi ripping the shirt off of him, like some visual forerunner to male rape, gloatingly asks Poelzig if he's ever seen an animal skinned, before informing him that that is what is going to happen to him – *"Tear the skin off you, bit by bit!"* **17** Shot in shadow, the scene offers off screen moans and groans and close-ups of Poelzigs' writhing hand that leave little to the imagination. Cuts to the film include the Alisons' wedding in Vienna at the beginning of the film which had a homosexual photographer, another scene set on the Orient Express where the Maitre d' Hotel (Herman Bing) tries tempting the newlyweds with food, and a brief scene showing Peter Alison brow beating Poelzig's Hungarian servants.

Yet it could have been a lot different if E.M. Asher had not been left in charge of production whilst the Laemmles were away. It was he who had a meeting on Monday 26th February with Joseph I. Breen of the P.C.A. (Production Code Administration), who advised for caution on 19 different aspects of the script, including the above-mentioned cuts as well as the skinning scene and Werdegast's killing of the cat. Alfred Easher states that:

> *"Ulmer's "complete freedom" came to a screeching halt when Universal execs saw the filmed footage and script. Lugosi's hero rapes the heroine, the heroine occasionally turns into a black cat, and Karloff's Poelzig is skinned alive and last seen crawling on the floor with his skin hanging from his body as Lugosi's mad hero laughs hysterically. All of these scenes were cut from the film and, par the course at that time, were destroyed. There are conflicting accounts as to whether the scenes were shot and then burned, or merely scripted and axed[3]."* **18**

---

3. From the unpublished screenplay:
I-29 INTERIOR CONTROL CHAMBER
   MEDIUM CLOSE SHOT.

   Werdegast lying wounded on the floor
   As Poelzig falls into the scene near him.
   Werdegast raises himself to one elbow and stares at Poelzig.
   He laughs hysterically, insanely; his eyes wander up and out and
   CAMERA PANS swiftly in the direction of his eyes to center
The switchboard at the other end of the room.

This led to Ulmer summoning cast and crew back for three and a half days of retakes and alternate scenes at a cost of $6,500 which brought the total budget to $95,745.31. Also gone in this re-shoot was Lucille Lund's *'The Cat People'*[4] inspiring characterization of Karen, to a more child-like innocent [This change might have been down to her refusal to sleep with the director[5]19], and Lugosi's madness induced rape of Joan and other aspects of his

---

This IS after Werdegast has flayed Poelzig and it is clear that Poelzig has fallen from the embalming rack.

I-32 INTERIOR CONTROL CHAMBER
MEDIUM CLOSE SHOT.

CAMERA moving over Werdegast as he approaches the switchboard, throws the switch. He turns into CAMERA and, as he looks back at Poelzig, CAMERA SWIFTLY AROUND TO SHOW Poelzig from Werdegast's angle. Poelzig, with the last vestige of his strength, turns and starts crawling towards Werdegast.

This scene is definitely scripted but whether it was filmed is uncertain as there are no photographs showing this and none of the cast EVER commented on this scene in any interview.

4. Lund was originally going to turn into the Black Cat of the film, not unlike Simone Simon in *The Cat People* (RKO 1942. Directed by Jacques Turner, written by DeWitt Bodeen. Released December 2nd. 70mins).

5. Speaking to Gregory William Mank in Women in Horror Films, 1930s, Lund would recount: "One day, Ulmer said, "I'd like to take you to dinner tonight, to Sardi's in Hollywood; I'd like to talk to you about the picture." So I was young, and new in the business, and I thought, 'Fine – why not?' So I went with Mr Ulmer to dinner. Now, with all due respect to this gentleman, he never laid a hand on me. But he said, in essence, "If you will be my girlfriend (so to speak), we would be a combination like Dietrich and von Sternberg!" And I said, "Well, thank you, that's very flattering, but I am not interested in such a situation with you." So we went back to shooting – and everything was different. That's when the horror started – and it was not in the script, believe me!" (McFarland & Company, Inc., Publishers 1999. Pg.252.)

darker side. Yet these re-takes, re-shoots and re-editing came with a price with the film lacking a clear-cut storyline; character motivations become questionable and Ulmer's dream film becomes something completely different than what its director originally envisioned.

Universal, determined that the film was going to be a hit, utilised their two horror stars as their main selling point. Film posters screamed out *"It's tremendous! Frankenstein Karloff, plus Dracula Lugosi, plus Edgar Allen Poe"* and three of the leads, Lugosi, Karloff and Wells made a personal appearance at the premier of the film on May 3rd 1934 at the Hollywood Pantages Theatre.

Despite all this, the film opened to mixed reviews. Variety stated that *"... skinning alive is not new ...[A truly horrible and nauseating bit of sadism, its inclusion in a motion picture is dubious showmanship... Karloff and Lugosi are sufficiently sinister and convincingly demented. Jacqueline Wells spends most of her footage in swoons."* **20** Newsweek said*: "Two major monsters perform all the ... antics of deviltry ...which has little to do with Edgar Allen Poe's brainchild. Karloff as High Priest of a cult of devil worshippers and hangs women by their hair ... but even this can't save him from Monster Bela Lugosi, of Dracula fame, who succeeds in skinning him alive. Bizarre modern settings and a dynamite-filled cellar in Karloff's home add to the eeriness of the situation ... utmost in sinister atmosphere is created by the cameraman who achieved foggy photographic effects that enhance the acting."* **21**

When released in England, all references to Satanism were cut from the film and were substituted to sun worship as it was felt the former reference would be too strong for the British audience to handle and the film was re-titled *The House Of Doom*. Spanish cinemas screened the film as *Satan*. It also had a name change when it was re-issued to television as *The Vanishing Body*, so as not to be confused with the 1941 film of the same name, which also featured Lugosi, though in a supporting role. Italy, Finland and Austria banned the film outright, while censors in other territories required cuts to the more gruesome sequences.

Speaking in 1966, Ulmer would have this to say about The Black Cat:
> "On the Black Cat, I designed the sets, that 'way out' house, and if you want to really know, Mr. Karloff's wardrobe. At the time, as he still does today, Mr. Karloff kept insisting that he didn't want to make any more horror pictures ... That he was tired of scaring people. As you know, he didn't quit; anyway the point I was aiming at was this... one of the things he found most exciting in the film was the wardrobe ... his outfits in particular. He knew he would be playing 'KARLOFF', but also felt in these duds, he could employ a sort of 'out of this world' appearance. That, as you know, was exactly as he appeared. In preparing the script, which I also had a hand in, we had come up with some very interesting, very supernatural undertones that had to be cut from the original. Censorship in the thirties was even worse than now, and people couldn't take things like the character of Karen resembling the physical characteristics of a cat. There were several other items of important interest to the story, that have been cut, and for me, let us say, how I feel, this has injured the story in many ways."[22]

Due to its short running time, *The Black Cat* cannot be classed as a major Hollywood film, but more of a 'B' movie, or in some respects a vignette, as so much more could have been realized if the original version had not been cut and drastically altered. But in that time frame the audience is subjected to scene after scene of Satanism, sadism, necrophilia, homoerotica and are completely overwhelmed by the sense of death and decay that wraps itself around the two central characters from beginning to end. For their first collaboration Lugosi and Karloff give their everything and deliver one of their most chilling performances to be filmed, thus raising *The Black Cat* from an average 'B' movie into a classic of the Horror Genre.

End Notes

1: Mank, G.W. *Bela Lugosi and Boris Karloff: The Expanded Story of a Haunted Collaboration, with a Complete Filmography of their Films Together* McFarland & Company, Inc., Publishers. Revised Edition.
2: Aldrich, R. & Bogdanovich, P. *Who the Devil Made It.* Ballantine Books, 1998.
3: The Black Cat. 1934 Dir Edgar G Ulmer. Universal.
4: Mank, G.W. *Bela Lugosi and Boris Karloff: The Expanded Story of a Haunted Collaboration, with a Complete Filmography of their Films Together* McFarland & Company, Inc., Publishers. Revised Edition. 158.
5: The Black Cat. 1934 Dir Edgar G Ulmer. Universal Studios.
6: The Black Cat. 1934 Dir Edgar G Ulmer. Universal Studios.
7: Peary, D. 1988. *Cult Movies #3.* Fireside.
8: Bojarski, Richard 1980. *The Films of Bela Lugosi.* Citadel Press.
9: Lennig, Arthur 2003. *The Immortal Count: The Life and Films of Bela Lugosi.* The University Press of Kentucky. 168.
10: The Black Cat. 1934 Dir Edgar G Ulmer. Universal Studios.
11: The Black Cat. 1934 Dir Edgar G Ulmer. Universal Studios.
12: The Black Cat. 1934 Dir Edgar G Ulmer. Universal Studios.
13: The *Times* Newspaper, Monday September 3rd 1934. P10.
14: Skal, D. J. *The Monster Show: A Cultural History of Horror* (London: Plexus, 1993) 178.
15: Bernstein, Rhona. J. *Attack of the Leading Ladies: Gender, Sexuality and Spectatorship in Classic Horror Cinema* (New York: Columbia University Press, 1996) 98.
16: The Black Cat. 1934 Dir Edgar G Ulmer. Universal Studios.
17: The Black Cat. 1934 Dir Edgar G Ulmer. Universal Studios.
18: http://366weirdmovies.com/edgar-g-ulmers-the-black-cat-1934/

19: Mank, G.W. *Bela Lugosi and Boris Karloff: The Expanded Story of a Haunted Collaboration, with a Complete Filmography of their Films Together* McFarland & Company, Inc., Publishers. Revised Edition. 173-74.
20: *Variety* as quoted in Bojarski, Richard & Beals, Kenneth 1974. *The Films of Boris Karloff*. Citadel Press. 97.
21: *Newsweek* as quoted in Bojarski, Richard 1980. *The Films of Bela Lugosi*. Citidel Press 97-100
22: *Modern Monster Magazine* August 1966, No.3 Pg.18 Edgar G. Ulmer Interview

"Poe, You are Avenged!"
Sex, Sadism, a Stuffed Bird and a Two Year Ban
The Raven – Re-examining a Horror Classic

Driving a long a wet and muddy road Jean Thatcher (Irene Ware) crashes her car. At the hospital, the doctors all agree that the only person that can save her is Dr. Vollin (Bela Lugosi) as she has damaged the nerves in her neck. Reciting Poe's "The Raven" to a museum representative, who is interested in buying his Poe collection, Vollin receives a telephone call from the hospital. The hospital explains the situation with regards to Jean Thatcher, but he refuses to help so Judge Thatcher (Samuel S. Hinds) takes the telephone and begs for him to save his daughters' life – the doctor again refuses, stating that the other doctors are equally qualified to perform the operation. Refusing to take no for an answer Judge Thatcher goes to Vollin's house and pleads with him in person; playing on his ego, he persuades the doctor to perform the operation, which he does successfully.

In a café in town, notorious murderer Edmond Bateman (Boris Karloff) is given Vollin's address and he makes his way to the house.

After noticing how his daughter is beginning to become infatuated with Vollin, despite her being engaged to Jerry Holdan (Lester Matthews), Judge Thatcher requests that he gently let his daughter down and not to encourage the blossoming relationship. Incensed at this request as he has fallen in love with her, Vollin refuses and demands that the Judge brings his daughter to him. The Judge, shocked at his attitude and demands, states that he cannot do it as he believes him to be mad and leaves!

Edmond Bateman (Karloff), a murderer on the run, comes to Vollin's house and demands that the surgeon gives him a new face so that he may live in anonymity. The doctor then hatches a plan to use Bateman to exact his revenge on those he feels have denied him his greatest love. He admits to not being a plastic surgeon, but states that he can help him, if he (Bateman) helps him in getting revenge on the Thatchers, which Bateman refuses. Vollin performs the surgery and turns Bateman into a disfigured monster, so that he has no choice but to do the doctor's bidding since Vollin has promised to re-operate and make his face normal again once his revenge is complete. On this condition, Bateman reluctantly agrees.

Vollin hosts a weekend dinner party inviting several friends and including Jean and Jerry. The Judge turns up to take his daughter home but is persuaded to stay after the doctor apologises for his earlier behaviour. Later that night, the three guests are caught in the Poe-inspired traps, with the Judge strapped under the swinging pendulum and Jean and Jerry trapped in a room with walls that slowly come together. Bateman is shot by Vollin as he rescues Jean and Jerry but throws Vollin into the shrinking room where he is crushed to death, and the guests escape.

If *The Black Cat* was not the critical success that Universal wanted, it was certainly the commercial success that they were expecting. It was therefore decided to bring Lugosi, Karloff and Poe back together for another outing. This time poem 'The Raven' and the short story 'The Pit and the Pendulum' were to be the inspiration, (the studio also had elements of 'The Gold Bug' in mind, but that idea was dropped), and instead of the dark melancholy essence of the former film, the only essence that *The Raven* captured was that of insanity and sadomasochism. Like its predecessor, *The Raven* has little to nothing to do with Poe's writings.

The script went through numerous drafts before one was found suitable. Guy Endore submitted a nineteen-page treatment on 31st August 1934. Michael Simmons and Clarence Marks submitted a fuller treatment on 1st October and fashioned a screenplay in November. Then Jim Tully submitted two treatments in December and a screenplay in January 1935. These were all discarded, and David Boehm wrote three screenplays in January and one was chosen to be filmed. As William K. Everson points out: *"In fairness to Hollywood (and to Britain, France and Germany, other countries that have made films from his works), Poe is not easy to adapt to film. Although his writing is full of marvellous visual images, it is less strong on the clear-cut narrative style required by the average movie."* [1]

Between scripting and the beginning of production, Universal announced in mid–February that the two horror stars would be starring in another Poe thriller, as Jimmy Starr in the *L.A. Evening Herald Examiner* for February 27th 1935 states:

> *Boris (Scare' Em) Karloff and Bela (also Frighten 'Em) Lugosi are again teamed in Universal's chill-getter, The Raven, a little spook thing Mr. Poe thought up.* [2]

Joseph Breen of the P.C.A. (Production Code Administration) had a meeting with Louis Friedlander and other Universal executives on March 14th 1935 to discuss the script. Amongst their concerns and demands were that no shots of Vollin operating on Bateman could be shown, blood could only be shown in a 'flash shot', the pendulum blade could not touch Thatcher's body, no improper dress or contact in the bedroom scenes and that Bateman's face not be 'unhumanly repulsive'. On the 19th March, Boehm handed in his final shooting script and Breen warned the studio that: *"We...deem it necessary to* *remind you that because of the stark realism of numerous elements in your story, you are running the risk of excessive horror!"***3**

Production began on March 20th on an allotted budget of $109,750 and was completed on schedule on April 5th with the final budget being around $114,209.91. A month earlier on February 6th David Diamond took the job as producer and he hired the 34-year-old Louis Friedlander (later Lew Landers) as director. This would be his first feature film directorship, having directed Universal serials. Irene Ware would portray Jean Thatcher, having starred opposite Lugosi three years earlier as Princess Nadja in *Chandu the Magician* (Fox 1932) and Samuel S. Hinds would portray her father, Judge Thatcher. There were a number of changes to the casting in as much as the character of Jerry Halden was originally meant to be played by Chester Morris but changed to Lester Matthews and the film historian Ron Borst in his book *Graven Images* states that Universal originally wanted Karloff for the role of Dr. Vollin! Karloff in passing playing the main villain may have thought that by playing the monstrous Bateman, he may steal the show – but Lugosi was not going to let that happen. Karloff again received top billing as just KARLOFF and Lugosi was billed second. Karloff may have received $10,000 for his work on the film to Lugosi's $5,000 – but *The Raven* was to be Lugosi's film from beginning to end. To add to the hype around the film, Universal informed the press that copies of the script had been sent to The Poe Memorial Trust for feedback – but as to which version of the script was sent is hard to tell.

Following on from the minimal, open spaced design of *The Black Cat*, Albert S. D'Agostino[6] and his technicians created sets that not only harkened back to Universal's Gothic tradition of sets, even incorporating a standing set from *The Bride of Frankenstein*, they incorporated the 'less is more' concept of

---

6. Albert S. D'Agostino 27th December 1892 – 14th March 1970. Nominated for an Academy Award an impressive five times for set design. The first time being for *The Magnificent Brute* (1936).

the former film: the most impressive set being the torture chamber, which is a mixture of medieval masonry and sleek scientific machinery, with the set dominated by the giant pendulum that swings down. To achieve the even rhythm of the swing, a large clock was built above the set and the pendulum attached. Previous attempts to get the pendulum effect to work had failed, and the only other option had been to film these sequences with trick lighting.

Jack Pierce and Otto Lederer created the make-up for Bateman's character, which unfortunately looks more like a fried egg stuck to his face than the tampering of nerve endings to create something monstrous. Charles Stumar[7] did the cinematography and Clifford Vaughan scored the film. He cleverly included pieces that represent both Vollin and Bateman with "The Raven theme" (for Lugosi) and "The Bateman theme" (for Karloff), with the Raven theme first introduced as Lugosi is out of shot, the focus being a stuffed raven in silhouette as he recites the poem. Here it is interesting to point out that in all the shots of Lugosi up until the operation scene, either he or the stuffed raven or the two together are continually in shot – thus emphasising that the raven and Vollin are in some respect the same – harbingers of death – *'Death is my talisman'***4** he states.

The film was released on July 22nd, having previewed at the end of May, beginning of June, to near negative reviews. For instance, in The *Times* 5th August 1935 under the banner 'New Films in London' they state: *"Mr. Peter Lorre and Mr. Boris Karloff are to be seen on the London screen this week, each in a melodrama: Mr. Lorre in The Hands of Orlac, Mr. Karloff in The Raven. Neither, however, has been given a character worth establishing."***5** In their review, they state: *"It is no more than a suggestion for what Poe made horrible in prose and haunting in verse has on the screen become merely*

---

7. Charles J. Stumar Born 1891 – died 29th June 1935 in an aeroplane accident. His genre film credits include *The Hunchback of Notre Dame* (1923 un-credited) *The Mummy* (1932) and *Werewolf of London* (1935). *The Raven* was his penultimate film.

*fantastic and dull. [ ] Like any chamber of horrors, there is neither life nor horror in this film."***6** *Time* Magazine for 17th June stated: *"The Raven…suffers chiefly from the obligation its producers felt to give it more blood-curdling situations and paraphernalia than The Black Cat. Consequently, the picture is stuffed with horrors to the point of absurdity."***7**

With a running time of a mere 61 minutes, *The Raven* is the shortest of the three Universal Karloff / Lugosi collaborations, but it is well-scripted and fast-moving, and in many ways is, in places, if not theme, a mirror reflection to *The Black Cat*. For example, both films start with a crash, which leads the female character into the clutches of the main villain. In both films the men are ineffectual against those they are pitted against – a case in point is when Jean's room is elevated down to the torture chamber, Lester Matthews runs to her aid, only to nearly topple into the void where her room had once been [apparently audiences laughed at this point!]. Both heroines flirt with the protagonist – Jacqueline Wells' character in contrast to Irene Ware's is possessed by the black cat, thus adding some 'supernaturalism' to the former film. Jean Thatcher, on the other hand, is infatuated with Vollin and she actively bolsters his ego and encourages his interest in her:

Jean: You're not only a great surgeon, but a great musician, too. Extraordinary man; you're almost not a man. Almost…

Vollin: A God?

Jean: Yes.

Vollin: A God with the taint of human emotions. **8**

This slight flirtation and ego bolstering comes after Vollin has played her a piece of music on his piano. He then checks her scar from the operation and the flirtation continues:

Vollin: A month ago I didn't know you.

Jean: And now I owe my life to you. I wish there was something I could do.

Vollin: There is…

Jean: Tell me…

Vollin: The restraint that we impose upon ourselves can drive us mad. **9**

Here she breaks away from Vollin's hold, stating that she doesn't know what he means; thanks him for giving her bland fiancé a job and as she leaves, asks if he is coming to see her dance the following night to which he replies: '*Nothing can keep me away.*' **10** She then tells him that she is going to have a surprise for him and departs. It is at this point in the shooting script that Vollin "*pulls her toward him in an embrace*"**11** and goes on that "*she gives him a 'quick impulsive' kiss.*" **12** Both these scenes were either not filmed or deleted. Had they been left in, the desire that Vollin has for her would have been better established, as it would have shown that he believed that she reciprocated his feelings. Jean's 'special' surprise for him is a dance especially prepared for his enjoyment, entitled *The Spirit of Poe* which she performs as the poem is recited[8]. This seals Vollin's desire for her and when she asks him if he liked the performance, he responds, almost lovingly, "*Whom the Angels call Lenore.*"**13** This is noted by Judge Thatcher and it is here where the film begins to change gear and becomes a twisted tale of torture and revenge, as Judge Thatcher is not going to allow Vollin to have his daughter and Vollin is not going to let anyone or anything stop him.

Judge Thatcher visits Vollin and informs him that his daughter is in danger of becoming infatuated with him because he saved her life!

Vollin: You think it's only in gratitude she feels?

Thatcher: I came to you once and asked you when death was near to save Jean. I come to you again. But this time instead of from death –

Vollin (*interrupting*): You want to save her from me?

---

8. Choreographed by Theodore Kosloff (Fyodor Mikhailovich Koslov 22nd January 1888 – November 22nd 1956 aged 74. Ballet Dancer, Actor, choreographer) Performed by Nina Golden (un-credited).

Here Vollin crushes a test tube that he had been holding and seeing Thatcher's reaction to this, continues, "Now that you know, you still say that your greatest wish is for her to marry Halden?

Thatcher: More than ever. There's no point in saving Jean's life if we're to sacrifice her happiness. You mustn't see her again.

Vollin (*reacting to this*): You drivelling fool. Stop talking…

Thatcher (*interrupting*): Be careful Vollin.

Vollin (*continuing*): Not see her again! Listen, Thatcher, I'm a man who renders humanity a great service. For that my brain must be clear, my nerves steady, and my hand sure. Jean torments me. She has come into my life, into my brain.

Thatcher: Forget it, man. Forget it.

Vollin: Judge Thatcher, there are no two ways. Send her to me.

Thatcher: Do you know what you are saying?

Vollin: There are no two ways. Send her to me!

Thatcher: You're mad.

Vollin: I am mad. And I tell you the only way you can cure –

Thatcher (*cutting in*): I can't talk to you, Vollin. I came here with a perfectly reasonable objection, and I expected you to be reasonable and instead I find you stark, staring mad. Good day Dr. Vollin.

Thatcher leaves with Vollin's response hanging in the air, "Send her Judge Thatcher, I warn you…" **14**

What we, as an audience are left to ponder as it is not clearly defined in the script is why it is Judge Thatcher has a problem with the doctor. He is obviously wealthy and has good standing both at the hospital and, from that we can surmise, the town/city and until this conversation he [Thatcher] has no idea of Vollin's ego (or madness), as up until Thatcher says *'more than ever'* **15** he had been quite reasonable. It is also not established as to whether the Judge is acting on his own behalf or his daughter's and regardless to either, I would suggest that the real issue here is that he had to beg Vollin, not once, but twice to save his daughter. The first time is at the hospital, where he takes the telephone from Jerry and Vollin refuses him twice and hangs up. Not taking this lightly, Thatcher decides to make a personal visit to the doctor, where he is rejected again, but he persists:

Thatcher: But you can't say no.

Vollin: I have said it.

Thatcher: I'll pay you any amount of money, Dr. Vollin.

Vollin: Money means nothing to me.

Thatcher: But someone is dying. Your obligation as a member of the medical profession –

Vollin: I respect no obligation. I am a law unto myself.

Thatcher: But have you know human emotion? My daughter is dying.

Vollin: Death hasn't the same significance for me as it has for you.

Thatcher: You're the one chance she's got.

Vollin (*sneeringly*): Doctors Cook and Hemmingway are 'competent' doctors.

Thatcher: Competent! It seems that competence is not enough. Cook, Hemmingway and Halden, they say you are the only one.

Vollin (*his face joyous*): So they do say I am the only one!

Thatcher: Yes. I beg you for my daughter's life.

Vollin: Very well, I will go. **16**

For a man of social standing as a judge it must have been demeaning – yet he was told twice by Vollin that the other doctors were just as competent to perform the operation. It is this scene that I suggest implanted Judge Thatcher's dislike of him. Furthermore, we have to ask why didn't Jerry Halden, Jean's fiancé intervene, if not with Vollin, with Jean? To be frank, Boehm's script is so hurried that it leaves too much out and doesn't sit well. As Lennig points out with regards to the love triangle: "[ ]*the film omits the tension she {Jean} must be feeling, torn as she is between the brilliant older man and her uninteresting and bland, but loving fiancé Dr. Jerry Halden. She gives no indication of having to choose between her two admirers. That she doesn't have any mixed emotions is what makes the film more of a melodrama than a study of the human condition.*" **17**

Enter Boris Karloff – first seen getting Vollin's address, disguised in a big shaggy beard. No-one seems to be able to recognise him as the violent criminal that he is, except for Vollin, who automatically recognises him. In an almost 'spoilt child' mode, he (as Bateman) asks Vollin to change how he looks – who after a moments' thought agrees to do so if Bateman will do something for him. Bateman enquires as to what it is:

Vollin: It's in your line.

Bateman: Like what?

Vollin: Torture and murder.

Bateman protests, so Vollin continues:

Vollin: You shot your way out of San Quentin. Two guards are dead. In a bank in Arizona a man's face was mutilated – burned – cashier of the bank –

Bateman: Well he tried to get me into trouble! I told him to keep his mouth shut. He gets the gag out of his mouth and starts yellin' for the police. I had the acetylene torch in my hand…

Vollin: So you put the burning torch into his face. Into his eyes!

Bateman (*petulantly*): Well sometimes you can't help things like that … **18**

Before Vollin operates on him, Bateman is almost like a sulky child, making his excuse for his crimes by uttering: *"Maybe if a man looks ugly, he does ugly things!"* **19** The point here is that until Vollin alters his face on the operating table, Bateman looks 'normal' and isn't ugly! In their first scene together both actors are perfectly balanced with dialogue and screen shots. On the one hand you have the tortured criminal Bateman, who believes his actions are down to how he looks and on the other hand you have the sadistic Vollin, who not only seems to relish in Bateman's crimes, but is busy formulating his own plan.

Vollin proceeds with the operation and in a scene a la *Frankenstein*, he gently removes the bandages from around Bateman's face, answering Bateman's question of does he look different with a 'Yes' before leaving the room. Feeling his face, Bateman looks puzzled, then curtains swish open revealing mirrors that reflect Bateman's face to him. It is here that Karloff's performance makes Bateman a simplistic and non-effective variation of the Frankenstein monster, growling and stomping around. His face hampered by make-up that looks like a fried egg or two stuck to his face – this is one of Jack Pierce's lesser make-ups – far removed from the Frankenstein Monster or The Mummy. Boehm's script describes Bateman's new face in detail:

> *'His face is a horror. Certain muscles have been paralyzed through cutting of the nerve ends. Certain others have been permitted to remain – giving life to the part of the face they control, so that here is a face – a crazy quilt of death and life. One part of the face remains in a horrible dead grimace, while the other remains alive – side by side with the corpse. One eye remains open, un-blinking – staring straight ahead.'* **20**

And whilst Bateman is shooting the mirrors, growling and becoming the monster, Vollin, safely watching from a grill overhead, laughing manically, states: *"You're monstrously ugly. Your monstrous ugliness breeds monstrous hate. Good. I can use your hate."* **21**

Bateman pleads with Vollin to change his face back, which he agrees to do, but only after Bateman has helped him in his plan – as he says: *"I can't use my hand to do it. My brain, your hand."***22**

Later, as Vollin shows Bateman around his Poe-inspired torture chamber, he lies on the table under the bladed pendulum and, seizing his chance, Bateman pulls the lever that straps Vollin to the table and starts the pendulum swinging. This scene is an opposite reflection of the scene in *The Black Cat* where Werdegast has Poelzig trapped on his embalming rack. Poelzig is hanging in a variant crucifixion pose; Vollin is lying down in the same position. Poelzig is skinned alive by Werdegast, just as Vollin is going to have his flesh cut by Bateman. Bateman only releases Vollin once he is reminded that only he [Vollin] can fix his face. In contrast, there is no escape for Poelzig, as he has to pay for his crimes; Vollin's crimes are yet to be committed.

Sometime later, Vollin's guests arrive for the weekend. They include Mary Burns (Inez Courtney), 'Pinky' Geoffrey Burns (Ian Wolfe), Colonel Bertram Grant (Spencer Charters) and his wife Harriet Grant (Maidel Turner). As for their performances, they could have been cut as they add nothing to the unfolding drama other than offer some light comic relief that almost derails the entire film. In many ways the comic relief here is as ineffectual as it is in *The Black Cat* with the two bickering police officers (Albert Conti and Henry Armetta), arguing over whose town is better. Jean Thatcher has decided to accept Vollin's invitation despite her father's reservations and brought along her ineffectual fiancé too! Judge Thatcher arrives to get his daughter but is persuaded to stay after Vollin apologises to him.

At one point when Jean is in her bedroom, Bateman enters, and this scene again replicates a similar scene in *Frankenstein* – she screams and runs off – but she does later apologise to Bateman for her behaviour and so ingratiates herself with him. During the course of the evening Vollin is questioned by a suspicious Thatcher as to why his interest in Poe. The response is revealing:

> Vollin: Poe was a great genius. Like all great geniuses, there was in him the insistent will to do something big, great, constructive in the world. He had the brain to do it. But – he fell in love. Her name was Lemore…Something happened. Someone took her away from him. When a man is denied of his great love, he goes mad. His brain instead of being clear to do his work, is tortured, so he begins to think of torture. Torture for those who have tortured him! My interest in Poe, the way I speak about torture and death, you people being laymen perhaps do not understand. As a doctor, a surgeon, I look upon these things differently. A doctor is fascinated by death – and pain. And how much pain a man can endure. **23**

The intensity of Lugosi's performance shows Vollin's descent into the madness that destroyed Poe (according to the script) and captures brilliantly the fine line between sanity and insanity and sets in motion the twisted act of revenge. Poe's greatness was destroyed by the loss of Lenore, Vollin's infatuation with Jean threatens his [greatness] and so she has to be destroyed, and the film very nearly brings off this notion, but as Carlos Clarens points out: "*When the script has him (Lugosi) exulting in such lines as 'Poe you are avenged' without a shadow of tongue in cheek, the movie becomes its own deadly parody.*" **24**

Yet is that a fair comment? By all accounts Lugosi carried the film single-handedly. It is his portrayal of Vollin that is remembered and not Karloff's as Bateman. It is here in this film that we can see the two different acting 'methods' that they brought to each of their roles.

In a 1964 issue of *Screen Facts* magazine, the author William K. Everson analysed Karloff's acting style: "*He [Karloff] also developed two very *distinct approaches to acting. Roles that he obviously respected – through the years these ranged from The Mummy to The Body Snatcher – he played seriously and creatively – and The Mask of Fu Manchu and The Raven are key examples – he saw as basically idiotic but great fun, he played in marvellous bravura style, revelling in every absurd line."* **25**

Karloff himself responded to the question about his acting technique: *"It isn't that I have any particular aversion to rehearsing; on the contrary, I study and memorise every line I have to speak and every gesture I have to create, but I do it with the minimum of physical effort. I find myself better able to grasp a situation and character by the sole method of concentration."* **26**

In contrast to Karloff, Lugosi took every role that he undertook with seriousness, as he explained in an interview in *The New York Times,* July 7th 1935: *"You can't make people believe in you if you're playing a horror part with your tongue in your cheek. The screen magnifies everything, even the way you are thinking. If you are not serious, people will sense it. No matter how hokum or highly melodramatic the horror part may be, you must believe in it while you are playing it."* **27**

Karloff was less than impressed with the project from the start and after having read the screenplay said, *"Here was an attempt to pile on the thrills without much logic."* **28** By the time that Karloff was cast in *The Raven* he was thoroughly disillusioned with Universal. The Laemmles had reneged on contracts with him, causing him to leave the studio in 1933 and freelance. Universal were impressed with several of his other performances and so drew up another contract, including a pay rise to lure him back. Obviously seeing how they (the Laemmles) had treated Lugosi, Karloff had a provision in his contract that he could still freelance, whilst being attached to the studio. It is possibly this disenchantment with the studio that makes his performance here so sterile. According to the actor Ian Wolfe, when he asked Karloff where the toilet was, Karloff's response was allegedly, *"This whole place [indicating Universal] is a toilet."* **29**

From here the film accelerates towards it conclusion. The guests retire for the night and Vollin sends Bateman to get Judge Thatcher and bring him down to the torture chamber, which he does. Thatcher is manacled to the slab under the pendulum, his eyes full of fear, which Vollin soaks in. Looking up he sees the pendulum:

Thatcher: What's that thing?

Vollin: A Knife.

Thatcher: What's it doing?

Vollin: Descending.

Thatcher: What are you trying to do to me?

Vollin: Torture you.

Thatcher: Oh, try to be sane, Vollin.

Vollin: I'm the sanest man who ever lived. But I will not be tortured. I tear torture out of myself by torturing you! **30**

Here in the script, Vollin becomes Poe or at least in his mind. He thinks / blames Thatcher for Jean's sudden disinterest in him, failing to realise that she is betrothed to Jerry Halden. As previously stated, her turmoil over each man is never made clear, which inhibits Vollin's actions to a degree. In the full throes of his Poe-inspired madness, Vollin pulls a lever and Jean's room (in reality a lift) descends down. Iron shutters slam down and seal the house off. Jerry, along with Mary and Geoffrey, find their way down to the torture chamber and both Jerry and Jean are forced into a room where the walls close in. As the walls close in on them, a triumphant Vollin shouts: *"What a torture! What a delicious torture, Bateman! Greater than Poe! Poe only conceived it, I have done it, Bateman. Poe, you are avenged!"* **31**

Bateman, having received kindness from Jean (even admitting to her that Vollin had changed and distorted his face) pulls the lever that stops the walls from closing in on the trapped couple and releases them. Vollin shoots Bateman, who then overpowers him and throws him into his own torture device and pulls the lever. The doctor screams and falls to the floor as the walls close in. Bateman collapses and Jean and Jerry rush to the Judge's aid and rescue him, ignoring Vollin's screams. This begs the question as to whom is the actual monster – Bateman is a monster because his preconceived concept of how he looks makes him do the things he has done *"maybe if a man is ugly, he does ugly things"* **32**; Vollin is a monster because he has been driven mad, not only by his obsession with Poe, his isolation from society, but his unrequited love for Jean –*"If a man is denied his great love, he goes mad."***33** But what about the Thatchers and Halden? Surely, they are the biggest monsters of the film! Judge Thatcher basically badgers Vollin into saving his daughter, when the other three doctors are more than competent to do the job; his daughter leads him on, so that he believes that he has a chance with her, and then both take that away from him. Once free from Vollin's insanity, they just leave him to be crushed to death, ignoring his screams. In fact, all the 'normal' people actually end up being monsters – none release Vollin once he's been disarmed, despite his screams and no-one attends to the fatally wounded Bateman. Again, the lesser characters are useless as they (Mary and Geoffrey) just huddle together and do nothing. Both Vollin and Bateman are left to die. In a warped sense, they both have an excuse for what they do, but the others do not. And in what must be the worst epilogue in cinematic history – in a scene of Jerry and Jean driving, the following conversation takes place:

Jean: Poor Bateman.

Jerry: Yes darling. He saved us from being crushed. (He puts his arm around her) I think I better finish the job – don't you? Only a little more gently.

Jean (*flirtily*): So you're the big bad raven!

Jerry: *Hmmmmm.* **34**

And thus, ends a lost opportunity.

Released to a barrage of mixed reviews, many negative, the effect of *The Raven* on the British cinematic audience's sensibilities was to hasten a two-year ban on American Horror films by the British Board of Film Censors.

The debate over what was seen as 'sordid films' did not start or end with *The Raven*. It may have been the catalyst that caused the banning of American horror films for two years, yet the studios were well aware that by pushing the boundaries of what was considered decency, they were living on borrowed time, especially in regard to the horror genre. On January 5th 1931, Edward Shortt[9], President of the British Board of Film Censors[10] released a circular letter to film companies stating:

> *"In our last reports attention has been drawn to the tendency to produce incidents of prolonged and gross brutality and sordid themes, which it must be admitted are unwholesome and repugnant ... [ ] No modification, however drastic, can render such films suitable for public exhibition. In consequence, the Board takes the opportunity of notifying the trade that in future no film will receive the Board's certificate in which the theme, without any redeeming characteristic, depends upon the intense brutality or unrelieved sordidness of the scenes depicted."* **35**

Yet eleven months later on December 1st, horror films were in the news again with an American Newsreel featuring an end shot of ..."*one of the lynched kidnappers of Mr. Hart hanging from a tree surrounded by a howling mob.*"**36** At this point the B.B.F.C. did not have any jurisdiction over the content of newsreels and so children were able to view this material. By December 5th,

---

9. Under Shortt's seven year Presidency nearly one hundred and forty films were banned. According to Keith Seacroft, Shortt also arranged for the Board to see film scripts so that producers would not make films that would not be distributed. In 1931, Shortt gave an outright ban on 34 films. He banned what are now considered two classic horror films both from 1932 – Tod Browning's *Freaks* and Bela Lugosi's *Island of Lost Souls*. The former was not seen for fifty years and the latter was finally released in Britain in 1958.
10. The British Board of Film Censors was established in November 1912 by the joint efforts of Cinematograph Film Manufactures and Exhibitors as an independent examiner of films. The first director was Mr G.A. Redford and had the approval of The Home Office.

though, this newsreel had been withdrawn from circulation, but due to its very nature, questions were raised in the House of Commons. The Home Secretary[11] hinted that there may be 'corrective powers' to sort out scenes of horror and violence in newsreels. As The *Times* states on December 5th:

> *"The extension of the voluntary censorship to news films would present certain difficulties, because of the element of time; but an official censorship would entail far more. This letter is the ultimate weapon of a hostile public opinion, and the film industry should not delay to seek the protection that the Board affords against risk of rousing such hostility."* [37]

It was a delay that Hollywood was going to push to the limit and the man that had first issued the stark warning, Edward Shortt, died on November 10th 1935, aged 73. He had been President of the B.B.F.C. since November 1929, on the death of former President Mr. T.C. O'Connor. Three months prior to Shortt's death, the *Associated Press* (of America) finally ran a headline that the studios had been aware of, yet ignored the possibility to: *"Horror Films Taboo in Britain – 'The Raven' – Last"* [38]

Between *Dracula* (1931) and *Dracula's Daughter* (1936) Hollywood (and in particular Universal Studios) produced over forty horror films and through these films the depiction of horror, decency, depravity and sexuality had become more and more predominant. Warnings were no longer adhered too (despite the fifty year ban on *Freaks* {1932}) gambles were taken and the studios lost. Lord Tyrrell (10th August 1866 – 14th March 1947) was appointed President of the B.B.F.C. at 69 years of age on November 26th 1935. It was under his guidance that a new certificate was introduced in early 1936. The 'H' for 'Horrific' certificate banned anyone under the age of 16 from seeing the film, with Karloff's *The Walking Dead* being one of the first films

---

11. Sir John Gilmour Home Secretary 1st October 1932 – 7th June 1935.

to receive this certificate[12]. This was a disaster for the Studios as they lost a major part of their ticket buying audience. While this debate raged on in Britain and production of horror films decreased in America, *The Raven* continued to show in UK suburbs and provinces, keeping the argument fresh in people's minds. As the *Observer* newspaper said of the film on January 19th 1936: "[ ] *A charming and sadistic little trifle, compounded in equal parts from 'The Raven" and 'The Pit and the Pendulum.' Boris Karloff and Bela Lugosi play the leading murderers, and as one trade review has it, "Karloff and Lugosi are one hundred per cent assurance that you're in for an evening of unadulterated horror."***39**

Despite being cut from 61 minutes down to 57 minutes, *The Raven* still received complaints as The *Times* stated on May 18th 1936, *'[ ] The Raven, as to which complaints or representations of various kinds were made.'***40**

Despite criticisms of the film, it is Lugosi's performance that holds the film together from beginning to end; even Karloff fails at every point to upstage him. For their next 'official' collaboration, Karloff would claim his position as the Number One horror star. Not only did *The Raven* close Universal's Poe trilogy (following on from *Murders in the Rue Morgue* (1932), and *The Black Cat* (1934)), it brought about a two year ban on horror films in the United Kingdom which effectively killed Lugosi's career. Yet in this film, for one fleeting moment he was able to shine again as he did in *Dracula*.

---

12. In his first speech to the Cinematograph Exhibitors Association, Lord Tyrell, in his first major talk held at Eastbourne on June 24th 1936 stated that "the horrific category of films had now ceased to exist."

End Notes

1: Everson, William K. 1974. *Classics of the Horror Film*. Citadel Press. Pg. 218.
2: Starr, J. *L.A. Evening Herald Examiner* February 27th 1935 as quoted in Mank, G.W. *Bela Lugosi and Boris Karloff: The Expanded Story of a Haunted Collaboration, with a Complete Filmography of their Films Together* McFarland & Company, Inc., Publishers. Revised Edition. Pg. 240.
3: Mank, G.W. *Bela Lugosi and Boris Karloff: The Expanded Story of a Haunted Collaboration, with a Complete Filmography of their Films Together* McFarland & Company, Inc., Publishers. Revised Edition. Pg. 246.
4: The Raven. 1935. Dir. Louis Friedlander. Universal.
5: The *Times*, 5th August 1935 Pg. 8 'New Films in London'.
6: The *Times*, 5th August 1935 Pg. 8 'New Films in London'.
7: *Time* Magazine, 17th June 1935 as quoted in Mank, G.W. *Bela Lugosi and Boris Karloff: The Expanded Story of a Haunted Collaboration, with a Complete Filmography of their Films Together* McFarland & Company, Inc., Publishers. Revised Edition. Pg. 263.
8: The Raven. 1935. Dir. Louis Friedlander. Universal.
9: The Raven. 1935. Dir. Louis Friedlander. Universal.
10: Lennig, Arthur 2003. *The Immortal Count: The Life and Films of Bela Lugosi*. The University Press of Kentucky. Pg. 227.
11: Lennig, Arthur 2003. *The Immortal Count: The Life and Films of Bela Lugosi*. The University Press of Kentucky. Pg. 227.
12: Lennig, Arthur 2003. *The Immortal Count: The Life and Films of Bela Lugosi*. The University Press of Kentucky. Pg. 227.
13: The Raven. 1935. Dir. Louis Friedlander. Universal.
14: The Raven. 1935. Dir. Louis Friedlander. Universal.
15: The Raven. 1935. Dir. Louis Friedlander. Universal.
16: The Raven. 1935. Dir. Louis Friedlander. Universal.
17: Lennig, Arthur 2003. *The Immortal Count: The Life and Films of Bela Lugosi*. The University Press of Kentucky. Pg. 223.

18: The Raven. 1935. Dir. Louis Friedlander. Universal.
19: The Raven. 1935. Dir. Louis Friedlander. Universal.
20: Mank, G.W. *Bela Lugosi and Boris Karloff: The Expanded Story of a Haunted Collaboration, with a Complete Filmography of their Films Together* McFarland & Company, Inc., Publishers. Revised Edition. Pg. 256.
21: The Raven. 1935. Dir. Louis Friedlander. Universal.
22: The Raven. 1935. Dir. Louis Friedlander. Universal.
23: The Raven. 1935. Dir. Louis Friedlander. Universal.
24: Clarens, Carlos. 1967. *Horror Movies: An Illustrated Survey*. London: Secker & Warburg Revised edition 1968. Pg. 96.
25: Everson, William K. 1964 *Screen Facts*. As quoted in Mank, G.W. *Bela Lugosi and Boris Karloff: The Expanded Story of a Haunted Collaboration, with a Complete Filmography of their Films Together* McFarland & Company, Inc., Publishers. Revised Edition. Pg. 252.
26: Bojarski, Richard & Beals, Kenneth 1974. *The Films of Boris Karloff*. Citadel Press. Pg. 24.
27: *New York Times,* July 7th 1935 as quoted in Mank, G.W. *Bela Lugosi and Boris Karloff: The Expanded Story of a Haunted Collaboration, with a Complete Filmography of their Films Together* McFarland & Company, Inc., Publishers. Revised Edition. Pg. 249.
28: Nollen, Scott. A. *Boris Karloff: A Critical Account of his Screen Stage & Radio, Television and Recording Work* McFarland & Company, Inc., Publishers. 2008. Pg. 127.
29: Mank, G.W. *Bela Lugosi and Boris Karloff: The Expanded Story of a Haunted Collaboration, with a Complete Filmography of their Films Together* McFarland & Company, Inc., Publishers. Revised Edition. Pg. 257.
30: The Raven. 1935. Dir. Louis Friedlander. Universal.
31: The Raven. 1935. Dir. Louis Friedlander. Universal.
32: The Raven. 1935. Dir. Louis Friedlander. Universal.
33: The Raven. 1935. Dir. Louis Friedlander. Universal.
34: The Raven. 1935. Dir. Louis Friedlander. Universal.

35: The *Times*, January 5th 1931 Pg. 10 'Sordid Films to be Banned'.
36: The *Times*, December 1st 1933 Pg. 14 'Horror in News Films'.
37: The *Times*, December 05 1933 Pg. 15 'Films and Censors'.
38: Skal, D. J. *The Monster Show: A Cultural History of Horror* (London: Plexus, 1993).
39: The *Observer* Newspaper, January 19th 1936 Pg. 14 'Suburbs and Provinces'.
40: The *Times*, May 18th 1936 Pg. 11 'Valuation and Rating'.

Other Sources

The *Times*, Thursday January 2nd 1913 Pg. 2 'Censorship of Cinema Films'.

The *Times*, Monday January 5th 1931 Pg. 10 'Sordid Films to be Banned'.

The *Times*, July 28th 1932 Pg. 10 'Rules for Exhibition of Film Posters'.

The *Times*, Friday December 1st 1933 Pg. 14 'Horror in News Film'.

The *Times*, Tuesday December 5th 1933 Pg. 15 'Films and Censors'.

The *Times*, Friday June 18th 1935 Pg. 8 'Censorship of the cinema'.

The *Times*, Tuesday November 26th 1935 Pg. 14 'New Film Censor'.

The *Manchester Guardian,* December 28th 1935 Pg. 8 'The Child and the Horrible'.

The *Observer* Newspaper, January 19th 1936 Pg. 14 'Suburbs and Provinces'.

The *Times*, May 18th 1936 Pg. 11 'Valuation and Rating'.

The *Times*, Thursday June 24th 1936 Pg. 13 'Censorship of Films'.

The *Times*, July 11th 1936 Pg. 12 'Ban on "Horrific Film".

The *Times*, Thursday July 30th 1936 Pg. 12 'Another "Horrific" Film'.

The *Times*, Thursday June 24th 1937 Pg. 13 'Censorship of Films'.

The *Times*, July 11th 1947 Pg. 5 'Children in Cinema'.

The *Times*, Monday February 28th 1955 Pg. 7 'News in brief'.

The *Times*, Monday October 6th 1958 Pg. 4 'Campaign against Horror Films'.

The *Times*, Friday October 30th 1959 Pg. 7 'Poster for Horror Films Banned'.

The *Times*, Thursday September 6th 1962 Pg. 14 'Mr. Boris Karloff on Horror Films'.

The *Times*, 4th February 1969 Pg. 1 'Boris Karloff gave the Monster a soul'.

The *Times*, 4th February 1969 Pg. 10 'Obituary: Mr. Boris Karloff'.

Male, Andrew Back to the Suture. The *Observer* Newspaper, January 5th 2000 Pg. D8.

Seacoft, Keith. *Insight: UK Film Censor Edward Shortt.* The Journal March 20th 2012.

Rukh's in the Closet: Glowing hands, homosexuality and Radium X The Invisible Ray: Re-Examining a Horror Classic

> "It isn't blood-curdling to the point achieved in some Hollywoodian efforts, but it is different and fairly entertaining… [Karloff] and Lugosi stand away out in an otherwise average cast." 'Char,' Variety.[1]

In the heart of the Carpathian Mountains, in a castle fit for Dracula himself, lives Dr. Janos Rukh (Boris Karloff), his mother (Violet Kemble Cooper) and his wife Diane (Frances Drake). Janos has developed a telescope that can not only study the stars but is able to 'read' the light that emanates from them and so he can see what has transpired millions of years ago. Therefore, he can see the developments of the universe as they happened. Through this discovery, he has learned that a meteor fell to Earth millions of years ago, crashing into Africa. He has invited a group of scientists who have derailed his theories before, to show them the truth of what he has said.

Sir Francis Stevens (Walter Kingsford), his wife Lady Arabella Stevens (Beulah Bondi) along with their nephew Ronald Drake (Frank Lawton) and Dr. Felix Benet arrive at the castle. Rukh shows them the proof of his theories, though Drake is more interested in Rukh's wife, and the scientists agree that they were wrong to misjudge him and arrange to go into the heart of Africa on an expedition to find the remains of the crashed meteor.

In Africa, we find that Rukh has gone off and left the party to their own devices, with Sir Stevens bemoaning about the heat, the food, and everything else. Lady Stevens actively encourages both her nephew and Diane to commit adultery, as they both swan around each other, denying their feelings. Dr. Benet is healing sick children and handing them back to their parents with a look of distain. Meanwhile Rukh has found the remains of the crashed meteor in an extinct volcano and has managed to reclaim some of the said meteor, which he names Radium X.

Radium X despite its healing properties is a deadly substance and Rukh has unbeknownst to himself absorbed poison from it. Not only does he glow in the dark, he learns that his touch brings instant death. Already a little neurotic, the poison begins to affect his brain. He goes to Benet, who makes a temporary antidote for him, but it is too late as Rukh is consumed by jealousy that his wife now loves another (as she believes that he doesn't love her), and that his fellow scientists have deceived him and stolen his discovery. Benet tries to reassure him that this isn't the case, but Rukh doesn't listen.

Rukh returns home, his wife goes off with the Stevens and Benet goes back to Paris, where he uses the healing properties of Radium X to cure people of their various maladies. Unable to contain his madness, Rukh goes to Paris and once he sees what is happening with his discovery, he goes completely over the edge and sets out to kill those he feels have stolen from him. His first step is to fake his own death, then he kills Sir Francis Stevens (off-screen). But clever Benet thinks there is something amiss and using a special camera takes a photograph of Stevens' eyes, and in development sees the image of Rukh coming in for the kill captured in the dead man's eye. In shock, Benet drops the slide and it shatters.

To add to the fear that is spreading throughout Paris that a murderer is at large, Rukh also uses Radium X to melt statues of Saints outside a church, thus creating a city that is teetering on the edge of chaos. Benet, along with Drake who has now married Diana, and the police arrange for a seminar to discuss Radium X, knowing that Rukh won't be able to keep away. They make it known that it is a seminar of fellow scientists and is by invitation only.

Rukh drugs one of the scientists and steals his invitation, kills Benet in the laboratory, when he (Benet) reaches into his pocket for his gun and then goes to kill his wife, whom he is unable to murder. Mother Rukh turns up, on the request of Drake, and reprimands her son for breaking the first rule of science and destroys his antidote. Rukh apologises to his mother before turning into a ball of flame as he throws himself out of a window.

That is a basic outline of what is a precursor to the science fiction films to come in the 1950s. The film has echoes of *The Invisible Man* (1933), in which a scientist's physical and mental health is affected by his experiments and driven insane:

Benet: Do you intend to kill us all?

Janos: Yes.

Benet: I felt it was better to let things alone when you were first poisoned. I warned you about your brain.

Janos: It began to affect my brain almost immediately. I could feel it coming, crawling for cells.

Benet: Aren't there ever moments when you think as you used to think? When you're human?

*Janos: Not often now, not often.***2**

The New York Times, January 11th 1936 stated that it was '*...just another case of a man's manager bringing him along too fast.*'**44**

To capitalise on the success of their previous two Karloff – Lugosi vehicles, *The Black Cat* (1934) and *The Raven* (1935), Universal released *The Invisible Ray* in January 1936, having announced its production in August the previous year. As it was the third major pairing between Karloff and Lugosi it was accorded an upper-class B status and production values, and Universal shrouded the production in secrecy due to the special effects.

Although now considered lost, there was a serialised film called *'The Invisible Ray'* released through The Frohman Amusement Corp on 1st July 1920, directed by Harry A Pollard. Its storyline of a mineralogist discovering a ray with extraordinary powers and a group of scientists who seek to use it in a criminal scheme may well have influenced the writing of the later film. Whatever the case may be Universal purchased *The Death Ray* (as it was known then) in May 1935 and it underwent some changes before production began. For instance, Rukh in the original script was called Koh, a Belgian, who goes to Africa, discovers a meteor and becomes radioactive. He goes to the expedition doctor, Dr Morceau, who gives him an antidote. As in the later film, his wife deserts him believing he is uninterested in her and there is a change in the end, whereas in the original script Koh accidentally kills his wife before succumbing to the radiation, in the final version, she lives as Rukh cannot kill her. Carl Laemmle Jr. possibly fearing a further backlash after *The Raven* chose to produce a science fiction bonanza in *The Invisible Ray* and wanted it to be taken seriously – rather than seen as a piece of fantasy, he wanted it to be seen as a film of actual possibility: *"Every scientific fact accepted today once burned as a fantastic fire in the mind of someone called mad. Who are we on this youngest and smallest of planets to say that the invisible ray is impossible to science? That which you are now to see is a theory whispered in the cloisters of science. Tomorrow these theories may startle the Universe as a fact."***3**

Directed by Lambert Hillyer, a Western specialist, he would direct *Dracula's Daughter* the same year, replacing Stuart Walker1[13], who dropped the project due to dissatisfaction with both the script and the shooting time. The film was

---

13. "Walker reported to the trades: 'I am very enthusiastic about the story and the cast but I did not feel that I could do the studio or myself justice under the conditions that came up suddenly. So far as I was concerned I needed more time and, as this could not be arranged, I suggested that some other director would be better for the assignment. It was not a matter of "walking out..."'" (Universal Horrors: The Studio's Classic Films 1931 – 1946. T Weaver, M Brunas, J Brunas Pg.115).

originally titled *The Death Ray* and was scripted by John Colton, based upon a short story by Howard Higgins and Douglas Hodges. The special effects were done by John P Fulton, who added the glowing effect on Karloff directly onto the film negative. In fact Universal claimed that it took six weeks to perfect Karloff's glowing hands and face. Yet records show that the trick only cost $250.00 to do. *Photon's*[14] Paul Mandell was given a more thorough explanation of how the effects were achieved by David Horsley:

> *"Mr. Fulton had plenty of time to think this one over, and he discussed the problem with Frank Williams, who had the patents on the traveling matte processes and at the time was operating his laboratory in Hollywood. Frank suggested that John use a bi-pack film in photographing Karloff, using a suitable make-up, so that the hands and face would sort of separate out of the rest of the scene. One part of the bi-pack record would be used to print the regular scene, and the other half would be used to take-off the mattes for the glowing effect. John agreed to do this, we made some tests, and they looked pretty good... We shot two days with (the bi-pack stock) before the lab discovered they could not get enough exposure and develop enough image on the pieces to make the system work (this was old film, quite old)... so we had to go ahead and photograph the film, and Fulton had to figure out a way to ink the mattes after it was finished. And that was what was done. I actually had the task of compositing all of those shots of Karloff glowing ... We had a crew of girls working around the clock, three eight-hour shifts. We had three stands, these were overhead cameras projecting down onto animation boards. The girls would pencil-in the hands and face, one frame at a time, and these would be painted onto cells so that the hands and face were black. There was well over a thousand feet of these mattes, so this involved more than sixteen thousand of these drawings. I was there every four hours, day and night, from the time the job started until the time all the mattes were inked and painted."* **4**

---

14. *Photon* film magazine. 1963-1977 Editor/Publisher Mark Frank. 27 issues published.

Fulton's special effects on the birth of the Universe and meteor crash were considered the best of their time. The effects for Karloff melting a boulder to scare his native workers and his disintegration at the end of the film only cost $700. As The *Los Angeles Times* on October 27th 1935 announced: *"Karloff Made Luminous: A feat in photography was successfully accomplished at Universal City when the hands and face of Boris Karloff were made to appear luminous when a motion picture in which he appeared was projected on the screen. Studio photographic experts worked on the problem for weeks. In 'The Invisible Ray', hands and face of the actor, supposedly poisoned by radium, glow in the dark."* **41**

Shooting began on September 17th 1935 with a budget of $166,875. It completed filming over schedule and budget on October 24th, 12 days later than anticipated and costing an extra $68,000. Karloff received $15,625 for five weeks work and Lugosi received a flat fee of $4,000. The film used a few standing sets from *Flash Gordon* as well as recycling the set of Lon Chaney Sr.'s Notre Dame Cathedral for the church where Diana Rukh and Ronald Drake get married. The film also utilised stock footage of electrical machines from *Frankenstein* (1931). Interestingly, stock footage of Karloff suited up and in the volcano is later reused in Universal's 1939 Lugosi serial *The Phantom Creeps*, with Karloff unwittingly doubling for Lugosi. As Rukh, Karloff would play a Hungarian and Lugosi would play a Frenchman! Furthermore, Frank Reicher's character 'Professor Meiklejohn' is correctly credited in the opening credits, but changed in the end credits to 'Professor Mendelsohn'. The film was scored by composer Franz Waxman, who also composed the score for *The Bride of Frankenstein* (1935) and the entire score lasts for 25 minutes.

The Invisible Ray was the first film to feature Karloff in a role he would play many times over in the coming years – the mad scientist. His career had been built up by his willingness to wear lots of make-up for roles, such as the Frankenstein Monster and Im-Ho-Tep in *The Mummy*, but for this film he just wore a curly hair wig and moustache. His performance remains the central core of the film and his initially dedicated scientist / later insane scientist created a template that many others such as Lionel Atwill, George Zucco and John Carradine would duplicate and can be seen in part as reminiscent of Doctor Mirakle in *Murders in the Rue Morgue* (1932).

Karloff though underplays the insanity of Rukh, probably not wanting to be compared to Lugosi's earlier portrayal of Dr. Vollin in *The Raven* the year before. Yet even before he is contaminated with the mysterious Radium X we learn that there is something that disconnects him from the rest of man, as his mother states when he agrees to go on the expedition to find the meteorite, *"You're not used to people, Janos. You never will be. Your experiments are your friends. Leave people alone."***5**

The Hollywood Spectator for February 1st 1936 was quick to pick this up and were less than flattering about Karloff's performance: '*…In this picture he is so intense from the start, so much the scientist absorbed by a single obsession, so completely the actor playing a role, I was not aware of his transition from sanity to insanity which explained his murderous impulses. If he had shaded his characterization somewhat, had been more human when sane, he would have been more impressive when he lost his mind. To me he did not seem normal from the start.*"**6**

Yet previously to that on the 11th of January 1936, *The Hollywood Reporter* had given a glowing review of Karloff: "*The part of the scientist is played by Karloff with moving intensity. This is a new Karloff in a new sort of role, full of vivid character contrasts, and will win him hosts of new admirers.*"**7**

If *The Black Cat* was Karloff's showpiece and *The Raven* was Lugosi's, then *The Invisible Ray* has to be seen as the equilibrium between the two actors as both demonstrate their versatility when it comes to acting. Despite having the lesser role, Lugosi's restrained performance proved what a versatile actor he was, but according to Carlos Clarens, '*Even Lugosi's non-villain roles he imbued with malevolence, as in The Black Cat and The Invisible Ray.*'**8**

Lennig contradicts this: *'Lugosi fans were disappointed in The Invisible Ray, for their hero was placed in an uncharacteristic role as a mild and reasonable scientist instead of a crazed monomaniac.'***9**

Disagreeing with both these later comments, *The Hollywood Spectator* wrote, "*In sharp contrast with Karloff's performance is the smooth, human and intelligent one of Bela Lugosi. He is an artist who conceals all evidence of his art, never for a moment suggesting the actor playing a part. I cannot understand why we do not see him on the screen more ofte*n."**10**

For their third venture Karloff dominated Lugosi not only in the film but in the publicity too. Karloff's surname big and monolithic dominated 'and Bela Lugosi'. It was as though Lugosi was just 'inserted' into the script, rather than have the script worked around the two horror stars as had their previous teaming. Gary Rhodes suggests that, "*His [Lugosi's] minimal role and screen time probably stem from story development that had to force in a part for him.*"**11** Lennig points out that '*...and Dr. Morceau's part was enlarged, and his name changed to Dr. Benet...*' **12**

Before being recalled to Universal, Lugosi had planned to return to Hungary for the first time in 16 years after he completed Hammer's *The Mystery of the Mary Celeste* (1935). Universal sent Lugosi a telegram summoning him back (possibly at the same time as they announced that production was to begin), thus forcing him to cancel the trip. According to Lillian Lugosi, "*Universal said we had to get back immediately for The Invisible Ray and they really made a stink about it. Bela was heartbroken that we wouldn't have the time to take the trip to Hungary. Then, when we finally did get back in late August, they told us that production wouldn't begin for at least another month! That really set Bela off, but by then it was already too late. The damage had been done.*"**13** Gary Don Rhodes speculates that Lugosi may have never wanted to see his homeland again: "*Though he definitely had other opportunities to visit his homeland, Lugosi never did. Perhaps he feared that too many changes had occurred. Budapest remained important to his memories; he* *did not want to ruin it by seeing the city's and country's changes."* **14** Further to this, Gregory W. Mank suggests that Lugosi's anger over this cancelled holiday was nothing but pretence and kept it up to fool his wife! It seems highly unlikely that Lugosi would pay for a holiday that he knew he wasn't going to take and it was announced in *The Hollywood Reporter* for June 19th 1935 that he was due back to begin shooting on September 1st. It is possible to speculate that Universal's summoning may have been a surprise to Lugosi, who believed that he had time to take this trip and that his anger may have been towards his management, who would have been aware of this. It would appear that Lugosi was represented by Collier and Flinn, Ltd. from 1930/31 through to January 1937, when it was announced that he was now represented by John Zanft Agency. It is unclear who represented him at Collier & Flinn Ltd., but it is possible that his agent, having secured the role for him, either failed to inform him of the shooting schedule or gave him the wrong dates, thus leading him to believe he could take the holiday. Further to this, Mank points out that as early as 18th May 1935, in her column, Louella Parsons' wrote, *"Bela would play The Invisible Ray's 'Uncanny hero'."* **15** From this we can speculate that perhaps Lugosi thought that he was going to play Rukh and not the Benet character. This could have brought Lugosi home too – to sort out with his agents as to why his part had been changed to a minor one. Further to this, The *Washington Post* for September 11th 1935 announced that *"…Bela Lugisi is back on the West Coast and will begin work on 'The Invisible Ray' with Boris Karloff."* **37** Whatever the case may be Lugosi was always scheduled to be a part of *The Invisible Ray.*

Gloria Stuart was originally cast in the role of Diana Rukh, but she was fed up with being a Universal contractee who was mainly cast in B movies, despite having played leading roles in 1932's *The Old Dark House* (with Karloff) and 1933's *The Invisible Man*. Stuart did co-star with Karloff and Lugosi in Universal's 1934 film *'The Gift of Gab.'* Her agent got her released from her contract and she immediately signed with 20th Century-Fox who offered her *The Prisoner of Shark Island* (1936), directed by John Ford. Frances Drake was brought in to replace her, following her successful role as the object of desire for Peter Lorre's obsession in *Mad Love* (1935). Under the banner *'Francis Drake Signed.'* **38** The *Los Angeles Times* for September 30th announced that *'Francis Drake has been engaged for the leading feminine role of The Invisible Ray.'* **39** The *Chicago Defender* for November 9th 1935 stated that: *"Daniel Hayes[15], noted actor and singer is now playing in his third motion picture since his coming to California a few months ago. It is Universal's new mystery-film, title 'The Invisible Ray' co-starring Boris Karloff and Bela Lugosi."* **40** Though both these articles appear during and after production we can deduce that there were many changes going on behind the scenes, both with cast and script.

Drake recounts in *Karloff and Lugosi: The Story of a Haunting Collaboration by Gregory William Mank*, working with Karloff on *The Invisible Ray*: *"Boris was a darling man...He was so good-natured, too."* **16** She also recalled her scene with Karloff when he rages against the scientific community with the angry vow, *"They'll never laugh at me again,"* and she ruined the first take by giggling. *"It was my first day, and Karloff was in his laboratory, and I had to go in and call his name. Well, I hadn't realized that he had a slight speech impediment - a lisp. And when he launched into his speech, and I heard the lisp - I had to laugh! Well, it was the first day, so fortunately we just put it down to "first day nerves!"* **17**

Universal intended to make another film: *The Man in the Cab* with Karloff and Lugosi, based on a similar theme, but with Karloff portraying an electrical man! It was based on the story *The Electric Man* by Harry J. Essex, Sid Schwartz and Len Golos and was bought by Universal on 1st August 1935. Whether the studio (under the Laemmles) thought it was too similar to *The Invisible Ray* or for some other reason, the project was shelved and did not

---

15. Rev. Dr. Daniel L Haynes, despite being publicised for his role in TIR was un-credited in the end. He came to prominence in the lead role in the 1929 film 'Hallelujah' which was the first all-black film. He died on July 31st 1954, aged 60.

see production until 1941 when it was released on March 28th as *Man Made Monster* (aka *Atomic Monster*) with Lon Chaney Jr. and Lional Atwill in the Karloff / Lugosi roles respectively.

It is very hard to classify *The Invisible Ray* as it is too dated to be classed a science fiction classic and not Gothic enough to be classed a Horror film. Due to its very nature, it falls somewhere in-between. The *Hartford Courant* for May 16th 1936 said that it *'succeeds in becoming a pseudo-scientific murder picture of the first magnitude.'*[42]

Not since *Dracula* (1931) has a 'horror' film contained more off-screen action. The murder of Sir Francis and a Parisian derelict (Walter Miller) both take place off screen, Lady Arabella's death is described in a newspaper montage as are the desecrations of the six religious statues that Rukh, in his madness, sees as the six from his African expedition. Even the death of Professor Meiklejohn towards the end of the film is almost off-screen, as all we are permitted to see is the professor hidden by his umbrella, accept a drink from Rukh and then collapse! So where does that leave *The Invisible Ray*? It is a hybrid of ideas that are not fully explored as the science gone mad element is bogged down by the continual set changes; Karloff as Rukh is no Colin Clive as Victor Frankenstein and the underlying story line of repressed homosexuality, adultery and insanity are not fully explored.

Another problem is it's clear Colonial racism haunts the Africa scenes – When Benet 'cures' a baby, he hands it back to its mother as though it's something disgusting. At the Mountains of the Moon, Rukh's servants want to leave, so he demonstrates the power of Radium X and melts a boulder into dust – *"You can all go if you want to – but you won't get far ... All that will be left of you will be like that"*[18] he snaps, while his 'men' wail and scream in absolute terror. Even the electrical equipment seems to scare them! Mank points out that a native (Fred Toones a.k.a. Snowflake) enters Rukh's tent later that night – sees him glowing (from the radioactive poisoning): *'and lets out a rolled-eye screech that offered comedy relief to the not-so-racially conscious audience of 1936.'* **19** Similarly to *The Black Cat* (1934), the script contained racist lines towards the natives, such as Rukh ordering one servant back: *'Come back here, you skulking black!'* **20** Thankfully all of this was cut before shooting. Other cuts included Drake saving Diana from a charging rhino and one or two romantic episodes between the pair. Another cut was a prologue conversation between Rukh's rivals on the way to his house.

In another way the film is fairly controversial for the time is in its depiction of the breakdown of a marriage and the subsequent affair that transpires through adultery. From the very beginning of the film, upon their first meeting, Ronald Drake flirts with Diana, though it could be construed as friendly banter. Yet at the close of showing his [Rukhs'] guests the meteor crashing into the Earth, Diana is clearly seen holding Drake's hand which she quickly drops and hurries over to her husband, having already implied to Drake that as her father had worked with her husband and died, she felt 'obliged' to marry him. *The Hartford Courant* picked up on this in their review: "*Ronald Drake (Frank Lawton) a nephew of Stevens, accompanies the two men and falls in love with the beautiful wife of Rukh. Diana Rukh (Francis Drake) married Rukh only because her late father, Rukh's former assistant, wished her to do so..[ ]*"**43**

This is also implied by Mother Rukh as he agrees to go to Africa. Once in Africa, Rukh leaves his wife in the hands of Drake and his Aunt and Uncle. Arabella states that the trip must be lonely for Diana and that it is all Drake's fault because of the way they both avoid each other. Drake admits to being in love with Diana, but that nothing can happen as she's married, but that sets Arabella off on a quest to put the two young people together, completely forgetting that Diana IS a married woman. Even her husband, Sir Francis, states that it is not her business to interfere – to which she retorts that it is and her excuse is that she is fond of Diana! But what really throws Diana and Drake together is Rukh's rejection of her when, confused, she rushes to his camp to get some form of reassurance that her husband does indeed love her. By the time she gets there, Rukh has realised that he has been contaminated and that if he touches her – she will die. He refuses to see her or allow her into his tent: *"This is no place for you! You must leave here at once"***21** he bellows. Devastated at his rejection, she rushes into another tent, crying. Rukh, following, hears this and is powerless to enter and comfort her. Even after Rukh has been given a temporary antidote by Dr. Benet, he still refuses to see or be with his wife. So when Benet delivers Rukh a letter from his wife, which states that she believes he does not love her and that she loves another, he goes mad:

Rukh: She doesn't believe I love her… She loves someone else … Drake?

Benet (softly): Yes.

*Rukh: You come like thieves in the night! You steal everything from me! Get out of here, Benet! Get out before I…?***22**

In reality Rukh has got no one but himself to blame. Had he been honest and told Diana of what had happened to him then this situation may never have arisen. In her eyes his utter rejection of her was the death knell of their marriage and gives her the opportunity to go off on a trip with the Stevens' and Drake, where their affair blossoms. Rukh returns home to continue with his experiments and to worry as to whether his sexuality will be 'outed'! Harry M. Benshoff points out: *"[ ] Benet [ ] is able to render Rukh temporarily 'normal' with a 'counteractive' serum. Like a homosexual with a double life, Rukh is adamant that his secret be kept in the closet: "Tell no one of this! Promise me!" Furthering the metaphor [ ] he solicits a man in the street in order "to do you a benefit – the greatest benefit one man can do another."***23** Originally the derelict was to have been killed in Rukh's hotel room thus emphasising the homosexual metaphor … why would a man pick up another man and take him to his room? The innuendo is that they are going to have sex! Furthering it even more are the African scenes where Rukh has surrounded himself with half-naked 'safari boys' and refuses to allow anyone to know where he has gone with them.

Due to the changes in the script, which originally portrayed Rukh as a tender, loving husband from the start – the film depicts him as reclusive, embittered, and vindictive towards those who have doubted him. This change in character from script to film opens up a whole new area, as Benshoff explains: '[ ]*The teaming of Boris Karloff and Bela Lugosi in the mid-1930s in a series of horror vehicles furthered the concept of a monstrously queer sado-masochistic male couple. This type of queer couple, unlike their domestic counterparts, was not interested in creating life together but rather in torturing one another to death.*'24

This is certainly true of both *The Black Cat* and *The Raven* where any potential homosexual desire falls into a sado-masochistic dance of death, where the queer couple have to die so the heterosexual couple survive, the subtext being that heterosexuality endures whilst everything other than leads to death. Unlike both those films, there is no clear cut sado-masochistic couple in *The Invisible Ray*. Rukh has already been 'homosexualized' by his domineering Mother, who rules his life and marriage. Fraying points out that, "*Throughout the film, she [Mother Rukh] has functioned – with cameo brooch and crucifix – as Janos Rukh's conscience: 'My son will not learn until too late I fear that ... there are some secrets we are not meant to probe.*'"25 She demeans him in front of his prospective colleagues by stating that no good will come from going to Africa, that he isn't good with people, to leave them alone, and that his experiments are his only friend. In the end she comes to Paris to enforce parental discipline upon her son, stating that: "*It is my duty to be here. My son, you have broken the first law of science...*"26 Mank points out that after having confronted Diana and unable to kill her, and then confronted by his Mother: '*Ashamed that Diana and now his beloved mother have seen the freakish monster of science he has become, Karloff rolls his eyes, and wrings his hands in shame and [ ] turns into a cringing, pitiful Mama's boy.*'27 Mother Rukh then destroys his antidote, thus condemning her son to death and as his body disintegrates due to her actions, Rukh states to his mother, "*It's better this way ... Goodbye, Mother.*"28 Metaphorically speaking, the insinuation is that he should not have explored his sexuality! The price for doing so is death, thus allowing the heterosexual couple to live happily ever after. In later dialogue between

Drake to Diana, he states *"You never belonged to him,"* **29** thus the implication is that the marriage was never consummated. Mank backs this theory by saying of Rukh, *"[ ] apparently never 'touching' his foxy wife – providing [ ] Hollywood's first 'sexually confused' horror villain."* **30** Yet only *The New York Times* points out his motives for killing: *"[ ] he decides to rid the earth of his wife, her lover and the woman whom he suspects fostered their romance."* **45**

Benshoff points out, *"Usually the plots of these films revolve around the attempts of medical science to cure the monsters [ ], somehow to make them "normal" enough to be integrated into society."* **31** Eleven days prior to the beginning of filming, on September 6th 1935, Dr. Louis W. Max at a meeting of the American Psychological Association informed them that he had "successfully cured a 'partially fetishistic' homosexual neurosis with electric shock treatment delivered at 'intensities considerably higher than those usually employed on human subjects." This is the first documented case of aversion therapy being used to 'cure' homosexuality. Therefore, the film can be seen as a metaphor for 'curing' homosexuality, with Dr. Benet working through the night to find a cure for his friend's latent homosexuality and once given the treatment, Rukh is temporarily cured:

Rukh: I can touch people now?

Benet: Yes. But remember what I told you. Nothing can ever cure you …And now that the counteractive has gone into your bloodstream, you can only live if you use a small amount of it at regular intervals – all the days of your life.

Rukh: And if I exceed the time?

Benet: Your body again becomes the deadly machine it was. Your touch will kill… **32**

This emphasises that his 'homosexual' nature must always be kept in check otherwise it will re-emerge to the detriment of society. When confronting his wife, Diana, at the close of the film, John Colton wrote a masterful piece of prose showing the inner struggles that are present in Rukh, his love for his wife, and his abhorrence to what has become of their marriage / his sexuality and his hatred of the man that he considers stole her away from him:

> *"I want to get my eyes full of your loveliness first, full of your loveliness. Cool hands – put them close to my forehead – but don't touch me, don't touch me. All the fires that burn inside my head are going, going. There's only a little time left for me, only a little time. Don't move, Diana, don't move... I want to hold you in my arms, just once. I want to destroy you, but I can't, I can't...you are too beautiful to kill – but he – he must die-"***33**

Most of this was cut from the final print of the film, just leaving, *"I want to kill you, but I can't, but he must die."***34**

Like *Frankenstein* (1931) and *The Invisible Man* (1933) before it, *The Invisible Ray* has hints of a morality play where man is unable to cope with his own devices and is corrupted by the very science that he is exploring. But it is the juxtaposition between Horror and Science Fiction that makes *The Invisible Ray* a classic as it sits nicely in both camps, despite its faults.

The *Observer* for 17th July 1936 described it as *'Another gooseflesh drama from Messers Karloff and Lugosi, all about a murderous scientist who glows luminously in the dark.'***35**

In 1957, *The Invisible Ray* was part of 52 Universal titles released to television in their *Shock Theatre* package. With a running time of nearly 80 minutes, it was longer than either of the earlier Karloff/Lugosi films by 15 and 19 minutes respectively, was intelligently scripted and highlighted two actors at the top of their profession, and yet for Universal under the Laemmles' *The Invisible Ray* heralded the end of an era – It was the last of their Karloff and Lugosi collaborations and one of the last films they would produce before selling the studio. It is also historic as the last of their seven films together, for never again would they be treated as equals on the celluloid screen. Karloff would continue on his upward path, whilst Lugosi would see his film career erode. Denis Gifford sums it up perfectly: '*A set-piece finale to a historic double-act: Karloff and Lugosi would ride again but never as equal partners.*'**36**

End Notes

1: As quoted in Bojarski, Richard & Beals, Kenneth 1974. *The Films of Boris Karloff.* Citadel Press. Pg. 115.
2: The Invisible Ray. 1936. Dir. Lambert Hillyer. Universal.
3: The Invisible Ray. 1936. Dir. Lambert Hillyer. Universal.
4: As quoted in Weaver, T, Brunas, M, Brunas, J Eds. 1990 *Universal Horrors: The Studio's Classic Films 1931 – 1946.* McFarland & Company, Inc., Publishers. Pg. 155/156.
5: The Invisible Ray. 1936. Dir. Lambert Hillyer. Universal.
6: As quoted in Mank, G.W. *Bela Lugosi and Boris Karloff: The Expanded Story of a Haunted Collaboration, with a Complete Filmography of their Films Together* McFarland & Company, Inc., Publishers. Revised Edition. Pg. 299.
7: As quoted in Mank, G.W. *Bela Lugosi and Boris Karloff: The Expanded Story of a Haunted Collaboration, with a Complete Filmography of their Films Together* McFarland & Company, Inc., Publishers. Revised Edition. Pg. 299.
8: Clarens, Carlos. 1967. *Horror Movies: An Illustrated Survey.* London: Secker & Warburg Revised edition 1968. Pg. 96.
9: Lennig, Arthur 2003. *The Immortal Count: The Life and Films of Bela Lugosi.* The University Press of Kentucky. Pg. 241.
10: As quoted in Mank, G.W. *Bela Lugosi and Boris Karloff: The Expanded Story of a Haunted Collaboration, with a Complete Filmography of their Films Together* McFarland & Company, Inc., Publishers. Revised Edition. Pg. 300.
11: Rhodes, G.D., & Sheffield, R. 2007. *Bela Lugosi: Dreams and Nightmares.* Collectables® records Corp. Pg. 147.
12: Lennig, Arthur 2003. *The Immortal Count: The Life and Films of Bela Lugosi.* The University Press of Kentucky Pg. 203.
13: As quoted in Cremer, Robert 1976. *Lugosi: The Man Behind the Cape.* Henry Regnery Company. Pg. 168-169.

14: Rhodes, Gary Don 1997. *Lugosi – His life in Films, on Stage and in the Hearts of Horror Lovers.* McFarland & Company, Inc., Publishers. Pg. 20.
15: As quoted in Mank, G.W. *Bela Lugosi and Boris Karloff: The Expanded Story of a Haunted Collaboration, with a Complete Filmography of their Films Together* McFarland & Company, Inc., Publishers. Revised Edition. Pg. 276.
16: As quoted in Mank, G.W. *Bela Lugosi and Boris Karloff: The Expanded Story of a Haunted Collaboration, with a Complete Filmography of their Films Together* McFarland & Company, Inc., Publishers. Revised Edition. Pg. 282.
17: As quoted in Mank, G.W. *Bela Lugosi and Boris Karloff: The Expanded Story of a Haunted Collaboration, with a Complete Filmography of their Films Together* McFarland & Company, Inc., Publishers. Revised Edition. Pg. 282.
18: The Invisible Ray. 1936. Dir. Lambert Hillyer. Universal.
19: Mank, G.W. *Bela Lugosi and Boris Karloff: The Expanded Story of a Haunted Collaboration, with a Complete Filmography of their Films Together* McFarland & Company, Inc., Publishers. Revised Edition. Pg. 290.
20: Weaver,T, Brunas, M, Irunas, J Eds. 1990 *Universal Horrors: The Studio's Classic Films 1931 – 1946.* McFarland & Company, Inc., Publishers. Pg. 153.
21: The Invisible Ray. 1936. Dir. Lambert Hillyer. Universal.
22: The Invisible Ray. 1936. Dir. Lambert Hillyer. Universal.
23: Benshoff, Harry M. 1997.*Monsters in the Closet: Homosexuality and the Horror Film.* Manchester University Press. Pg. 90.
24: Benshoff, Harry M. 1997.*Monsters in the Closet: Homosexuality and the Horror Film.* Manchester University Press. Pg. 61
25: Frayling, C. 2005. *Mad, Bad and Dangerous? The Scientist and the Cinema.* Reaktion Books Ltd. Pg. 169.
26: The Invisible Ray. 1936. Dir. Lambert Hillyer. Universal.

27: Mank, G.W. *Bela Lugosi and Boris Karloff: The Expanded Story of a Haunted Collaboration, with a Complete Filmography of their Films Together* McFarland & Company, Inc., Publishers. Revised Edition. Pg. 296.
28: The Invisible Ray. 1936. Dir. Lambert Hillyer. Universal.
29: The Invisible Ray. 1936. Dir. Lambert Hillyer. Universal.
30: Mank, G.W. *Bela Lugosi and Boris Karloff: The Expanded Story of a Haunted Collaboration, with a Complete Filmography of their Films Together* McFarland & Company, Inc., Publishers. Revised Edition. Pg. 273.
31: Benshoff, Harry M. 1997. *Monsters in the Closet: Homosexuality and the Horror Film.* Manchester University Press. Pg. 90.
32: The Invisible Ray. 1936. Dir. Lambert Hillyer. Universal.
33: Mank, G.W. *Bela Lugosi and Boris Karloff: The Expanded Story of a Haunted Collaboration, with a Complete Filmography of their Films Together* McFarland & Company, Inc., Publishers. Revised Edition. Pg. 295.
34: The Invisible Ray. 1936. Dir. Lambert Hillyer. Universal.
35: The *Observer* Newspaper, *Films of the Week: Suburbs and Provincial.* July 12th 1936.
36: Gifford, D. 1973 *A Pictorial History of Horror Movies.* Hamlyn Publishing Group Ltd, London, Pg. 117.
37: The *Washington Post,* September 11th 1935. Pg. 9.
38: The *Los Angeles Times,* September 30th 1935. Pg. 8.
39: The *Los Angeles Times*, September 30th 1935. Pg. 8.
40: The *Chicago Defender* (National Edition), November 9th 1935. *The Pacific Coast Stage and Actors.* Pg. 8.
41: Scheuer, K.P. *A Town Called Hollywood: Karloff Made Luminous.* The *Los Angeles Times.* October 27th 1935. Pg. A3.
42: The *Hartford Courant. The Invisible Ray with Boris Karloff at Loew's* Theater. May 16th 1936. Pg. 20.
43: The *Hartford Courant. The Invisible Ray with Boris Karloff at Loew's* Theater. May 16th 1936. Pg. 20.

44: *New York Times. At The Roxy.* January 11th 1936. Pg. 9.

45: *New York Times. At The Roxy.* January 11th 1936. Pg. 9.

Other Sources

Schroeder, M. *Changing Social Attitudes in the United States: Increasing Acceptance of Homosexuals.* UW-L Journal of Undergraduate Research VII (2004).
http://www.uwlax.edu/urc/jur-online/PDF/2004/schroeder.pdf

Queer Heritage: A Timeline 1930s.
http://www.aaronsgayinfo.com/timeline/time30.html

The Site of Movie Magazines
http://www.moviemags.com/main.php?title=PHOTON&etos=%

The *Manchester Guardian,* July 31st 1954. *Played "De Lawd" in "Green Pastures."* Daniel Haynes obituary. Pg. 5.

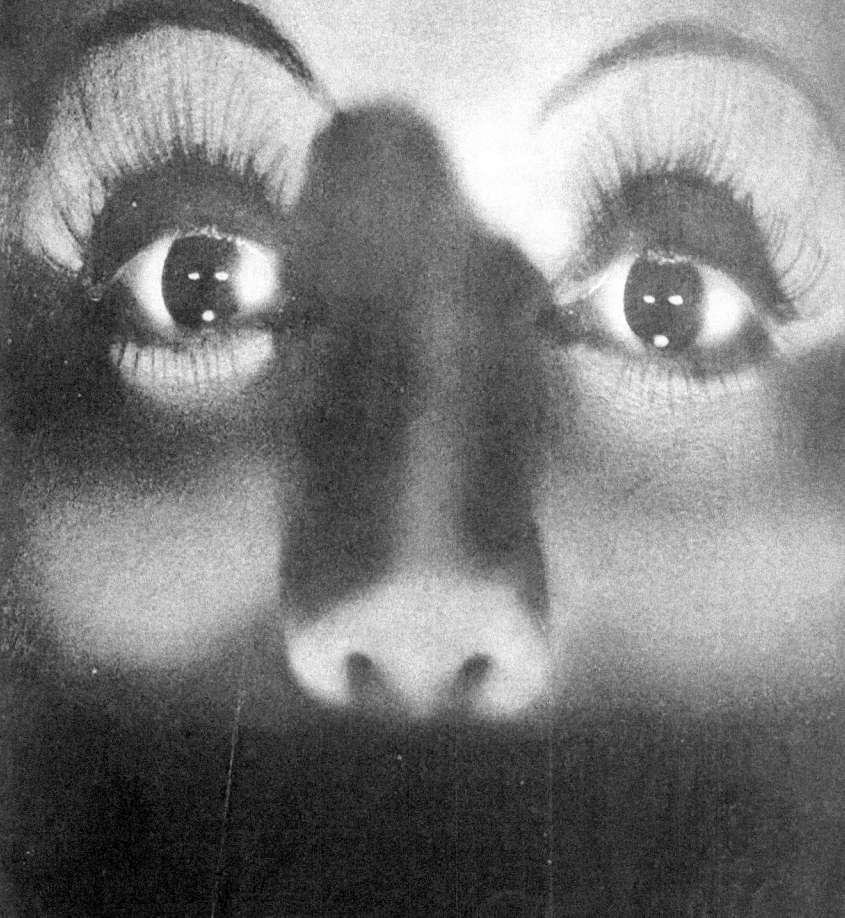

There are Bats in her Belfry, a monster in a closet and the Death of Universal: Dracula's Daughter: Re-Examining a Horror Classic

"Horror destined to end all horror pictures"**1** proclaimed *Photoplay* in July 1936. For Universal under the Laemmles', never a truer word was said. Not only did *Dracula's Daughter* end the first wave of horror films, it also saw the end of the Laemmles' at Universal. Four days after shooting was completed, on March 14th they lost their studio[16]. "After I won my Academy Award for

---

16. The Laemmles were always risk-takers and on more than one occasion their films had brought in enough revenue to stave off financial ruination. As Brunas, Brunas and Weaver point out: "(The Accounting Department's report for the nine months ending October 31st 1932, showed a net loss of $759, 646, a figure greater than the profit for the whole year of 1931.) [Pg.2] the ailing studio limped on, but on November 1st 1935, Laemmle Snr. Was forced into entering into a deal with J. Cheever Cowdin's Standard Capital Corporation and tycoon Charles R. Rogers to secure funds of $750,000 to keep the studio running. There was a clause in the contract: the two businessmen stipulated that they would have the option to buy the studio for $5.5 million within three months if Laemmle failed to repay the loan. Laemmle, confident that he could repay the loan and save the studio he founded, on the returns of a new slate of pictures agreed to the terms: "Its financing deal with Standard Capital and a financial group represented by Charles R. Rogers now set, Universal will immediately fix budgets on the next batch of important pictures on its schedule and start active productions."[*Motion Picture Daily,* Monday November 4th 1935]. It was a fatal mistake for Laemmle. Cowdin and Rogers amassed enough capital to buy 90 per cent of Universal stock. Laemmle not believing that they could raise that sort of capital within the designated time frame, lost his studio when the group foreclosed on their deal and took control of the studio.

'*All Quiet on the Western Front*' we went onto success with the Monster films *Dracula, Frankenstein* and *The Mummy*. I wanted to make sequels to all of them. I wanted James Whale[17] to direct them both and in 1933 we announced *The Return of Frankenstein* and *Dracula's Daughter*..."**2** reminisced Carl Laemmle Jr.[18] in 1971.

The 1933/34 *Universal Exhibitors* book has a poster for the film clearly stating that Laemmle Jr. was going to produce and Whale to direct, yet by the time the film eventually went into production neither was to be involved. *Dracula's Daughter* was meant to have helped save Universal, but the film appeared cursed from the beginning. By the time filming began on February 4th 1936, it had already cost the studio $20,000 for treatments and screenplays that were not used, $17,500 for a director who did not shoot a single frame and $4,000 to Bela Lugosi who was originally going to star in the film, but did not[19]. In fact, *The Fitchburg Sentinel* announced on January 18th

---

17. Author Ramsey Campbell in his introduction to the novelisation of *Dracula's Daughter* by E K Leyton (A Star Book published by W H Allen & Co Ltd. 1980), claims that Robert Florey was originally scheduled to direct (rather than Whale). I can find no evidence to support this.
18. Carl Laemmle Jr. American Film Producer and Studio Executive. April 28th 1908 – September 24th 1979.
19. Rhodes in Lugosi pg. 219 states "some reference works claim Lugosi was paid as much as $4,000 for his trouble even though he didn't appear in the film. This, however, seems unusual, given a one page letter agreement between the actor and Universal Studios dated February 20th 1936. In it, Lugosi allowed Universal to use his likeness for the wax bust, 'without compensation.'" In a private email to me Dr. Rhodes states: "There is no doubt that Lugosi was paid $4,000. Not only is this present on the budget, but also on a contract that exists. The latter contract became pivotal in the long running Lugosi v. Universal lawsuit, and as a result the payment to Lugosi has paved the way for all manner of subsequent actions on behalf of heirs against studios who were selling t-shirts or etc. of the old stars like The Three Stooges. In addition to surviving Universal paperwork, all of this became evidentiary in the Lugosi lawsuit, acknowledged in the court records."

1936 that, "Dracula's Daughter has been withdrawn from production at present... Bela Lugosi is without a role but the studio hopes to get one (for him) soon."3 The film had an original budget of $230,425 but by the time it was completed its costs had risen to $278,000, making it one of the most expensive horror films of its time. For her role as the Countess Marya Zaleska, Gloria Holden would receive $300 per week, totalling $1450 for four weeks and five days' work. Edward Van Sloan received $600 per week for reprising his role of Van Helsing, totalling $2400. Marguerite Churchill, $250 per week totalling $1125. Irving Pichel received a flat fee of $2950. Nan Gray[20] received $100 per week for two weeks work, totalling $200. The biggest earner was Otto Kruger, who received a whopping $2,500 per week, totalling $9583.30. Sherriff's fees as set out in the film's budget report: London payments $10, 932.62, studio payroll $4756.00 and transportation $961.95 totalling $16,650.57. Another writer who was brought on board, Finlay Peter Dunne, was paid $2350.00 for his services and Sutherland received $17,500 for 'retained time.' Director Lambert Hillyer, fresh from directing Karloff and Lugosi in *The Invisible Ray* for Universal received a salary of $5,400 and Garrett Ford, who was brought in to write the script (thus receiving sole credit) received $6,375. Universal also paid $5000 for the story and E. M. Asher received $3500 for 'idle time' that he had done whilst waiting for the project to go ahead.

II

The origin of *Dracula's Daughter* was a short story by Bram Stoker, published posthumously in 1914. It appeared in his third collection of short fiction under the title of 'Dracula's Guest.' The story itself is the much disputed and widely discussed edited early chapter from Stoker's 1897 novel, *Dracula*. It appeared in two American periodicals – *Short Stories* and *Weird Tales* in 1917 and 1927, respectively. The latter appearance in December 1927 coincided with Lugosi's triumph on Broadway with the play *Dracula*. It could be speculated that a young David O. Selznick may have come across the story at

---

20. Nan Gray, American Actress. July 25th 1918 – July 25th 1993. (Aged 75).

this point. The story itself has little to nothing to do with the final product and indeed, the only similarity could be Balderston's surviving treatment.

In 1933, producer David O. Selznick[21] having seen the success of the Universal horror cycle, arranged with Bram Stoker's[22] widow, Florence[23], to buy the rights to 'Dracula's Guest,' offering her a $500 advance against a purchase price of $5,000 for the film rights. Cleverly, Selznick placed two clauses in the contract, the first being that he had the rights to resell the rights if he so wished and the second was the approval to use the alternate title, *Dracula's Daughter*. He then hired Universal's screenwriter John L. Balderston[24] to write a screenplay treatment.

Balderston[25] had already written screenplays for *Dracula* and *The Mummy* and the composition for *Frankenstein*. Selznick tried to get MGM to produce it, but the studio was wary about the possibility of infringing Universal's copyright on both the character and name '*Dracula*.' Using the code name

---

21. David O. Selznick. American Film Producer & Studio Executive. May 10th 1902 – June 22nd 1965. (Aged 63, heart attack).
22. Abraham 'Bram' Stoker. Irish Author. November 8th 1847 – April 25th 1912. (Aged 64).
23. Florence Stoker. (Balcombe) Stoker's Literary Executor / Widow. July 17th 1858 – May 25th 1937. (Aged 78).
24. In their novel *Dracula: The Undead* (Harper, 2009, Pg. 408) Darce Stoker and Ian Holt state incorrectly: "The problems truly began when Hollywood wanted to make a sequel to that film based on 'Dracula's Guest.' The story goes that Florence Stoker would not sell the rights unless she was guaranteed more input in the creative process. It was in the midst of these negotiations that Bram's copyright was declared void by the U.S. Copyright Office. This left Hollywood free to develop the sequel they wished. With Florence demanding more control and Bela Lugosi demanding a large pay increase to reprise the role of Dracula, the decision was made to hire John Balderston to write *Dracula's Daughter*, thereby cutting Bela and Florence out of the process completely."
25. John L. Balderton American playwright & Screen writer. October 22nd 1889 – March 8th 1954. (Aged 64, heart attack).

'*Tarantula*' for their discussions, cables and letters went back and forth from studio heads and their lawyers. Eventually it was decided not to proceed with the production and face years of possible litigation, so Selznick went into negotiation with Universal, cleverly demanding and receiving a time statute, meaning that if Universal failed to produce the film by a certain date, the rights would revert back to him. In January 1934 Balderston delivered a twenty page treatment to Universal, accompanied by a strict critique as he felt that his previous horror assignments for them had 'dropped badly' in their last two thirds (particularly *Dracula* (1931) and *The Mummy* (1932)) due to scheduling and financial. Disgruntled, he gave instructions as to how he envisioned *Dracula's Daughter*:

> "Why should Cecil B. DeMille have a monopoly on the great box office values of torture and cruelty in pictures about ancient Rome, etc.? I want, especially in Part Two, to establish the fact that Dracula's Daughter enjoys torturing her male victims… and that these men under her spell rather like it. [ ] I want to see her (Dracula's Daughter's) loathsome deaf mute servants carry into her boudoir savage-looking whips, chains, straps, etc., and hear the cries of the tortured victims without seeing exactly what happens… I feel sure that so long as it is a woman torturing men, the thing is not too unendurable as it would have been had the man Dracula so treated his female victims. [ ] …we must rack the nerves of our audiences more than in previous horror films."4

The treatment as set out in Philip J. Riley's[26] book *James Whale's Dracula's Daughter* is in three parts, starting with the last scene in *Dracula* with the Count being staked in Carfax Abby. Van Helsing and company then discuss going to Transylvania to end the lives of Dracula's brides. The next scene is in a Transylvanian village where a grief-stricken mother is screaming that someone has stolen her baby and a young wife complains that her young husband has disappeared. Van Helsing and Dr. Seward emerge and promise

---

26. Philip J. Riley. American Author and Film Historian. January 21st 1948 - .

to end the horrors for them. At the castle, three women take form from a mist and a fourth enters and tosses them a bag which squirms as though there is something alive within. The three women whisper that they want love "as well as drink – love, give us love – you keep that for yourself, men, young men..."**5** The woman is furious and lashes out with a whip, stating that they are Dracula's wives and should be loyal to him, whilst she is his daughter. The three women descend upon the squirming bag, leaving the audience to assume as to what the bag contains. The scene changes to a small room in the castle, where a young man is desperately trying to escape. The door opens and Dracula's daughter enters. Upon seeing her, the young man becomes enthralled. She weakens his resolve to escape by whipping him. He crawls on his knees towards her, begging not to be drained of blood and as she swoops in towards his neck she murmurs 'blood is the life!'**6** The scene then dissolves into Van Helsing and Seward entering the castle and staking the three vampire brides. They find the body of the young man, but they do not discover the body of Dracula's daughter. They leave believing that they have killed all of the vampires.

The middle section is set in London. Countess Szekeley is the talk of London society with her late night parties and coterie of young men. At a dance floor in a hotel we meet Lord Edward (Ned) Wadhurst and his fiancée Helen Swaythling, and they are introduced to the Countess. Ned becomes strangely fascinated by her and she ends up seducing him. Later at Seward's, after examining the corpses of two young men who have bite marks upon their necks and were known lovers of the Countess, Seward realises that she is a vampire and sends for Van Helsing. Upon his arrival Van Helsing is attacked but not hurt by an escaped wolf. Chester Morris also arrives and he is furious with Ned because of the way that he is treating Helen, whom he is also in love with. Morris confirms that the Countess has closed her London home and disappeared.

In a scene reminiscent to one in *Dracula*, Ned admits to Helen that the Countess is a devil and has made him unclean and so unworthy of her and her love. There follows across the next few scenes his 'battle' with his 'vampiric desires' and his 'humanity.' Realising that time is short if he wants to live, Ned agrees to help the group find the vampire. Under her influence, Ned goes to the Countess, where she admits that she loves him and gives him the 'final' kiss. Van Helsing, Seward and Morris arrive in time to see the Countess vanish and Ned, realising what he has done, faints. Later, Van Helsing informs a repentant Ned that not only is he turning into a vampire, his soul is becoming one with that of the Countess. Under hypnosis Ned reveals that the Countess has fled back to her castle in Transylvania. They realise that they must follow her and destroy her before Ned becomes a vampire.

The final section is set in Transylvania, where we find the group at the inn. Ned is nearly a vampire and hypnosis no longer works, the locals steer clear of them and Van Helsing announces that they must search by night. So the group camps out near Castle Dracula. Van Helsing draws a protective circle around their camp using the sacred wafer. Later that night, Van Helsing handcuffs Ned to him, so as he cannot be drawn out of the circle. Three bats fly out from the castle towards the group and a large grey wolf circles the camp, making the horses whine and fretful. Morris, moving forward to shoot the creature, accidentally steps over the protective circle and is killed. Next night it snows, so Van Helsing quietly unlocks the handcuffs, and under the Countess' influence, Ned goes to her, only to return the following morning as though nothing had happened. Van Helsing is joyous as they can follow the footprints that are in the snow that Ned left during his night-time excursion. The footprints lead them to a hidden entrance. Inside they find a single coffin. Opening it, they see the Countess asleep and Van Helsing instructs Ned that he must drive the stake into her heart to redeem himself: "At the last moment the vampire's eyes open, Ned gathers all his strength and pounds the stake into her heart."**7** The scar on his forehead disappears with her passing and the group celebrate their victory.

This is the basic summary of Balderston's treatment dated January 1934. There is a problem with this, as we do not know if there is an earlier draft.

If this was the original that was written for David O. Selznick, then it not only violates Universal's copyright as it owes more to the novel *Dracula* rather than 'Dracula's Guest' and would have theoretically had both studios (M.G.M. and Universal) tied up in copyright litigation for years. It also violates the terms of agreement with Florence Stoker in that it would "employ no character or incidents from any other work by Stoker besides 'Dracula's Guest.'**8** The fact is, if this were optioned by M.G.M., it would never have been made. In the notes for this treatment, Balderston makes it clear that this is a direct sequel to *Dracula*: 'The plot and action follow naturally and plausibly from the close of the film 'Dracula', where the male vampire was destroyed in the cellar of an English suburban house."**9** Again if this was the treatment written for Laemmle Jr. then it is apparent that Lugosi was not considered at that point for any role in the film as there is no Count. This in itself contradicts reports in both *The Hollywood Reporter*, July 28th 1934 **10**, which announced that Universal had purchased the story *Dracula's Daughter* by John L. Balderston and would again star Lugosi; and a report in *Film Daily* for August 18th 1934 which states: 'With the winding up of *"The Return of Chandu"* for Principal Pictures, Bela Lugosi returns to Universal to play the lead in *"Dracula's Daughter."*'**11**

Things appeared to be quiet with the film for well over a year. *The Daily Film* **12** announced on Friday June 7th 1935 that Laemmle Jr., would produce *Dracula's Daughter*, with R.C. Sherriff[27] writing the screenplay and that James Whale[28] would direct. This echoed a report prior to that from *The Hollywood Reporter* 28th May 1935: "Laemmle, Jr., has picked his horror pic of '35-'36: *Dracula's Daughter*, a story John Balderston wrote for U. last year. Manuscript has been shipped to R. C. Sherriff in London, who will write a screen treatment. Lugosi will play Dracula."**13** The decision to include Lugosi

---

27. R. C. Sherriff: British playwright and screenwriter. June 6th 1896 – November 13th 1975. (Aged 79).
28. James Whale. British film director. July 22nd 1889 – May 29th 1957. (Aged 67, suicide).

again may have come from a letter in *The New Movie Magazine*, March 1935, where Adriana Leynaar wrote, "After having recently seen Bela Lugosi give a very fine performance in 'The Black Cat' I wonder why it is that we are not allowed more opportunities of seeing this actor. Why is it that the studios give one star too many pictures until movie-going public gets fed-up with seeing him or her, and allow another actor who could be just as successful, if not better, to fade away into obscurity by giving them nothing but a mediocre role now and then. Don't the studios believe that variety is the spice of life? I believe that many other people besides myself would enjoy seeing more of Bela Lugosi. He is the type of actor who helps make just an ordinary picture good because of his presence in it and a good picture excellent."**14** It is theoretically possible that this letter, coupled with the success of *The Black Cat*, and the runaway success of *The Bride of Frankenstein* may have contributed to Lugosi being attached again to the project. The studio would have realised the importance of having the principal players back, after witnessing the success of *The Bride of Frankenstein* (1935), which had Colin Clive and Boris Karloff reprise their respective roles of Henry Frankenstein and his creation. Further to this The *Los Angeles Times* for March 19th 1935 reported: "Carl Laemmle, Jr. has decided soon to produce Dracula's Daughter with a cast composed of Lugosi, Boris Karloff, Claude Rains and Colin Clive, and he feels he will be able to secure those players, famous in one respect or another from their horror impersonations ... It was because of the results attained in Bride of Frankenstein, which is now completed, that Laemmle decided to produce the new thriller film.[29]"**15**

---

29. Bela Lugosi, Hungarian / American Actor. October 20th 1882- August 16th 1956 (Aged 73, heart attack) starred as Count Dracula in *Dracula* (1931).
Colin Clive, British Actor. January 20th 1900 – June 25th 1937. (Aged 37, bronchial pneumonia / tuberculosis), starred as Doctor Henry Frankenstein in *Frankenstein* (1931).
Boris Karloff, British Actor. November 23rd 1887 – February 2nd 1969 (Aged 81, pneumonia) starred as The Frankenstein Monster in *Frankenstein* 1931.
Claude Rains, British Actor. November 10th 1889 – May 30th 1967 (Aged 77, abdominal haemorrhage) starred as Doctor Jack Griffin/The Invisible Man

Over the next few months there would be a mass of contradictory reporting over the film and those involved. The *Motion Picture Herald*[16] announced on 8th June 1935 that Lugosi would star in *Dracula's Daughter* and *Motion Picture Daily* for Wednesday August 28th that: "Bela Lugosi arrived on the Majestic yesterday after spending six weeks in London where he appeared in *'The Mystery of Mary Celeste'* for C.M. Woolfe[30], who recently formed General Distributors Ltd. He said Woolfe had offered him a contract for another three pictures, but signing of a deal depends on whether he can sandwich in the time between Universal pictures. Lugosi stated he will leave for Hollywood Sept.2 to begin work on *'The Invisible Ray,'* following which he will appear in *'Dracula's Daughter.'*" [17] What is clear up to this point is that Lugosi was led to believe, and indeed believed, that he was to star in the film[31]. Slightly contradicting this *The Hollywood Reporter* on August 29th 1935 noted that 'Lugosi was 'about to start *The Invisible Ray* for Universal' and that "they might option him for two more films: 'probably' *Dracula's Daughter* and 'maybe' *Blue Beard*."[18] Another contradiction came in late Autumn with *Motion Picture Daily* stating on September 27th that "R. C. Sherriff and Paul Robeson[32], both under contract to Universal, arrived here yesterday on the Empress of Britain. Sherriff will confer with Carl Laemmle, Jr. on the story called *'Dracula's Daughter!*'"[19] *Variety* for October 2nd states that "R.C. Sherriff arrived yesterday (mon) from London, reporting to Universal with completed screenplay of *'Dracula's Daughter,'* which Carl

---

in *The Invisible Man* (1933). All films were Universal productions under the Laemmles.

30. C M (Charles Moss) Woolfe. British Film Producer/Distributor. July 10th 1879 – December 31st 1942, aged 63. Credited with bringing film producer J.Arthur Rank into the film industry.

31. Robert Cremer in his biography of Lugosi also points out that *Dracula's Daughter* and "The Suicide Club," both to co-star Karloff were still in various stages of re-write and pre-production at the end of 1934" (Pg.158). Therefore it is clear that Lugosi was waiting for over a year to reprise his famous role.

32. Paul (Leroy) Robeson. American Actor, Singer, Social Activist, Lawyer. April 9th 1898 – January 23rd 1973 (Aged 77).

Laemmle, Jr. is slated to produce. Writer, under contract to U. for the past three years had provision in his contract allowing him to work on scripts in London."**20** On October 9th, *Variety* noted "Loan out deal on Bela Lugosi requires an early starting date for *'Dracula's Daughter.'* Under present plans the heavy budgeted pic will be washed up around Feb. 1."**21** With a script in disarray, shooting schedules here there and everywhere, *Variety* gloatingly reported on November 13th, "Howard Spurns *'Dracula.'* [ ]Carl Laemmle, Jr. and William K. Howard[33]couldn't get together after several weeks of dickering to have Howard direct *'Dracula's Daughter'* at Universal. Deal chilled on terms."**22** Finally, *Variety,* 20th November 1935 noted that Eddie Sutherland was to direct, having been transferred from *'Song of Joy'*[34] after "trouble between him and Paul Kohner[35], producer, regarding treatment of Marta Eggerth[36] story by Preston Sturges[37]."**23** with Lugosi to star; and that Universal slated *Dracula's Daughter* to go into production by December 1st due to a clause in the story's purchase, having already been given a two month extension. Realising that for Balderston's treatment to go into full production as a direct follow-on, Universal would not only need Edward Van Sloan[38] to be available (he was), they would also need Herbert Bunston[39] (*Dr Seward*),

---

33. William K, Howard. American Film Director, Writer, Producer. June 16th 1899 – February 21st 1954. (Aged 54, throat malignancy).
34. "Song of Joy" was to have been Marta Eggerth first film for Universal.
35. Paul Kohner. Producer. May 29th 1902 – March 16th 1988. Married to Lupita Tovar (July 27th 1910 - 2016) from 1932 – 1988. Tovar is best remembered for her role in the Spanish speaking version of *Dracula* that was filmed simultaneously as the Browning / Lugosi version.
36. Marta Eggerth. Hungarian born Singer / Actress. April 17th 1912 – December 26th 2013. (Aged 101).
37. Preston Struges. American Playwright, Screen Writer and Film director. August 29th 1898 – August 6th 1959. (Aged 60, heart attack).
38. Edward Van Sloan, American Actor. November 1st 1882 – March 6th 1964. (Aged 81).
39. Herbert Bunston, British Actor. April 15th 1874 – February 27th 1935. (Aged 60, heart attack).

Helen Chandler[40] (*Mina Seward/Harker*) and David Manners[41] (*Jonathan Harker*). Chandler was, according to Skal: "By the mid-1930s she was unemployable in films..."**24** possibly due to her alcoholism and addiction to sleeping tablets. In fact between 1935 and 1938 she made just two films (*It's a Bet* [1935] and *Mr. Boggs Steps Out* [1938] was to be her last celluloid appearance) and by 1945 was just a footnote in *Film Daily* 'Send birthday Greetings to'. In 1935,Manners retired from film making to concentrate on his writing, his last three films (*Lucky Fugitives, Hearts in Bondage* and *A Woman Rebels*) coming out in 1936, and Herbert Bunston would die at the end of February after completing *Clive of India* for 20th Century- Fox. Realising that there could be possible problems with the script, Laemmle Jr. sent in Sherriff's draft script and Balderston's treatment to the Breen Office on September 5th, for an 'off the record' response. Breen's response on September 13th stated, "This story contains countless offensive stuff which makes the picture utterly impossible for approval under the production code."**25**

Following this, Sherriff handed in a toned-down script on October 21st of which The Breen Office stated: "dangerous material from the standpoint of political censorship [ ] There still remains in the script a flavour suggestive of a combination of sex and horror." And went on to say, " ...in the early part of the script, where Dracula's soldiers sweep the countryside and bring to his castle a group of young women, with a sprinkling of men, that you affirmatively indicate that the purpose for which the young girls have been abducted is to provide dancing partners for the Count's assembled guests at the banquet ...[ ] We ask that you eliminate the shot of Dracula in his chamber 'crushing the limp figure of a girl in his arms' – this to get away from the definite sexual connotation. Maybe the scene could show the girls dancing."**26**

---

40. Helen Chandler, American Actress. February 6th 1906 – April 30th 1965. (Aged 59).
41. David Manners, Canadian / American Actor and Novelist. April 30th 1900 – December 23rd 1998. (Aged 98).

According to Riley, Whale was desperate to get out of filming *Dracula's Daughter* as he wanted to make *Showboat*. He secretly submitted Sherriff's first draft script to the Breen Office, on October 25th 1935, which was rejected conclusively. The problem seemed to be with the opening prologue sequence which would have starred Lugosi: Set in the Middle Ages, Dracula is a cruel nobleman, who sends out his troops to procure young virgin girls for the entertainment of his guests. At one of his parties, the guest who throws the highest number on a dice gets first option on the girls, but Dracula makes it very clear that all the noblemen will 'taste all the fruit' and to be gentle with them. Egged on he chooses one, who is sent to his chambers. Unknown to Dracula, the villagers are in uproar and a traveller listening to their commotion promises to help and contacts a wizard/warlock, who then goes to the castle. Upon seeing the debauchery going on he turns Dracula's guests into swine and then, turning to Dracula, places the curse of being a vampire upon him. As the castle crumbles around him, Dracula goes to his chambers and upon seeing the young girl that he had chosen goes to her and turns her into a vampire.

The Breen Office was incensed. Kidnapping, the insinuation of multiple rapes and black magic – it was all too much, and they made it clear that the film would never see the light of day. A further script by Sherriff, submitted in November, again proved too much and was rejected and Whale left the project. As Laemmle Jr. remembered in 1971: "James finally gave in on *The Return of Frankenstein* which after all the scripts turned in he changed the name to *Bride of Frankenstein* and as far as I was concerned we were going to start the *Dracula* sequel immediately after the *Frankenstein* picture. Jimmy wouldn't do it. He stalled, made outrageous demands and almost ruined our friendship. So I gave in and let him do his romances and *Showboat*."**27**

Motion Picture Daily[28] for Friday December 6th stated that '*Dracula's Daughter* got under way at Universal Dec. 2,' yet on December 24th *The*

Hollywood Reporter29 noted that Laemmle Jr. had relinquished supervision of *Dracula's Daughter* to E.M. Asher[42] and then announced on 26th December that 'there was a strong possibility that A. Edward Sutherland[43] was about to become Universal's first producer / director – the assignment being Dracula's Daughter.'**30** Two days later on December 28th they announced that Universal had discarded the idea of Sutherland producing and directing the film and that E.M. Asher was back to supervise. Universal were still, at this point, looking to casting the lead role. Gary Rhodes states that Tamara Drasin[44] was twice auditioned for the role and that by December 27th she was 'practically set' for a contract.**31** On December 4th *Variety***32** announced that she was being tested by Universal and we can suppose that it was for this role, but that had changed three days later when The *New York Evening Post*, December 30th 1935 announced: "Jane Wyatt[45] will be *Dracula's Daughter* with Bela Lugosi in his original role as the vampire gentleman, Count Dracula. Eddie Sutherland's assigned to direct. Miss Wyatt is going to do *'Reno in the Fall'* for Universal, too, and probably *'Strangers at the Feast.'*"**33** *Film Daily* on Tuesday January 7th 1936 contradicted this, saying: "Edward Sutherland, who directed 'Diamond Jim,' for Universal has bowed out of the direction of *'Dracula's Daughter,'* and is expected to announce a new affiliation shortly."**34** Yet on January 6th *The Hollywood Reporter* amended its early

---

42. E.M. [Ephriam Milton] Asher. American Film Producer. September 1st 1887 – October 29th 1937. (Aged 50, stroke).
43. A. Edward Sutherland, British Film Director. January 5th 1895 – December 31st 1973. (Aged 78).
44. Tamara Drasin (Swann) Ukrainian born American Actress. Born (Various dates are 1905, 1907 and 1910) – February 22nd 1943 in USO plane crash, aged 32 (According to The Billboard March 11th 1943, pg.27) Famous for performing the song 'Smoke gets in Your Eyes' in 1933. Her death was overshadowed by the death in the same crash of Arthur A. Lee, prominent distribution executive and former head of Gaumont British in the United States and the rescuing of seriously injured radio and stage singer Jane Froman, who had swapped seats with Tamara.
45. Jane Wyatt, American Actress. August 12th 1910 – October 20th 2006. (Aged 96).

report of December 28th, saying that "Sutherland 'asked to be relieved' of the project"**35** and gave the start date as January 25th. By January 4th 1936 Jane Wyatt was off the project as The *Los Angeles Examiner* reported that "Zita Johann[46] is being tested now for the lead in *Dracula's Daughter* at Universal City."**36** On January 8th, *Variety* not only announced that Universal had dropped 30 films in production slow-up, it went on to say, "However, there's doubt whether *'Dracula's Daughter'* will be produced at this time, in view of the fact that Edward A. Sutherland on Saturday (4) pulled out of the directorial spot. David O. Selznick released yarn to Universal with understanding that film would be made by certain date, but final extension ends Jan 25. Carl Laemmle, Jr. recently turned over production supervision to E. M. Asher."**37** Zita Johann was no longer associated with the project when on January 28th, *The Hollywood Reporter* announced that "Broadway actress Gloria Holden[47] has signed a term contract with U. and will star in *Dracula's Daughter*."**38**

On January 14th, E.M. Asher informed the Breen Office that it had completely scrapped the Sherriff scripts and was starting afresh and on January 15th *Variety* announced: *'Dracula's Dotter'* on Universal Sked Again. Universal

---

46. Zita Johann 1904-1993 played Helen Grosvenor/Princess Ankh-es-en-Amon in Universal's 1932 classic *The Mummy* opposite Boris Karloff.
47. Gloria Holden, British Actress. September 5th 1903 – March 22nd 1991. According to http://allanellenberger.com/gloria-holdens-birthday/ there is a discrepancy in Holden's actual age and birth year: There is an obvious discrepancy when it comes to Holden's year of birth. At the time of her death in 1991, obituaries gave her age as 73 and her year of birth as 1917 — which is the date on her grave marker. Recently that was amended to 1908 and is given as such on the Internet Movie Data Base and other sources. However, according to the census report of 1930, Gloria Holden's age is listed as 26 which means she was actually born in 1903 (the census was taken in April). She also had a son Marvin who was seven years old at the time so the 1917 date could not be possible since it's doubtful she gave birth to him at the age of seven. This information is also confirmed by the 1920 census when her family was living in Radnor, Pennsylvania and she was 16 years old, which would also validate the 1903 year of birth. When she died in 1991, Gloria Holden was in fact 87 years old and not 73.

has decided to make *'Dracula's Daughter'* after many script delays. New play is being prepared on formula of *'Invisible Ray'* under Lambert Hillyer's direction. Similar scientific approach to horror and thrill elements is being incorporated, eliminating the purely supernatural."**39**

Possibly fed up with waiting for the film to go into production, Lugosi signed up on 17th January to star alongside Phillips Holmes and Mae Clarke in Republic's *The House of a Thousand Candles. Film Daily***40** announced that he was still involved on January 22nd, but that all changed on January 25th, when it was announced that' "Fighting a bad cold throughout the first week of production, Bela Lugosi was finally forced to withdraw from the Republic feature, *"The House of a Thousand Candles,"* when complications set in. Irving Pichel has been signed to replace him."**41** As to what these 'complications' were, we can speculate. Lugosi, knowing from reports that *Dracula's Daughter* was due to start shooting on January 25th, may have used his illness as an excuse, hoping to get back on the Universal lot and recreate his most famous role, or as Dello Stritto and Brooks suggest 'an early, unexpected round of attacks from "the lightning pains."'**42** may have caused his exit. Whatever the case may be Lugosi was off the shoot by January 30th as *The Hollywood Reporter* revealed: "Dracula will stay dead in *Dracula's Daughter.* U. thought of flashing in Bela Lugosi in a prelude scene, but recent condemnations of undue horror stuff decided the studio to let him lay."**43** They also announced that they had borrowed Marguerite Churchill[48] from Warner Bros. to replace Jane Wyatt. Cesar Romero[49] was reported set for the male lead and Irving Pichel[50] was to play Sandor, the Countess's slave

---

48. Marguerite Churchill, American Actress. December 25th 1910 – January 9th 2000. (Aged 89).
49. Cesar Romero, American Actor. February 15th 1907 – January 1st 1994. (Aged 86, Bronchitis & Pneumonia).
50. Irving Pichel, American Actor / Director. June 24th 1891 – July 13th 1954. (Aged 63, heart attack).

(Universal had wanted Herbert Marshall[51].) *Variety*[44] for 29th January noted that Karloff had signed a one-year contract with Universal and also mentioned that Lugosi was no longer featuring in *Dracula's Daughter* (with Cesar Romero his replacement), but that he was "off" the Universal lot as well.

The Reporter[45] for 1st February noted that Otto Kruger[52] would be replacing Cesar Romero as he (Romero) was needed for another film[53]. *Film Daily* on February 10th announced that: "Marguerite Churchill has been lent by First National to appear again with Boris Karloff in *'Dracula's Daughter'* for Universal[54]."[46] This is the second time that Karloff's name appears in connection with *Dracula's Daughter*[55]. He had worked with Churchill previously

---

51. Herbert Marshall, British Actor. May 23rd 1890 – January 22nd 1966. (Aged 75).
52. Otto Kruger, American Actor. September 6th 1885 – September 6th 1974. (Aged 89).
53. It is interesting to note that *Variety* for Wednesday February 5th, Calendar of Current Releases (Pg.27) clearly states that Cesar Romero was still scheduled to appear in the film.
54. If this article is correct, this means that Karloff was associated with the production well after Lugosi was dropped and production had begun.
55. William K Everson states "The removal of Karloff from *Dracula's Daughter* was the reason for his appearance in the non-horror but quite interesting *Night Key*." (*More Classics of the Horror Film – 50 Years of Great Chillers*. Citadel Press, 1986, Pg.25). Everson's speculation is incorrect and has nothing to do with Karloff's involvement in *Night Key*. *Night Key*, released on May 2nd 1937, was a double 'first' for Karloff – It was the first time that he had returned to the Universal lot after completing *The Invisible Ray* (shooting from September 17th to October 25th 1935), which was released on January 20th 1936. It was Karloff's last film for Universal under the Laemmle regime. The Laemmle's lost control of the studio that they had founded on March 14th 1936, four days after *Dracula's Daughter* had completed production, to Standard Capital Corporation. It was his first film for 'New Universal' and a departure from his previous Universal productions as it was a thriller. The new owners vetoed any new 'horror' productions after *Dracula's Daughter* until *Son of Frankenstein* in 1939. *Night Key* went into production on January 18th 1937 and was completed

on *The Walking Dead* for Warner Bros. On February 24th, Gloria Holden and producer David Diamond dined with Lugosi in the Universal Studios Commissary, where several publicity shots were taken. It is also plausible that the 'on-set' publicity photographs were taken at that time.

Prior to that meeting, on Wednesday 12th February, *Variety* published a synopsis of the forthcoming film, which not only shows how the story was originally meant to have panned out, but also hints at what Lugosi could have become had he made the right decision over *Frankenstein*: "Story – Sequel to 'Dracula,' produced few years ago by U. with Bela Lugosi, at that time forerunner to cycle of horror pictures. New version depicts the curse of Dracula being carried over into the second generation. The daughter still feeling she has inherited the stigma of the vampire is not satisfied until she has the dead body of her father, cremated to erase all possible heritage. The professor, who in the original play tried to kill Dracula, extends his interest in the daughter and helps her regain respectable position in society and, of course, works up romance that ends with daughter commanding a high position in the world of art by becoming a painter. Sequel in no way contains the horror element that prevailed in the original. Instead it is a battle to wipe out the stigma of the father's depredations."* **47**

Possibly seeing this as yet another Universal rejection and another chance at regaining the stardom that he had once had at the studio may have embittered Lugosi as Paul Harrison noted in *Long Beach News* February 29th 1936 that, *"Dracula is dead and the chief celebrant at the obsequies is Bela Lugosi. Dracula is dead and Lugosi, who created the monster, hopes that all memories of Dracula will die, too. Dracula made Lugosi famous and then in true Frankenstein fashion, ruined him. That actor hopes now that he can go on being just an actor, not a horror-master. With movies' genius for reincarnation, nobody was sure that Dracula had drawn his last evil breath*

---

on March 20th. Karloff's triumphant return to the Universal lot after a fifteen month absence was marred by script complications, studio bureaucracy and Screen Actors Guild rules.

until Universal began filming *Dracula's Daughter*. Lugosi isn't even in it…So Lugosi seems to have shaken off Dracula's ghost."**48**

-III-

The film rushed into production without a working script shows at the beginning with the comedic antics of the two policemen. This opening is meant to set the pace and tone for the rest of the film which it fails to do:

Hawkins: Who is 'e in there?

Van Helsing: His name was Count Dracula.

Hawkins: 'Ow long 'as 'e been dead?

Van Helsing: About five hundred years.

Hawkins: Albert – 'and me them 'and cuffs!

Van Helsing: That won't be necessary, constable.

Hawkins: So you say. One bloke a-welterin' in 'his blood with a steak driven through 'is 'eart. A gentleman lying 'ere with 'is neck broke – by the way, who 'is 'e?

Van Helsing: A poor harmless imbecile who ate spiders and flies…**49**

Perhaps due to not having a completed script at the beginning of production and being written as it was filmed gives the film its disjointed feel. This again comes across in the performances of Otto Kruger and Marguerite Churchill, where they bicker like an old married couple, but that bickering detracts from the main drama. Furthermore, Churchill's character is so underwritten and not fleshed out, that she comes across rather like a petulant child. For example when Garth has gone to Zaleska's apartment for a scheduled appointment, Janet phones the apartment and speaks in a false German accent:

Dr. Garth: Yes? Dr.Garth speaking. Well who is this? What do you want?

Janet Blake: Please come right away. This is the zoo speaking.

Dr. Garth: The what? The zoo?

Janet Blake: Ja! One of our elephants is seeing pink men!

Dr. Garth: All right. Now listen to me, Janet, this has gone far enough! Well, there's nothing funny about it! I'm in the midst of a very serious...

[*Janet hangs up and laughs*]

Dr. Garth: HELLO?

[*hangs up*]**50**

It is a pity that Churchill is used for just childlike comic relief, when in fact she was a talented actress, having won the Wintrop Ames and the Otto H. Khan scholarship at the Guild Dramatic School at aged just 15. She later married the actor George O'Brien, whose first film was directed by Hillyer. Janet's jealousy towards Countess Marya Zaleska seems to be misplaced and she seems not to understand that Garth's interest in her might just be one of professionalism. Yet there is an implication that Garth may have cheated on Janet before, which would explain her behaviour that is not fully explored on any level.

Otto Kruger is an odd choice of leading man for at fifty-one he was old enough to be Churchill's father rather than her fiancé / lover and there appears to be little to no chemistry between them. Yet he brings a kind of downplayed intellectualism to the role, knowing that certain things cannot possibly be true but underneath knowing them to be so. Such as when Von Helsing explains that a vampire casts no reflection in a mirror, it dawns on Garth that he saw no mirrors in Zaleska's London apartment. He realises that she must be the vampire, for in an earlier conversation with her he says: "You know, this is the first woman's flat I've been in that didn't have at least 20 mirrors in it."**51** Edward Van Sloan fits nicely into the role of Von Helsing (though why his name has been changed from Van to Von is not explained) that he had played previously on the stage and in the original film *Dracula*. Gilbert Emery as Sir Basil Humphrey is just as ineffective as Herbert Bunston's Dr. Seward and one has to wonder if the role was actually written for the latter, given all the last-minute cast changes and script delays.

Yet the entire film rests firmly on the shoulders of Gloria Holden. In her performance as Countess Mayra Zaleska, she brings a dark, brooding intensity, grace and inner turmoil that dominates the entire film. Holden was born in London, England in 1903, but moved to the United States where she studied at the American Academy of Dramatic Art. In 1927 she came to the public's attention by winning the title of 'Most Tastefully Dressed American Woman' in a national contest to promote American designed clothes. On December 17th 1932 she married director and Columbia film scout Harold Wilson. M.G.M. director Clarence Brown invited her to come to Hollywood for a screen test, but ended up being too busy to shoot it. In the interim, Holden appeared as a villain on radio in *Stories of The Black Chamber*[56]. According to *Radio Mirror*, June 1935, Holden and her husband "occupy separate apartments, but manage to dine together every evening. They think living together inimical to their careers and maintain different households."**52** They would divorce in December 1937, after he deserted her on September 15th 1936. Here we could speculate that things may not have been going well in the marriage whilst the film was being shot and some of that pain was brought to the role.[57] At the age of thirty-three Gloria Holden landed her first and only major Hollywood starring role and it was one that she would, towards the end

---

56. *Stories of the Black Chamber* was an old time radio show about spies, murder and intrigue centered around the room (in Washington) where ciphers were broken in wartime. Described as 'An authentic serial which promises to keep you in gooseflesh three times a week.' It was broadcast on N.B.C. at 7.15pm Monday, Wednesday and Friday. Each episode lasted for fifteen minutes. It was co-authored by Major Herbert O. Yardley and sponsored by Ferhan Company, Inc.

57. *The Pittsburgh Press, Wednesday April 12th 1939, Pg.23 Broadway by George Ross*: 'Golden Boy': "William Holden, the lad just signed for the coveted lead in 'Golden Boy,' used to be Bill Beadle. And here is how he obtained his new movie tag. On the Columbia lot is an assistant director and scout named Harold Winston. Not long ago he was divorced from the actress, Gloria Holden, but carried the torch after the marital rift. Winston was one of those who discovered the "Golden Boy" newcomer and who renamed him – in honor of his former spouse!"

of her life, describe as 'that awful thing.'**53** As to why she felt that way about it, one can only speculate. Although the new people at Universal did not like 'horror' films, *Dracula's Daughter* appears to have been properly promoted[58] and indeed Lugosi came back onto the set and had lunch with the cast and posed for some publicity shots on February 24th. Henry Sutherland's column 'Hollywood Film Shop' in *Nevada State Journal* claimed that when Lugosi was seen with Holden, she introduced him as "My father." *Universal Weekly* on 7th March 1936, under the title "'Dracula's Daughter meets her 'Dad'" quotes Lugosi as saying, "This is the first time that anyone acquired a vampire daughter by way of the screen."**54**

Holden received positive reviews for her performance. *The New York Times* for May 18th 1936 said: "...Gloria Holden is a remarkably convincing batwoman..."**55** *Movie Classic*, July 1936 stated that: "...Gloria Holden as the vampire is startlingly impressive. She will hold every theatregoer spellbound with each of her scenes."**56** The *Albany Evening News* for July 13th states: "In

---

58. *Film Daily* for June 15th 1936 states that Hett Mannheim of Universal's exploitation staff was in Pittsburgh for a week doing advance work for 'Dracula's Daughter' which opened at the Alvin cinema. Further to this, on Monday July 27th 1936 *Film Daily* announced that 'Lurid Warning Plugs "Dracula's Daughter." According to the article the people of Mt. Vernon, Ind., were distributed to them when Louis Davis played the film. Printed on the envelopes were other directions such as, "This envelope contains wolfbane, the herb that vampires fear! If you meet Dracula's Daughter … if she seeks to give you the kiss of death, only this wolfbane can save your life! Bring it with you to the New Vernon when you see her story unfold." The article states that the envelopes actually contain, "The magic herb in each envelope consisted of a half-teaspoon of green tea." Davis went on to add to his promotion of the film, "Are you a sissy? Can you 'take it'? If you are a coward at heart, if you fear, then don't dare see the vampire picture 'Dracula's Daughter!'" Apparently the challenge was met by the 'young bloods' of the town and they showed up at the theatre to 'prove their heroism.' In the *Independent Exhibitor Film Bulletin* Wednesday May 6th 1936, Har Blair wrote, 2 Cash in on the popularity of the original 'Dracula.' This is its successor in horror. Wide selection of fine, creepy stills would be easy to plant because of unusual theme."

fact, Gloria Holden, a newcomer who plays the girl, makes her a rather pathetic figure as she seeks to rid herself of this soul torturing affliction. Miss Holden is a big addition to the screen pictorially and she has a deep rich voice. It is something to make *Dracula's Daughter* more impressive than the usually "boogy" man or woman of these cinemas."**57** Previous to that The *Albany Evening News* for Monday May 18th described Holden as having 'Shades of Theda Bara.'**58** One of her best reviews came from Paul Jacobs at *Hollywood Spec*: "Miss Holden upon whom lay the complete burden of producing reality from phantasy, achieved a brilliant blending of the human elements with the subtle aura of weirdly malign powers, the chilling sweep of things unspoken. Her work bears the stamp of unguessable abilities. She is definitely a great find…The student of cinema will find a wealth of study material in the penetratingly intelligent synthesis of Miss Gloria Holden."**59**

She had a successful career, spanning twenty-two years after *Dracula's Daughter* as a character actress in mainstream films as well as 'B' movies, yet she would never headline another major film; and it would take another sixteen years before she would work at Universal again in 1952's *Has Anyone Seen My Girl*. Just before the release of *Dracula's Daughter*, Holden would have a supporting role in *Wife vs. Secretary* starring opposite Jean Harlow, Clark Gable and Myra Loy for Metro Goldwyn Mayer, released on March 4th. Her following film 1937's *The Life of Emile Zola* in which she played Zola's wife opposite Paul Muni, went on to win the Academy Award for Best Picture. It appears that the tide against her first role began in the audition stages for her second major role as Louella O. Parsons pointed out in the *Milwaukee Sentinel* on Tuesday 16th February 1937 under the title: "Gloria Holden Tops All Tests for Zola Film." Parsons goes on to say, "Scoring a success in 'As Husbands Go' and in 'The Long Frontier' on the stage, Clarence Brown saw her and asked her to come to Hollywood for a test [ ] the test was never made, but she did go into *'Dracula's Daughter'* at Universal, which didn't do much for her or anyone else."**60** In June 1937, Charles E. Ford, Universal's new Vice-President in charge of production announced at a Sales Convention: "[ ] we have a large and growing stock company of young players, many of whom may develop into the stars of tomorrow ... [ ] other new players are [ ] Gloria Holden, Nan Gray ..."**61** Holden was obviously unhappy with the way things had progressed with her first starring role and dissatisfied with how Universal were treating her, for on August 14th 1936, *Motion Picture Daily* announced that "'Gloria Holden Quits Film.' Hollywood, Aug.13 – Gloria Holden Universal contract player has secured a release from her contract with this company."**62**[59]

The *Ballston Spa Daily Journal* for September 21st 1937, under the title '*Hollywood Roundup*' has the only (as far as I have found) mention of *Dracula's Daughter* by Gloria Holden. When discussing her part as Madame Zola, Holden stated, "I wanted a part with character for my second Hollywood assignment, especially since my first was the title role in the macabre *Dracula's Daughter*."**63** According to Mark Clark, Holden told reporters during production of the film, "I don't believe any woman has ever been asked to play such a poisonous role before. The screenwriter has made me an insatiable fiend."**64**

Holden was possibly worried that she would be typecast like Lugosi was as Count Dracula; indeed they may have even discussed it when he visited the set as they had worked together before in 1934's *The Return of Chandu*. Holden's co-star, Hedda Hopper, had worked with Lugosi in the 1930 film *Such Men are Dangerous* and both had travelled on the Aquitania on July 28th 1935, sailing from New York to England and it is plausible that the two actors had met on board. Therefore it is again plausible that the two actresses discussed Lugosi between takes. Certainly, Hopper[60] had a fond memory of Holden, for she said in her May 1936 *Movie Classic* column, "I had a bit of

---

59. Interestingly, both *Photoplay* and *Modern Screen* still had Holden's 'Address For The Stars' at Universal in December, despite having left four months previously.
60. Hedda Hopper (May 2nd 1885 – February 1st 1966) started her career as a Hollywood actress. The IMDb lists 146 credits to her name, starting her career in 1916 and ending with her death in 1966. She is most famous now for her gossip column and on-going feud with fellow gossip Louella O. Parsons

work in Dracula's Daughter at Universal. Gloria Holden plays the lead. She certainly looked spooky, but between scenes she sits and knits!"**65** Whatever the case may be, Holden's alleged worries proved to be founded, for like *Dracula, Dracula's Daughter* refused to die.

When it was released in America, the film did not set the box-office on fire as *Dracula, Frankenstein,* and *The Bride of Frankenstein* had before. It opened on May 15 at the Rialto Theatre, having been moved from The Roxy, to mainly positive reviews, especially for Holden. In fact *Variety*, America's leading Film and Entertainment magazine reviewed it thus:

> "This is a chiller with plenty of ice; a surefire waker-upper in the theatre and a stay-awake influence in the bedroom later on. Rates tops among recent horror pictures and, as such, figures to deliver nice grosses. Entire E.M. Asher production rates bows, from scenario groundwork up through the acting, direction and photography … The heavy portions are more than adequately handled by Gloria Holden, portraying Dracula's Daughter, and Irving Pichel, her jealous servant. Edward Van Sloan, who played the scientist in the original Dracula film, is ditto in this, and just as convincing…"**66**

Five months after its initial release, *Dracula's Daughter* was still opening in theatres around America. As the *Spokane Daily Chronicle* for Friday November 6th 1936, under the title, "Western Picture Lead at Empress [theatre]' points out: *"Dracula's Daughter,* a picture in which vampires play an important part, stars Otto Kruger and Marguerite Churchill."**67** For the next twenty years, *Dracula's Daughter* would play in theatres and drive-ins around America; for example *Niagara Falls NY Gazette***68**, August 11th 1949 has an advert for *Dracula's Daughter* playing at The Strand, in 1954 it was

---

(August 6th 1881 – December 9th 1972). Through their gossip columns Hopper and Parsons became the most powerful women in Hollywood.

playing at the Will Mills Drive-In Theatre and in October 1956 it was playing as part of a double bill with *The Indestructible Man* at the 211 Drive In[61]. In 1938 it played at the Capitol as part of a double bill with *The Bride of Frankenstein*, whilst the crowd-pulling film was *Girl's School*, which starred both Gloria Holden and Nan Grey! In England, the film was at the mercy of the censor and *The Times* for July 21st reported that the London County Council 'announces that it has classified the film entitled *Dracula's Daughter* as "horrific." All cinema licensees in the County of London have accordingly been informed that when this film is exhibited at their premises a notice, "This film is unsuitable for children," in letters not less than 1 1/2in. high, must be affixed to each category board at the premises during the whole time that the film is included in the programme. The film deals with the theme of human vampirism."**69** Following in the footsteps of America, in Britain the film refused to die: in January 1940 it was billed with *Son of Frankenstein* (1939) playing at the Rialto in London and eight years later it was at the Theatre Royal, double-billed with *Ghost of Frankenstein* (1942) in July 1948.

Over the years *Dracula's Daughter* has gained the reputation for being one of the first mainstream horror films to have an overtly 'homosexual' theme as well as the reputation for being one of the most accomplished and stylistic horror films of its era. In truth, it is a multi-layered, multi-themed masterpiece that can be viewed and read on many levels. It is one of the most influential vampire films, whose influence is still felt today in film and litera-

---

61. To give an idea of its longevity in the cinema, in 1939 it played as a double bill with *The Bride of Frankenstein* at The Strand, Albany and Mercury theatres. Played at The Colony in 1940 and in 1949 it played as part of a double bill with *Frankenstein Meets the Wolf Man* at Temple Theatre in July, as well as two other theatres in June and September, respectively. As part of Dr. Hess's Madhouse of Horrors at the Palace Theatre in 1951, played at Loews in 1952 as a double bill with *The Phantom of Paris* and played at the Hollywood Drive-In as part of a double bill with *Weird Woman* in 1958. This is just performances over the New York State and advertised in the many newspapers there.

ture, though not always acknowledged as such. Bernstein points out that, "At the most superficial level, Dracula's Daughter is a tale of heterosexual desire doomed to fail."**70** To some degree this observation is correct. The Countess is 'drawn' to Garth, but he is already engaged to his secretary, Janet. Thus the Countess then represents the 'psycho-mistress' (or 'bunny boiler'[62]), who when rejected and in an effort to win his love, kidnaps Janet. Garth is then given a choice – to either join her or allow Janet to die. Throughout the film, Garth is shown to be reliant on Janet. As his fiancée, she helps him to dress, she picks him up from his holiday, listens to his childish retorts (something that she herself does too), and as his secretary runs his day to day appointments, etc. Bernstein states that this perspective can represent an exploration of Garth's journey toward Oedipal adulthood as he moves from this childlike manner through to 'an adult, heterosexual position by its conclusion'**71** where the film's final image shows Garth holding Janet as she awakens from the Countess' spell, thus asserting his masculinity against her femininity – the hero rescuing the damsel in distress, thus reversing the dynamics of their relationship as previously shown. Bernstein continues to state that this heterosexual 'surface plot' was apparent to 1936 critics, citing Douglas Gilbert's review in which he states, "At a dinner party, she meets Garth, London's leading psychiatrist, and goes for him in a big way."**72** There are undercurrent hints throughout that Garth's interest in Zaleska may not be as professional as he tries to make out and it is left to the audience to decide whether they have gone beyond. Benshoff states that "The film also conflates unproblematically a romantic interest between patient and doctor and a professional one: Garth and the countess have a strong sexual interest in each other, as their many pointed gazes that cinematically dissolve into a fireplace make apparent."**73**. For example: upon Zaleska's arrival to a London party:

Janet (*to Garth, who is staring at Zaleska*): Don't you know it's very rude to stare at strangers.

---

62. This type of character would be firmly established by Glenn Close in 1987's *Fatal Attraction*, where as a spurned lover she does indeed boil a bunny!

Garth (*snappily*): Thought I'd gotten rid of you for a while.

Janet (*retorting*): Not while there's a dangerous-looking brunette like that around.

They (Garth and Zaleska) are introduced and just stare at each other (fadeout)**74**

In another later scene when Garth is getting ready to go and see Zaleska, Janet takes the opportunity to bring up her worries:

Janet: You were the only person at Lady Esme's party to whom she paid the slightest attention.

Garth (*brushing off both Janet and the conversation*): Perhaps I'm intelligent!

They then fall into childish bickering.

Janet (*tying Garth's bow tie*): I have never seen you in such a dither. I must have underestimated the lady's attractions.**75**

After Garth has been to Zaleska's apartment, he confronts Janet over her telephone calls to him and she informs him that she has handed in her notice, which he readily accepts. On her way out, she is confronted with Zaleska coming in. Zaleska asks where Garth is and Janet responds that he has already left. A nurse then calls out to Garth and Zaleska looks shocked at Janet who in turn looks ashamed at being caught in her lie:

Zaleska: Why was it necessary to lie? Dr Garth asked me to come this evening.**76**

Here is a clear division between the two central female characters; on the one hand we have the fiancée / wife figure fighting to save her relationship and on the other we have the femme fatale, the mistress. It is clear from Janet's various statements that she sees Zaleska as a major threat to her relationship with Garth and at no point does he give her any reassurance that their relationship is safe. Furthermore Janet, even though she is a baroness, knows that the Countess is of a higher rank socially, and as she has to work and the Countess does not, must add to her insecurity. The only time that we truly see Janet state her position is near the end of the film. The Countess is waiting to see Garth, looks out of a window and telepathically summons Sandor. Janet comes into the room and Zaleska approaches her:

Zaleska: Won't you sit down. I'd like to talk to you.

Janet (*scoffs*): Well, I'm sure we've nothing to discuss, Countess Zaleska.

Zaleska: We might talk of Dr Garth. He's interested in … (*gloatingly*) both of us.

Janet: I'm quite aware of his interest in you, Countess… as a psychiatrist.

Zaleska shocked at being put in her place looks at Sandor, who has entered the room.

Zaleska: Sandor.

Sandor overpowers Janet.

Zaleska: Take her to the car, this way.**77**

Though Zaleska attempts to imply that there is more going on between her and Garth, thus adding to Janet's growing insecurity over her relationship with him, it is she who firmly puts Zaleska in her place by stating that Garth is only interested in her as a patient. Zaleska is fully aware of their (Garth and Janet's) relationship and as she is the outsider and emotionally unstable has no choice but to take Janet at her word. This leaves her with no alternative (in her mind) but to use Sandor to kidnap Janet and thus (so she thinks) force Garth into her plans for him. Throughout the course of the film, whether Garth has led her on or not, Zaleska has pursued him despite knowing that he had a fiancée and once rejected forces him to her will. It is only through Sandor's jealousy that both Garth and Janet survive, as he shoots Zaleska with an arrow that was actually meant for Garth. It is not a case of 'heterosexual desire doomed to die,'[78] it could be argued that it is a moral statement that adultery is wrong and like *Fatal Attraction* fifty-one years later, the end result is those that try to break up a marriage/relationship must pay the ultimate price for doing so. Yet the Countess represents a lot more than just a femme fatale – she represents the 'outsider' who is desperate to join and become integrated in society.

Benshoff, in his study of homosexuality and the horror film points out that from the 1920s onward, homosexuality was believed to be a mental illness that could be "cured (or at least understood) through psychological means"[79] and "Like the debate over homosexuals, monsters were increasingly figured as a problem best approached through medical and/or psychiatric intervention, rather than legal or religious means."[80] This opens up *Dracula's Daughter* into several different avenues to be explored. Firstly, is she really a vampire? The script never makes it clear as to whether Zaleska is Dracula's biological daughter or not, nor is it clear if she is really a vampire. There is no supernatural element at all in the film – there is no changing into either a wolf or bat, no visual draining of blood or attempt to as in *Dracula*; she even needs a jewelled ring to hypnotise people. When the villagers see a light shining from Castle Dracula they fear that the Count has returned, not his son or daughter. This implies that the villagers are either unaware that Dracula 'sired' any children or that they feared him more than his 'children.' Further to this we see her holding a crucifix aloft and is seen with a cup of tea. This all implies that Zaleska may be human and delusional – with that delusion being fed by Sandor himself, whose appearance is more vampire-like than that of the Countess. In fact he does not want Zaleska to be cured at all and does everything he can do to undermine her at every given opportunity and that makes him the worst kind of enabler – feeding Zaleska's delusion for his own ends. The question here is why did Zaleska not fulfil her 'promise' to make Sandor a vampire? Did she fear that he would no longer assist her and that he would, once given the 'gift,' reject her?

If that is the case and the Countess is human, then what does she wish to be cured of? It is here that the question of sexuality raises its head, with many film theorists and critics claiming that Zaleska is a lesbian as Benshoff writes: "Perhaps because of her female status, Dracula's daughter, the countess Marya Zaleska[ ] is one of the most equivocal monsters of the classical period; in fact, she actively desires to be cured of her condition. This 'condition' is directly expressed in terms of her queer sexuality, her non-traditional gender role [ ]"**81** There are two scenes in question that imply this and I shall discuss these later.

Throughout the film it is clear that she wishes to be cured of her (alleged) vampirism. This paves the way for another avenue of exploration, which is that the Countess is truly a vampire and desperate to be cured of her 'vampirism' (which can be seen as a metaphor for repressed sexuality). She states after cremating the remains of Dracula, "Free – Free forever. Do you understand what that means Sandor? Free to live as a woman, free to take my place in the bright world of the living instead of among the shadows of the dead."**82** With the utter destruction of Dracula's body, Zaleska believes that the 'spell' of vampirism is broken, but Sandor is unsure as is pointed out the following night:

Zaleska: Why are you looking at me that way?

Sandor: I'm remembering last night … and waiting.

Zaleska: You think this night will be like all the others, don't you? Well, you're wrong. Dracula's destroyed. His body's in ashes. The spell is broken. I can live a normal life now, think normal things, play normal music…

Zaleska starts to play a lullaby on the piano, which reaches a crescendo of dark notes…

Sandor: That isn't the music of freedom [ ] It is the music of the dark. *83*

At this, Zaleska realises that she has not escaped the curse of the vampire. Yet what sort of vampire is she? Von Helsing offers up an explanation in the film: "How can a vampire have a daughter? I thought they were only legends, for now I must begin to doubt. One says that her mother became Dracula's victim while she was carrying the child, so that it was born neither human nor vampire. There are other different tales. But this is what it means for you, friend Jeffrey: the Countess will return to Castle Dracula. She must think of that as her home."**84**

So, if she is truly a hundred-year-old vampire as later stated in the film, then surely she would have realised that there is no cure. In fact the whole exorcism speech takes the vampire mythos into several different areas that are away from the common assumption / concept of a vampire and what it is:

> "Unto Adoni and Asteroth, into the keeping of the lords of the flames and lower pits, I consign this body, to be forever more consumed in this purging fire. Let all baleful spirits that threaten the souls of men be banished by the sprinkling of this salt. Be thou exorcised, O Dracula, and thy body, long undead, find destruction throughout eternity in the name of thy dark, unholy master. In the name of the holiest, and through this cross, be the evil spirit cast out until the end of time."**85**

This is the first vampire film to imply that vampirism is not only possession by an evil spirit, but a state caused by magic and / or a form of mental illness. Zaleska exorcises Dracula's corpse of an 'evil spirit,'86 then informs Sandor that 'The spell is broken' **87** and finally informs Sandor, after a meeting with Garth, "He can help me, Sandor. This time I'm sure."**88** [This last quote implies that she has tried various other medical solutions to find a cure.] It is these inconsistencies that have made *Dracula's Daughter* so influential. If *Dracula* opened up the first wave of the horror cycle, then *Dracula's Daughter* closed it. What is overlooked is that *Dracula's Daughter* is in many ways a mirror reflection of *Dracula*. For instance when we first meet Dracula, he is the driver of a coach, with only his eyes showing; similarly when we first meet Zaleska we only see her eyes, the rest of her face is covered. As Mina is being urged to remember a nightmare by Van Helsing, when asked whose face it is she saw, Dracula is announced as having arrived, and at a party in *Dracula's Daughter*, Zaleska's arrival is announced in similar fashion. Also at the party, when offered a drink, she reiterates her father's famous quote of "I do not drink wine."**89** Zaleska's relationship with Sandor is the reverse to that of Dracula and Renfield – even down to the killing of the 'partner' – Dracula kills Renfield, believing him to have betrayed him and Sandor kills Zaleska out of jealousy as she is going to give immortality to Garth and not him. The scene where Zaleska 'picks up' a gentleman is similar to the scene in *Dracula* where the Count attacks a flower girl. Even the scenes of her rising from her coffin are shot in the same fashion as that of *Dracula*. As Gary D. Rhodes points out in his book *Tod Browning's Dracula*: "Another reason that *Dracula's Daughter* closely echoes its predecessor is the decision for its narrative to begin immediately after the climax of the 1931 film. [ ] The opening scenes thus attempt to connect the two films plausibly and continue the same narrative. Later scenes also recall Dracula, particularly the Main Hall of Dracula's castle in Transylvania, which closely (even if not precisely) recreates the *mise-en-scène* of the original. [ ] even repurposes footage from its predecessor: a high-angle long shot of a teaching space in a hospital in which a physician discovers punctures in the neck of a victim."**90**

There are two scenes in *Dracula's Daughter* where critics have stated categorically that the implication is lesbian in tone, and although I can see what they are saying, I disagree and I shall explain why. The first scene is the attack upon the artist model Lili. When asked to lower her straps Zaleska's resolve fails and she attacks – the camera staying steady on her face then cuts to a grinning mask on the wall and we hear Lili scream. The Breen Office saw fit to be worried about the Lili scene as they suggested that: "The present suggestion that the girl Lili poses in the nude will be changed. She will be posing her neck and shoulders, and there will be no suggestion that she undresses, and no exposure of her person. …The whole sequence will be treated in such a way as to avoid any suggestion of perverse sexual desire on the part of Marya

[Zaleska] or of an attempted sexual attack by her upon Lili."**91** Workman and Howarth have stated that: "The most widely noted (and disputed) aspect of *Dracula's Daughter* is the above noted, barely-veiled lesbianism of its title character. There's no doubt both that it's there and Universal knew it when they cooked up the tag line 'save the women of London from Dracula's Daughter!' [ ] Actually, it takes a conscious effort to not read the film as an anti-homosexual diatribe (though a masterfully constructed and extremely engaging one) in which Zaleska's lesbian nature is coded as vampirism. [ ] Zaleska desperately wants to be rid of her vampire/ homosexual inclinations and turns to the then-new science of psychiatry (which, in the 1930s was just beginning to view homosexuality as a curable mental condition) to end her vesication. When Dr. Garth learns the truth about her, he is disgusted, a common reaction towards gays during that period."**92**

It is interesting to note here that in 1935's *Mark of the Vampire* there is a similar scene where the character of Luna (Carroll Borland[63]) goes in to bite the neck of Irena Borotyn (Elizabeth Allen[64]) and there appears to be no controversy over that and it certainly has not been labelled a 'lesbian scene.'

The Lili scene is itself a direct parallel to the scene in *Dracula*, where Mina attacks Harker on the balcony. The camera keeps a steady shot of her face as she moves up to attack him and we hear his reaction off screen. The reverse here is that one stays with the attacker and the other with the victim. The second scene which has a lesbian undertone is when after kidnapping Janet and returning to Castle Dracula, Zaleska hovers over the unconscious body of Janet, slowly descending as if to give her the kiss ... but pulls back on Garth's entrance. It was once described as 'the longest kiss never filmed.'**93** This replicates the scene in *Dracula* where a drugged Renfield collapses in his room after fending off a bat. The door swings open and Dracula's brides enter

---

63. Carroll [Carol] Borland, American Actress, Professor, Writer. February 25th 1914 – February 3rd 1994. (Aged 79).
64. Elizabeth Allen, British Actress. April 9th 1910 – July 27th 1990. (Aged 80).

and they advance towards the fallen man. Dracula enters through the French windows, signals the brides to leave and then goes down onto his knees and slowly ' leans in towards Renfield in as the screen fades out. I can find no reference to this scene being homosexual in nature and yet it obviously is. This raises the question as to why one version is seen as heterosexual (*Dracula*) and the other as 'queer / lesbian?' (*Dracula's Daughter*). In fact, this scene in *Dracula* must be seen as homosexual in nature, not just because it is with two men, but because it was deliberately filmed as such, for in the script, this scene is entirely different:

A-59 INT. CLOSE SHOT RENFIELD AT WINDOW

As he looks down a mist comes rushing in, and with it a gigantic bat.

Renfield, dizzy from the blow, recoils and in doing so, strikes his head

Against the window and collapses, unconscious, upon the floor.

CAMERA MOVES BACK TO LONG SHOT

A-60 LONG SHOT

The three women who had been watching all this enter – go

To Renfield with a curious, measured cat-like tread.

FADE OUT 94

Rhodes points out that: 'Browning's decision was likely made due to a set that did not allow for that chasm to be visualized, but also helps to clarify Dracula's control over Renfield for the rest of the film. It also directly contravenes Junior Laemmle's suggestion on a Bromfield-Murphy draft of the script that Dracula should "go only for women and not men." And, rather bravely, the implications of the new narrative action ignored the Code of Ethics for the Production of Motion Pictures as adopted in 1930, which claimed, "Sex perversion or any inference of it is forbidden."'**95**

In contrast, the Spanish version of *Dracula,* filmed simultaneously to Browning's, filmed the same scene as above, but the fade out is when the 'brides' descend upon Renfield's unconscious form. Another scene that has a homosexual undertone is when Zaleska is out prowling the streets and picks up a man. Vito Russ speculates that this could be seen as a parallel to the gay cruising scene, rather than lesbian. To be fair, Universal took full advantage of this idea of sexuality in its promotion of the film, with headings such as *'She gives you that weird feeling'***96** and *'Save the women of London from Dracula's Daughter.'***97** Even the press book added to this with advertisements screaming out *'Women obeyed her commands! Men feared her power!'***98** As Vito Russo wrote: *"Gays as predatory, twilight creatures were a matter of style and personal interpretation in the horror films of the 1930s. The equation of horror and sins of the flesh is easily seen in monster movies of the period."***99** What is not taken into account is that although Zaleska attacks Lili and later kidnaps Janet; her two main victims are men. Furthermore, she does everything in her power to entice Garth and when Rhonda J. Berenstein sums up *Dracula's Daughter*: "But to characterize Zaleska as lesbian or bisexual in a conventional sense is to misread the transgressions performed by monsters. Monsters do not fit neatly with a model of human sexuality. Instead, they propose a paradigm of sexuality in which eros and danger, sensuality and destruction, human and inhuman, and male and female blur, overlap, and coalesce. In this schema, sexuality and identity remain murky matters, steeped in border crossings and marked by fuzzy boundaries."**100** I have no choice but to agree with her.

IV

Dracula's Daughter has like early twentieth century women struggled to find emancipation from the yoke of the male-led Hollywood. That is not to say that it should outweigh the importance of those lesser known movies told through a more feminine filter. For all its faults *Dracula's Daughter* stands the test of time and as with *Dracula*, only truly falters when Zaleska is not on the screen – just as Lugosi holds *Dracula* together, Gloria Holden holds *Dracula's Daughter* together with her impressive performance. Sadly, without a 'name' star to bring in the audience, the film failed to impress at the box office. Yet this has not stopped it from being one of the most influential vampire films of all time. It is the first to feature a vampire wanting to be cured of their ailment. Although later films such as 1945's *House of Dracula*'s Baron Lathos, Barnabas Collins in both *House of Dark Shadows* (1970) and *Dark Shadows* (2012) and the vampires in *Near Dark* (1987) all seek a 'blood cure' for their 'vampirism' rather than a 'matter of will' cure – this wanting a cure is all part of her legacy. Zaleska is the only vampire on screen to have held a crucifix, it would take another thirty-six years before a vampire would touch a crucifix again and unlike Zaleska, he would be burnt for his efforts in Hammer Films' *Dracula AD 1972*. The scene in question is when Dracula has Van Helsing's granddaughter lying on an altar and he goes in to take his revenge by turning her into a vampire, and her cross slips out from the side of her neckline. With a guttural howl of pain, Dracula rips the crucifix from her neck, burning his hand in the process, just as Van Helsing arrives to save the day.

Gloria Holden's performance would have a lasting effect on a nine-year old Anne Rice[65] and that influence would change the vampire in both visual media and literature. *Interview with the Vampire* is the second most read vampire novel after *Dracula* and it started its life as a short story that was written in 1969. Following her daughter's death in 1972, aged 5, Rice reworked the story into a novel. With regards to Holden's influence, Rice said "That's the first time I saw vampires as a kid. I loved the tragic figure of Dracula's daughter as a regretful creature who didn't want to kill but was driven to do it. The tragic dimension is at its fullest most eloquent and articulate in Dracula's daughter because she herself was articulate and intelligent."**101** On her Facebook page in 2013 Rice wrote, *"Dracula's Daughter.* One fateful night in my childhood, I went to the Grenada Theater two blocks from my house and paid the admission of 12-cents to see this 1936 film. It must have been the early 40's. It was old then. I never forgot it. The elegant and beautiful Gloria Holden as *Dracula's Daughter* swept me away. Decades later, remembering the tragedy, that romance, that elegance, I sat down to

---

65. Anne Rice, American Novelist. October 4th 1941 -

write a book called *'Interview with the Vampire'* and capture the same ambience."**102** Further to this Rice said in a 2011 interview, "As a child, I saw this beautiful film, *Dracula's Daughter*, and it was with Gloria Holden and was a sequel to the original Dracula. It was all about this beautiful daughter of Dracula who was an artist in London, and she felt drinking blood was a curse. It had beautiful, sensitive scenes in it, and that film mesmerized me. It established to me what vampires were—these elegant, tragic, sensitive people. I was really just going with that feeling when writing *Interview with the Vampire*. I didn't do a lot of research."**103** Whilst the dark brooding intensity of the film and the melancholic nature of Zaleska are beautifully captured in the novel and the character of Louis (who Rice modelled on both herself and Holden's character), it is with *The Queen of the Damned*, the third novel in the "Vampire Chronicles" as they have now become known, that the influence of *Dracula's Daughter* is most felt. Not only did Rice name a bar in the book 'Dracula's Daughter,' she used the idea of an evil spirit/demon possessing the body of a person, thus turning them into a vampire.

In *The Queen of the Damned*, Rice describes the origin of the vampires. Akasha is a Queen in a land called Kemet (Egypt), thousands of years ago. It is during her reign that two powerful witches, Maharet and Mekare, live in the mountains and are able to communicate with invisible entities, gaining simple favours from them. A bloodthirsty spirit known as Amel frequently pesters the two witches, continually asking if they need his assistance, which they decline. When the witches' village is destroyed, they are imprisoned by the King and Queen, who desire their knowledge. The witches offend Akasha, and she condemns them. After being brutally raped the witches are cast out into the desert. While making her way back home with a pregnant Maharet, Mekare curses the King and Queen secretly with the bloodthirsty spirit and this spirit inflicts such torment that they demand advice and help from the two witches.

Whilst the Queen and King attempt to exorcise Amel, they are assassinated by people unhappy with their reign. As they lie dying, the evil spirit sees its chance to ensnare the soul of the dying Queen and pulls it back into her body. The spirit combines itself with her flesh and blood, transforming her into a vampire, the mother of all vampires in fact. Akasha allows the King to drink her blood, which saves his life. They then order their servant to find the witches and bring them back to Egypt so that they could use their knowledge of spirits to help them, as they feel guilty because of their thirst for blood.

So not only does Rice successfully use the concept of an evil spirit being the cause of vampirism, she throws in an extra nod back to the source that influenced her writings by doing so. Rice breathed new life into a concept that had been left untouched for fifty-two years in both literature and visual media. It would take another nine years until visual media would take up the mantel that *Dracula's Daughter* set in motion and that Rice brought into the mainstream – that vampires were in fact corpses inhabited by evil spirits – *Buffy the Vampire Slayer.*

Buffy the Vampire Slayer ran for seven seasons from 1997 to 2003 and its cross-over show *Angel* ran for five seasons from 1999 to 2004. The programme was created by Joss Whedon and was based upon his earlier film of the same title. Both Whedon and fellow writers would make reference within the confines of the show to the vampire genre either in parody of, or homage to that which had gone before it; for example in *Lie to Me* Lugosi's *Dracula* is playing in the background of a club full of vampire wannabes; in *School Hard* Angel and Spike discuss Anne Rice's vampire novels:

Spike: People still fall for that Anne Rice routine. What a world! **104**

However, in the Season One opener *The Harvest* (Part Two), the character of Giles explains the origins of vampires:

Giles: The Books tell us that the last Demon to leave this reality fed off a human, mixed their blood. He was a human form possessed –infected – by the Demon's soul. He bit another, and another…and so they walk the earth, feeding. Killing some, mixing their blood with others to make more of their kind. Waiting for the animals to die out, and the Old Ones to return.**105**

In Season Two, Episode Three, *School Hard*, the character of Spike re-enforces the fact that vampires are demons. When in a confrontation with Angel, Angel states that things change, Spike responds: "Not us! Not demons! [ ]"**106**

Not only does this reference Anne Rice, it shows just how influential *Dracula's Daughter* has become. The whole concept is less than a sentence, yet its power has reverberated down through the years. Further, in the exorcism speech, Zaleska implies that Dracula has a soul, "Let all baleful spirits that threaten the souls of men be banished by the sprinkling of this salt."**107** Not only does it imply that Dracula has a soul, but that the evil spirit has control not only of his body, but his soul as well. This idea of a vampire with a soul was successfully adapted in both *Buffy* and *Angel* – with the character of Angel – a vampire cursed by gypsies after he has murdered their daughter. This curse returns his soul to him, thus forcing him to relive every murder that he has committed. Furthermore I would suggest that the character of Angel was modelled on Louis from *Interview with the Vampire* – a reluctant vampire who refuses to feed from mortals. In the script for *Welcome to the Hellmouth*, Angel is described as, 'strikingly handsome, with intelligence and a kind of distance in his eyes.'**108** As the character of Louis was partially based on Zaleska, then her influence/persona must be partially accredited to the character of Angel as she is the original source for the reluctant, dark and brooding vampire. This image of the vampire would be seen again in the Canadian television series *Vampire High* which ran for 26 episodes from 2001 to 2002. Jeff Roop played a variation of the Angel character called Drew French. In fact I would go so far as to say that Drew was modelled on Angel from the outset. On the official website for *Vampire High*, Jeff Roop says this about his character:

"Um, Drew I guess is basically the, I mean he's the romantic essence of it, of the show. He's the one that comes closest to typifying, sort of, the artistic, poetic notion of what a vampire is. Romantic, passionate, emotional, uh, torn between his, his hatred of who he is and sort of, he's trying to accept who he is and hating it, but also loving it at the same time. In terms of the group, he's probably the one who's the biggest loner. The one who's most apart from them. Who, um, has the hardest time fitting in, and who really doesn't wanna fit in. I think he's the one who comes closest to sort of the Count Dracula notion of a vampire."**109**

Even the concept of being set in a school / college and the love between mortal and vampire seems to have been lifted from *Buffy*. The main difference is that his love interest Sherry Woods (Meghan Ory) is not a slayer, but a fellow student. Both shows deal with teenage angst that owes its heritage to *Dracula's Daughter* and her desire to live a normal life, to love and not be on the outside. Everything is a variation of a theme and the essence stems directly from *Dracula's Daughter*.

For over seventy-eight years *Dracula's Daughter* has been influencing the vampire genre, whether it be the novels of Anne Rice through to television shows like *Buffy the Vampire Slayer, Angel* or *Vampire High* or films like the sexploitation films of the 1960s and 1970s such as *The Vampire Lovers* (UK, 1970), *The Velvet Vampire* (US, 1971), *Les lčvres rouges* (*Daughters of Darkness*, Belgian 1971), and *La novia ensangrentada* (*The Blood Spattered Bride*, Spain 1972), each and every one of these owes a nod to the first fully multi-layered vampire film, which, though it failed on its initial release, has dominated the vampire culture ever since, and long may that influence continue.

End Notes

1: *Photoplay,* July 1936. Pg. 116.
2: Riley, P. Ed *James Whale's Dracula's Daughter.* Kindle Edition.
3: The *Fitchburg Sentinel.* January 18th 1936.
4: Riley, P. Ed *James Whale's Dracula's Daughter.* Kindle Edition.
5: Ibid.
6: Ibid.
7: Ibid.
8: Skal, D. *The Monster Show: A Cultural History of Horror.* Plexus, London. 1993. Pg. 198.
9: Riley, P. Ed *James Whale's Dracula's Daughter.* Kindle Edition.
10: *The Hollywood Reporter,* July 28th 1934.
11: *Film Daily,* August 18th 1934. Pg. 3.
12: *Film Daily,* Friday June 7th 1935.
13: *The Hollywood Reporter,* May 28th 1935.
14: *The New Movie Magazine,* March 1935. Pg 63.
15: The *Los Angeles Times,* March 19th 1935 as quoted in Jacobs, S. *Boris Karloff: More Than A Monster.* Tomahawk Press, 2011. Pg. 177.
16: *The Motion Picture Herald,* June 8th 1935.
17: *Motion Picture Daily,* Wednesday August 28th 1935.
18: *The Hollywood Reporter,* August 29th 1935.
19: *Motion Picture Daily,* September 27th 1935.
20: *Variety,* October 2nd 1935.
21: *Variety,* October 9th 1935.
22: *Variety,* November 13th 1935.
23: *Variety,* November 20th 1935.
24: Skal, D. *The Monster Show A Cultural History of Horror.* Plexus, London. 1993. Pg. 196-197.
25: Ibid. Pg. 198.
26: Ibid. Pg. 198-199.
27: Riley, P. Ed *James Whale's Dracula's Daughter.* Kindle Edition.

28: *Motion Picture Daily,* December 6th 1935.
29: *The Hollywood Reporter,* December 24th 1935.
30: *The Hollywood Reporter,* December 26th 1935.
31: Rhodes, Gary. D. *Dracula's Daughter Scriptbook.* Bear Manor Media. 2015.
32: *Variety,* December 4th 1935.
33: The *New York Evening Post,* December 30th 1935.
34: *Film Daily,* Tuesday January 7th 1936. Pg. 10.
35: *The Hollywood Reporter,* January 6th 1936.
36: The *Los Angeles Examiner,* January 4th 1936.
37: *Variety*, January 8th 1936.
38: *The Hollywood Reporter,* January 28th 1936.
39: *Variety*, January 14th 1936.
40: *Film Daily*, January 22nd 1936.
41: *Film Daily,* January 25th 1936.
42: Stritto, F.D & Brooks, A. *Vampire over London – Bela Lugosi in Britain.* Cult Movies Press. 2001. Pg. 175.
43: *The Hollywood Reporter,* January 30th 1936.
44: *Variety,* January 29th 1936.
45: *The Reporter,* February 1st 1936.
46: *Film Daily,* February 10th 1936. Pg. 7.
47: *Variety,* Wednesday February 12th 1936.
48: Harrison, P. *Long Beach News* February 29th 1936. "Dracula is dead" as quoted in Cremer, R. *Lugosi: The Man Behind the Cape.* Henry Regnery Company. 1976.
49: Hillyer, L Dir. *Dracula's Daughter.* Universal, 1936.
50: Ibid.
51: Ibid.
52: *Radio Mirror,* June 1935. Pg. 89.
53: Mank, G.W. *Women in Horror Films, 1930s.* McFarland & Co. 1999. Pg. 350.
54: *Universal Weekly*, March 7th 1936.

55: *The New York Times,* May 18th 1936: http://www.nytimes.com/movie/review?res=9E00EFDF1230E13BBC4052DFB366838D629EDE. Accessed 05/11/2013.
56: *Movie Classic,* July 1936. Pg. 60.
57: The *Albany Evening News,* July 13th 1936. Pg. 5.
58: The *Albany Evening News,* May 18th 1936. Pg. 20.
59: Jacobs, Paul. "Hollywood Spec" as quoted in *Motion Picture Review Digest* Vol. 1, June 29th 1936. Pg. 35.
60: The *Milwaukee Sentinel,* Tuesday 16th February 1937. Pg. 3.
61: *Motion Picture Daily,* Wednesday June 17th 1936.
62: *Motion Picture Daily,* August 14th 1936.
63: The *Ballston Spa Daily Journal,* September 21st 1937. Pg. 4.
64: Clark, M. *Smirk, Sneer and Scream: Great Acting in Horror Cinema.* McFarland & Company, Inc., 2004. Pg. 185.
65: Movie Classic, May 1936. Pg. 57.
66: *Variety* as quoted in *Motion Picture Review Digest* Vol. 1, June 29th 1936. Pg. 35.
67: *Spokane Daily Chronicle,* Friday November 6th 1936.
68: *Niagara Falls NY Gazette,* August 11th 1949.
69: "L.C.C. and Horrific Films": *The Times.* July 21st 1936. Pg. 14.
70: Berenstein, Rhona J. *Attack of the Leading Ladies. Gender, Sexuality, and Spectatorship in Classic Horror Cinema.* Columbia University Press, New York. 1996. Pg. 24.
71: Ibid. Pg. 93.
72: Ibid. Pg. 24.
73: Benshoff, Harry M. *Monsters in the Closet: Homosexuality and the Horror Film.* Manchester University Press, Manchester and New York.1997. Pg. 81.
74: Hillyer, L Dir. *Dracula's Daughter.* Universal, 1936.
75: Ibid.
76: Ibid.
77: Ibid.

78: Berenstein, Rhona J. *Attack of the Leading Ladies. Gender, Sexuality, and Spectatorship in Classic Horror Cinema.* Columbia University Press, New York. 1996. Pg. 24.
79: Benshoff, Harry M. *Monsters in the Closet: Homosexuality and the Horror Film.* Manchester University Press, Manchester and New York.1997. Pg. 77.
80: Ibid. Pg. 77.
81: Ibid. Pg. 77.
82: Hillyer, L Dir. *Dracula's Daughter.* Universal, 1936.
83: Ibid.
84: Ibid.
85: Ibid.
86: Ibid.
87: Ibid.
88: Ibid.
89: Ibid.
90: Rhodes, Gary, D. *Tod Browning's Dracula.* Tomahawk Press, 2014. Pg. 291-292.
91: Berenstein, Rhona J. *Attack of the Leading Ladies. Gender, Sexuality, and Spectatorship in Classic Horror Cinema.* Columbia University Press, New York. 1996. Pg. 26.
92: Workman, C. & Howarth, T. *Tome of Terror: Horror Films of the 1930s.* Midnight Marquee Press, 2015. Pg. 183.
93: Hanson, Ellis, Ed. *Outtakes, Essays on Queer Theory and Film.* Duke University Press, 1991, Revised 1999. Pg. 198-199.
94: Riley, Philip, J. Ed. *Dracula: The Original Shooting Script.* MagicImage Filmbooks. 1990. Pg. 121.
95: Rhodes, Gary, D. *Tod Browning's Dracula.* Tomahawk Press, 2014. Pg. 163.
96: http://www.zomboscloset.com/zombos_closet_of_horror_b/2012/08/draculas-daughter-pressbook.html. Accessed 25/01/2014.
97: http://www.zomboscloset.com/zombos_closet_of_horror_b/2012/08/draculas-daughter-pressbook.html. Accessed 25/01/2014.

98: http://www.zomboscloset.com/zombos_closet_of_horror_b/2012/08/draculas-daughter-pressbook.html. Accessed 25/01/2014.
99: Russo, Vito. *The Celluloid Closet*. Harper & Row, Publisher. 1981, Revised 1987.
100: Berenstein, RhonaJ. *Attack of the Leading Ladies. Gender, Sexuality, and Spectatorship in Classic Horror Cinema*. Columbia University Press, New York. 1996.
101: Ramsland, K. *Prism of the Night: A Biography of Anne Rice*. A Plume Book, Penguin Books USA 1991 (Revised 1994). Pg. 40-41.
102: https://www.facebook.com/annericefanpage/posts/10151869644695452. Accessed 23/06/2014.
103: http://www.thedailybeast.com/articles/2011/11/23/anne-rice-on-sparkly-vampires-twilight-true-blood-and-werewolves.html. Accessed 24/06/2014.
104: Various. *Buffy the Vampire Slayer The Script Book Season Two, Vol. 1. School Hard*. Pocket Pulse, Pocket Books. 2001. Pg. 47.
105: Various. *Buffy the Vampire Slayer The Script Book Season One, Vol. 1. The Harvest*. Pocket Pulse, Pocket Books. 2001. Pg. 5.
106: Various. *Buffy the Vampire Slayer The Script Book Season Two, Vol. 1. School Hard*. Pocket Pulse, Pocket Books. 2001. Pg. 50.
107: Hillyer, L Dir. *Dracula's Daughter*. Universal, 1936.
108: Various. *Buffy the Vampire Slayer The Script Book Season One, Vol. 1. The Harvest*. Pocket Pulse, Pocket Books. 2001. Pg. 38
109: www.vampirehigh.co.uk/drew-french. Accessed 27/06/2014.

"Princes', Mord, Princes'!" – A Bald Executioner, A Handsome Richard III – The completely Horrid History of Tower of London – Re-Examining a Horror Classic.

Horror films had been the main winner at the box-office for Universal since Chaney's two Gothic masterpieces *The Hunchback of Notre Dame* (1923) and *The Phantom of the Opera* (1925). In 1931, though, Universal launched the first horror cycle with Bela Lugosi in *Dracula* (1930), yet within six years the public had grown weary of such pictures and with 1936's *Dracula's Daughter*, saw not only the end of the first horror cycle but the Laemmle reign at Universal, the studio that they had founded. The new proprietors at Universal had no interest in making horror films and the genre remained in the shadows. That would change in 1939, when after a successful reissue of both *Dracula* and *Frankenstein* (1931), the Heads at Universal decided to give the go-a-head for a new Frankenstein film and that film was *Son of Frankenstein* (1939). It was a huge success and opened up the second wave of horror films. Basil Rathbone, who starred in the film was having an excellent year too and by the end of 1939 had starred in six blockbusters: four for Universal and two for Twentieth Century-Fox: *The Hound of the Baskervilles* and *The Adventures of Sherlock Holmes* for the latter and *Son of Frankenstein, The Sun Never Sets, Rio* and *Tower of London* for the former. Due to there being an overlap of scheduling between the filming of *Rio* and *Tower of London*, Rathbone had to spend a week working on both films. Furthermore, RKO wanted Rathbone for a pivotal role of Frollo in their upcoming remake of *The Hunchback of Notre Dame*, but Universal, who had him under contract refused to release him and the role of Quasimodo's protector and later betrayer went to Cedric Hardwicke.

Roland V. Lee's next film for Universal had been knocking about for a few years after the director had visited England for some historical research. The screenplay would be written by his brother Robert N. Lee, who would later say in an interview: "We agreed that we wanted to use the roughest, most hard-boiled period of all time [ ] Row was for the Stuart era but I held out for the time of Richard." (Brunas, Brunas& Weaver, 201) "Many people think research experts do all the work on historical films, but the directors must study intensely themselves. The director can't achieve the correct historical tone unless he makes himself an authority on his subject. I know English history quite well except for the 15th century. I'm learning about that now for work on Tower of London which deals with the period from 1475 to 1485, sometimes known as the horror decade ... The metabolism of people must have been different in those days. Those crudities that amused them then – we just couldn't take them today." (*Washington Post*, August 27th)

Indeed, Universal were happy with Lee's output for them, despite both his previous films (*Son of Frankenstein* and *The Sun Never Sets*) overshot their budgets and shooting schedules, and in fact as early as April 17th 1939 *Tower of London* was mentioned as a Rathbone vehicle with Lee as director and producer. On June 21st*Variety* announced that the film should start production around about August 1st and that Rathbone and Karloff would star. Interestingly, though the director had fought hard for Lugosi on the *Son of Frankenstein* production, the actor was nowhere to be seen in this follow-on production! *Motion Picture Herald* announced on July 22nd that Universal had purchased the screenplay from the Lee brothers. By August 12th both Barbara O'Neill and Nan Grey had been added to the cast on the same day as Vice-President Matthew Fox 'singled out Tower of London' with Boris Karloff and Basil Rathbone as a picture worthy of comment *(Motion Picture Herald, August 12th)*. Indeed, the picture was worthy of comment for the previous day the studio had given the production a budget of $500,000 and a 36 day shooting schedule.

Lee wanted and demanded that his film be as authentic as possible and so Jack Otterson, the art director went to work immediately, reproducing the 'Tower' on the studio's back lot, using the original 13th century blueprints as well as consulting historical records to make it as accurate as possible. The completed structure, standing over 75 feet tall, would be used in various other Universal genre films and the prop department accurately recreated various torture devices as showcased in the script. [The tower set was finally removed circa 1988 to make way for the construction of the Earthquake show building, which has replaced it.]

For whatever reason, filming did not start on schedule and in fact began a week later on August 19th, when *Motion Picture Herald* announced that Universal had begun production on two films: "Unquestionably the more important is 'Tower of London,' in which Basil Rathbone, Boris Karloff, Ian Hunter, Nan Grey and Barbara O'Neil will be the principals." Filming had begun and at the end of lunch that day, Karloff received a telegram from his wife Dorothy under the guise of their daughter Sara Jane: "Excitement of your starting picture produced first tooth – love – Sara Jane." A delighted Karloff turned the Western Union form over and in pencil wrote – "Sara Jane Karloff, 2320 Bowmont Dr. Beverly Hills. Upper or Lower. Suspense holding up production. Congratulations and love, Daddy." He wired the 'message from the studio at 3.02pm' (Nollen, S.A., 123) Karloff, thrilled with his new role, plotted to have a father – daughter project and shaved his daughter's hair so they looked alike and when Dorothy saw the pair, according to Cynthia Lindsey: "She absolutely flew off the handle. She was furious. She said 'Boris, how dare you? It's going to take years to grow out.' Well, it didn't, and she looked kind of cute, but it wasn't really the thing to do – but it amused him to do so. Whether he'd done it to annoy Dorothy, or to make her laugh – she did not laugh – I don't know." (Nollen, S.A. 124)

Yet it was not a tooth or a haircut that was to cause the production endless problems and worries. The growing political unease in Europe with the rise of Nazi Germany and the imminent threat of war was sending a resounding shockwave throughout filmdom as *Variety* on August 23rd noted on its front page: "English Leading Men in U.S. Would be Hit by a War" and went on to state: "Growing possibility of war in Europe is causing some uneasiness in show biz circles. Fear is that a number of English players on Broadway and the Coast would rush back to London to join the army. In several cases actors are known to have made tentative preparations for just such action. [ ] There is a large English contingent in Hollywood, many of whom were in the last war and are still young enough to be called for service if hostilities break out again. Some of the prominent actors who might go include Charles Laughton, Basil Rathbone, David Niven, Errol Flynn, Boris Karloff [ ]" While the threat of war was on everyone's mind, on the set Lee was facing his own war, with the extras. "Nearly 500 years after they were originally fought, the historic English battles of Tewkesbury and Bosworth were re-waged in part last week for Universal's new drama, 'Tower of London.' More than 450 extras took part in the four-day campaign filmed near Tarzana, Calif." (*Syracuse Herald Journal*, Sept 18th 1939)

For filming on 19th August, over three hundred extras were given a 4 am call, which required them to travel to a ranch located in Tarzana, 20 miles north of Hollywood. Once there they had to get ready to re-create the Battle of Bosworth and the climate conditions in which it was fought. Despite assembling the fog machines early, the morning winds wrecked such havoc that the filming for these scenes had to be postponed. Lee then decided to film the Battle of Tewkesbury, which required the battle to be shot in rainy conditions. As production began on this, the water pump on the rain machines broke, leaving 300 odd people to melt in the 100+⊠ heat and when the water was turned back on, the cardboard armour and helmets the extras were wearing soon dissolved. Having been hit by driving morning winds, drenched, then left to dry out in sweltering heat, only to be drenched again, as well as a 4 am call out and to only be getting $11.00 for the whole working session, the extras were more than miffed and made all aware of their unhappiness as the assistant director M F Murphy "noted in his daily report that 'a group of unruly, uncooperative and destructive extras dressed in helmets and armour made this one of the most unsuccessful days the studio had with a large crowd of people in many years.'" (Brunas, Brunas, Weaver, 298) The *Los Angeles Evening Herald Express* columnist Harrison Carrol reported on August 21st that Rathbone was 'ready to collapse from nerves' as he beheld the make-believe beheading of his real-life son and this was reiterated in October's *Photoplay* when it stated that the execution scene of Lord De Vere (John Rodion) took several takes: "Visitors on the 'Tower of London' set watched Basil Rathbone as Richard the Third order executioner Boris Karloff to cut off his victim's head. Take after take was made, with Basil growing paler and paler beneath his make-up as the gory scene was enacted. The scene finally completed, Rathbone staggered from his seat and called his victim to him. "Good work," he smiled, a little wanely, "but it was getting me down fast." The victim smiled back at his father. He was Basil's son, Rodion." Also for Rathbone there seemed to be some serious behind the scenes concerns, as Donnie Dunagan would later recollect: "On *Tower of London*, I saw Mr. Rathbone angry several times. He would walk around with the heavy script and talk to people who were obviously in charge ... what happened *may* have been somebody changing the storyline and/or scripting and/or dialogue as we went along. I remember very explicitly that Mr. Rathbone was very "out of character" for him, taking this big pile of typed papers and patting them in the way you do when something's wrong, and pointing here and pointing there, and big discussions that four or five people would join in on. He was unhappy with that film. *Very* unhappy. I could tell because he was always super-super-nice to me [on *Son of Frankenstein*], and on *Tower of London* he did not have the smiles on, he did not come by or pat me or invite me to ice cream or stuff he used to do." (Brunas, Brunas, Weaver, 206)

Lee tried again to shoot additional battle footage on August 22nd, but again the weather was against him and brought production to a halt. *Variety* for August 30th announced that fifty extras had walked off the film: "Fifty of 200 extras working in battle scenes for Universal's 'Tower of London' were replaced Monday [August 27th] after producer-director Rowland Lee notified the front office that the supes refused to co-operate and tossed away their spears, helmets and other equipment in the thick of fighting. Protest was filed with the Screen Actors Guild and an investigation is underway." The same issue announced that Universal had signed a five-year acting deal with Barbara O'Neil and was still worrying over the effects of war if British actors, directors, writers and technicians were called in, stating "[ ] practically every studio in Hollywood would be hit by an outbreak in Europe."

Universal started to worry about the many delays to the film and reacted by trying to cut corners and one scene in particular that they wanted cut was the marriage scene between the baby Prince Richard and Lady Mobray. They argued that it would cut $10,000 off of the budget, but Lee was adamant that the scene should stay and agreed to compensate for the $10,000 layout by quickly completing all the scenes with the higher-paid actors, starting with Karloff: "The youngest matrimonial match ever screened found five-year-old Donnie Dunagan and six-year-old Joan Carroll being married with all the pomp of the 1400's for a colourful scene ...[ ] Donnie, as the Duke of York, and Joan as Lady Mowbray, are participants in a matrimonial alliance designed to strengthen the throne of Edward IV, against the plots and intrigues of Richard III, England's infamous 'Crookback King.'" (*Syracuse Herald Journal*, November 30th, 1939) There were other problems on the set too. Jimmy the Raven, who is first seen sitting on Karloff's shoulder, and when Lee called "action" the bird would fly up into the corner of the soundstage. It would remain there until its owner could cajole it down. In his biography of Karloff, Jacobs states that the bird's owner claimed that its disobedience was down to professional jealousy!!

August 30th saw the notice that Harold Schuster was 'England-bound to supervise the filming of background footage for Universal's 'Tower of London', currently in work here,' and on September 1st, it was announced in the Trade papers that Universal was 'increasing production budgets of 'Tower of London' by $300,000 [ ]' and 'Additionally, a maximum budget of $100,000 is being allotted for Trade paper and consumer promotional campaigns to back up the forgoing big pix.' (*Film Daily*, Sept 1st)

The film officially wrapped on September 4th. Yet it is interesting to note that the *Syracuse Herald Journal* for September 13th made this announcement: "Tower of London: Ernest Cossart, character actor, and Ronald Sinclair, juvenile player, have been added to the cast of [ ] Universal's horror drama featuring Basil Rathbone and Boris Karloff."

It was ten days over schedule and had exceeded its budget by almost $80,000. On October 17th Ford Beebe, a serial producer (*Flash Gordon's trip to Mars* (1938) and *Buck Rogers* (1939) to name a couple) was brought in as second unit director to complete a few remaining shots, which were completed by October 21st and the film then went into post-production.

It is here that another pivotal role seems to have been cut. Anne Neville (Rose Hobart) vanished from the screen after becoming betrothed to Richard! There is no explanation as to where the character has gone and the audience is left pondering as to whether or not she has been 'bumped off'! Hobart would later suggest that, "Some of my scenes must have been cut, I worked on Tower of London for almost six weeks. When I see it now I think 'They could have shot that in three days.'" (Brunas, Brunas & Weaver, 204) On September 30th *Motion Picture Herald* printed one of the first previews for the film that was scheduled for release on October 6th: "Melodramatic, political, military and personal events of English history in the exciting years 1471-1483 will be pictured in 'Tower of London.' Naturally the show will be a costume production, and the scale upon which Universal is making it may be realized from the importance of the names it will present, the great number of persons who will be used, the scope, size and authenticity of settings, the prestige of the principal and the repute of the producer-director Rowland V. Lee." Despite this, the studio was still unhappy, finding fault with the film's soundtrack. They were disgruntled with the historically accurate medieval music and had it removed, only to be replaced with Frank Skinner's score from *Son of Frankenstein*.

The basic plot goes like this: Edward IV (Ian Hunter) has made himself King by imprisoning Henry VI (Miles Mander), but he fails to realise the ambitions of his brother The Duke of Gloucester (Basil Rathbone), who is sixth in succession and aims to be first. When Henry VI's exiled son The Prince of Wales (G.P. Huntley) leads an invasion from France, Richard releases the old king and manipulates him into leading an attack upon his son. The Prince is killed in battle and upon his return, Richard orders Mord, his faithful executioner to murder Henry VI. Then in a drinking competition for "the whole of the Warwick estates" (Lee, 1939), Richard loses to the Duke of Clarence (Vincent Price), who he then, with Mord's help, drowns in a vat of wine. Edward VI dies and Richard becomes protector of his brother's young sons. He has them taken to the tower for their protection and once there, under his orders, Mord murders them too. Richard becomes King, and two years later is killed as is Mord in a battle against Henry Tudor.

The story, based on (alleged) historical fact is the rise to power of Richard the Third through manipulation, deceit and murder: "In spite of its factual pretentions, Lee deliberately simplified historical incidents and carried off each gruesome beheading, drowning, stabbing, etc. in the manner of a Karloff – Lugosi vehicle." (Borjarski, Beals. 147) – "[ ] Tower of London [ ] which brought the mechanics of horror to historical spectacle and was, in essence Shakespeare's Richard the Third minus the text with every beheading, drowning, stabbing, and smothering lovingly intact.[ ]" (Clarens, 125).

Taking the title role was Basil Rathbone, who clad in a red wig and with a slight deformity, played the role as a handsome but sinister and manipulative character. It would be with Lawrence Oliver's 1955 portrayal of Richard and later Vincent Price who would capture the public's imagination as Richard being a grotesque hunchback.[66]

---

66. In fact, due to recent research and the discovery of Richard the Third's body, we now know that Rathbone's physical portrayal is more accurate than what has been perceived to be true. As Vincent Price would say: "Basil gave an excellent performance and, in the light of modern research on the subject, was probably more correct in his interpretation of Richard than either Olivier or myself." (Druxman, 231) (Before Rathbone's performance there had been four previous cinematic portrayals of Richard III. Firstly

Tower of London previewed at the Alexander Theatre, Glendale, California on November 16th and the reviews came in. *Film Daily* stated on November 21st: "Hollywood Preview – Outstanding Historical Drama Brilliantly Played [?] With his vivid picturization of the 15th Century, when cunning, heartless "Crookback" Richard III, Duke of Gloucester, fought to sweep away all human obstacles in his path for the throne of England, producer-director Rowland V. Lee has delivered one of the best historical pictures yet screened. He has gained brilliant characterizations from his cast and interest is held to the end. Topping the list of performances is that of Basil Rathbone as Richard III, while Boris Karloff is his loyal clubfooted executioner. Ian Hunter has never been better than as King Edward IV, while Barbara O'Neil is decorative and capable as his wife, Queen Elizabeth. Vincent Price does fine work...[ ] Jack Otterson's sets are eye-filling and impressive." On November 25th *Motion Picture Herald* followed suit with the praise: "...the effect of the barbarity, both raw and veneered, is made more striking by the portrayals of Basil Rathbone and Boris Karloff. Rathbone enacts the role of 'Richard,' Karloff that of 'Mord,' the clubfooted executioner and torturer of the Tower of London and they have a strange affinity for each other, the executioner sadistically bowing to the murderous whims of his master. [ ] Apparently having as his purpose the raising of the audience "gooseflesh," Rowland V. Lee succeeds admirably. From the start, which shows "Mord" grinning evilly as he whets his headsman's ax, to its climax at the battle of Bosworth, it is an audience-chilling spectacle." In contrast *Showman's Trade Review* for the same date was less than glowing: "This picture is so far under what it could have been that in most spots it cannot do better than a second feature, with Rathbone as its single drawing power. Production, particularly

---

in 1908, William V. Ranous [12/03/1857-01/04/1915] portrayed Richard in a USA silent short, 1911 saw Frank Benson [044/11/1857-31/12/1939] portray the character in a UK silent short. Frederick Warde [23/02/1851 – 07/02/1935] portrayed Richard in an early American feature length film. Originally believed lost, a print was donated by William Buffum to the American Film Institute in 1996 and is the oldest surviving American feature length film. In 1915, Rolf Leslie portrayed the character in a silent film based on the play by Nicholas Rowe – The Tragedy of Jane Shore.

the battle scenes, falls short and most of the actors exhibit a tendency to 'mug' entirely too much."

The film opened at the Paramount Theater, Los Angeles on December 7th and at the Rialto, New York on December 11th and such was the demand to see the picture that the cinema had to remain open all night: "Tower of London Clicks: Rialto Operates all Night – Universal's Tower of London registered such a strong opening yesterday [11th December] at the Rialto Theater, Broadway, that General Manager Arthur Mayer ordered the theatre to stay open all night. Late last night, house was heading for an all-time record. The SRO [Standing Room Only] sign was put up 12 minutes after the house opened" (*Film Daily*, December 12th), and the following day it was reported that "'U's Tower of London Sets Record at Rialto. In a 21-hour day, Universal's Tower of London broke an all-time opening day record at the Rialto Theater, Broadway on Monday. Ten complete shows were given to 6,000 patrons, it was reported. House seats 600." (*Film Daily*, December 13th)[67] On Friday 15th December the film opened at the Warfield Theater, San Francisco with personal appearances of Boris Karloff, Bela Lugosi, Mischa Auer, Nan Grey and John Sutton "for one day in connection with Tower of London. House should get fairly good $14,000 for the week." (*Variety*, December 20th) As late as February and March 1940, the film was still gaining reviews: "that superb actor Basil Rathbone gives a great portrayal of the ruthless Richard [ ] Splendid performances are given by Ian Hunter as King Edward IV, Vincent Price as the Duke of Clarence, [ ] and John Sutton and pretty Nan Grey[68] look

---

67. *Showman's Trade Review* for December 16th confirms this: "Tower of London Breaks Rialto Records" – An all-time record for one-day receipts was broken this week at the Broadway Rialto with the opening of Universal's Tower of London which grossed more than $2,000 in the 21 hour day, the 600-seat house playing to more than 6,000 people. Ten complete shows were necessary to handle the crowds."

68. In an interview in *Radio & Television Mirror* April 1940 Vol. 13, No. 6 Nan Grey talks about her love affair with Jackie Westrope and the article states: "She did not dream that six months hence she would wear a new name, Nan Grey, and be

after the romance. Boris Karloff as a ghastly, sinister executioner is not the type of person you'll want to meet in a dark alley." (*Silver Screen*, February 1940) "Tower of London: Fair. "Off with his head" seemed to be the favourite phrase used by those in command during the dark and bloody reigns of medieval English Kings. The famous Tower, in those days, was not only a prison, but the home of the ruling house and this film gives you an idea of how Richard the Third gratified his lust for power." (*Silver Screen*, March 1940) When the film was released in England, The *Times* had this to say about it: "With Mr. Boris Karloff present as an executioner, to drown the Duke of Clarence in Malmsey, polish off Henry VI, dispose of the princes in the tower, and flog, rack, and burn unfortunate prisoners, it is mildly surprising that this exuberant film has escaped a horror certificate. The executioner does all these unpleasant things out of regard for Richard of Gloucester, who, as Mr. Basil Rathbone plays him and the film shows him has nothing at all to do with the Middle Ages or with history, but nevertheless emerges as a man of a certain sardonic intelligence and distinction."

It is hard to define *Tower of London* as it sits across several genres. Firstly, due to its historical context it can be seen as a period drama, due to the battles it could be seen as a war film, with the intrigue and machinations it could be seen as a thriller and with the murders, beheadings and drowning could be seen as a horror. As we have seen, early reviewers were at a loss as to where the film sat, but as the film had Boris Karloff starring, had a plethora of murders and tortures, was made by Universal, who were known for their horror pictures, it is easy to see how it has fallen into this genre by default.

In his autobiography, Rathbone would rate this film as one of his best: "Other pictures of quality that I made between 1934 and 1946 were: [ ] For Universal:

---

under contract to a leading Motion Picture company in Hollywood. She did not know that she was destined to become one of the original 'Three Smart Girls,' or the heroine of such movies as 'Tower of London' or 'The Invisible Man Returns'." There is no mention of her pivotal scenes in 'Dracula's Daughter' (USA, 1936).

The Sherlock Holmes pictures and Tower of London, a historical picture in which I starred as England's Richard III." (Rathbone, 151-152) It is easy to see why he held this role with such regard – Not only was his son John Rodion (21 July 1915 – 22 August 1996) in the film, but Rathbone's portrayal of Richard is also sly, manipulative, ambitious without a moral code and yet slightly sympathetic in as much as he is a man of his time. He knows that he will always be seen as a misfit on a certain level due to his disability as he says to Mord: "Crook-back and drag-foot! Misfits, eh? Well, what we lack in physical perfection we make up here, eh? [Points at his brain]." It was a performance of a lifetime without the theatricalities of other Shakespearian performers. After the success of *Son of Frankenstein*, Universal signed Karloff for a further two films. The fictitious character of Mord the Executioner was probably written with him in mind, and as with the Frankenstein Monster, Karloff had to undergo a gruelling make-up session. His head, hands and wrists were shaved, leaving only his dark bushy eyebrows for contrast and were waxed and curled. His nose was built up and hooked and his ears were taped back. His clubfoot was created with a large shoe, not unlike the Frankenstein Monsters', with his right leg built up. Jensen asks, "Why is it that Mord, a minor character, is almost the only one to arouse a viewer's sympathy, even though he clearly enjoys his villainy? The reason is perhaps that the others are sane enough to know what they are doing, to recognise their weaknesses, and to scheme toward some goal. Unlike them, Mord acts instinctively and is incapable of comprehending, much less controlling, his desires and destiny." (Jensen, 118-119) Here Jensen has missed a major point, as religion was more important at that time than it is perhaps now, and many people have done a lot of things in the name of God and Religion and so when Mord states to Richard, "You are more than a Duke, more than a King – you are a God to me," he has given himself over to fanaticism, the lines between faith and morality are blurred to such a degree that Richard and Mord become the flip side of the same coin. Richard is the brain and Mord is the brute strength, both needing the other and in the end that need leads them both to their deaths in the same battle. There is a scene when after Wyatt has escaped, Richard realises that The Queen Mother has been conspiring against him and although she has sanctuary of the Cathedral, he can "crush her spirit for all time," and orders Mord to take the young Princes to 'the bloody tower.' As he turns to leave, some realisation dawns on Mord and there is a look that passes between the two men – an understanding of things said, but not.

There are three scenes that show the complexity of the character of Mord. The first scene is where Mord is introduced and comes three-and-a-half minutes into the film and the complexity of the scene is shown in a minute and seventeen seconds. The tolling of a bell fades into a close up of Mord grinding his axe, a raven on his shoulder and as he finishes that task and goes to leave, he crosses the torture chamber in a smooth tracking shot, stopping along the way to make a few adjustments to his victims: firstly he adds another heavy weight to someone who is being crushed, then crosses to a well to get some water and as he drinks, another victim being starved begs for water. Karloff gives him such a baleful look before throwing the contents of the ladle onto the floor, where the helpless victim throws himself in order to get a few drops of water. Mord exits. This scene shows a man who is dedicated to his craft, totally in tune with his working environment and is able to multi-task whilst on his way to do another job. The second scene is where after the young princes have been taken to the bloody tower, Mord carefully creeps into their chamber where they are sleeping. The younger prince is asleep in prayer and as he picks him up to place him on the bed, the young prince's arm trustingly goes around his neck. At this Mord's face softens, and as he lays the young prince down, his face is a symphony of emotions. He covers them up with a blanket, and here Karloff's acting really steps up a gear as you can see the inner battle of what he has to do and what he does not want to do. Then he visibly shuts down, his face becomes grim and he measures out the size of the young prince. Interestingly, Mord does not carry out the killings himself, but leads three others to do it on his behalf; whether this is a pricking of his conscience is up to the audience to decide. The final scene is near towards the end of the film, when Richard realises that Henry Tudor with the Royal treasure means war. Mord asks: "A battle?" "Yes." "You'll let me fight with you this time against many men?" to which Richard responds: "I may need every friend I have." Again there is a look that Mord gives that signifies an understanding, yet at the battle Bosworth, after seeing Richard slain, Mord goes to make his escape and is pursued and killed by Henry Tudor. It is the logical conclusion that Tudor should kill the two men who are one in the same – yet one dies heroically, the other cowardly.

Also appearing in the film was Vincent Price, in only his third film. His role as the Duke of Clarence was really a cameo and very nearly his last film as he would later elaborate on his near real death due to the practical joke of co-stars Karloff and Rathbone: "It was the scene where Basil and Boris drown me in the vat of wine. Being young and foolish, I insisted on going into the vat myself. The stunt co-ordinator instructed me to grab onto a bar at the bottom of the vat, count ten, then come up for air. The ten count would allow Basil to finish the take and, also, give the crew enough time to reopen the lid of the vat. Anyway, while I was down at the bottom of that tank ... holding onto the bar and counting ... I heard the crew breaking into the vat with axes. It seems that my friends Boris and Basil, had sat on top of the lid and the thing was stuck. Luckily for me, they got it open before I was in any serious danger." (Druxman, 234) Price really gives his all, petulant, arrogant, and devious and when in the drinking competition scene Richard revives, the utter shock and then anger that Price portrays before being knocked to the floor give an early insight into how great an actor he would become. As the Queen Mother, Barbara O'Neil brings to the role some sophistication and integrity. She was Price's on-again – off again fiancée and had entered films two years previously in 1937, following a successful Broadway career. O'Neil would find fame playing Scarlet O'Hara's (Vivian Leigh) mother in *Gone with the Wind* and would receive an Academy Award nomination in 1940 for *All This and Heaven Too*. Ian Hunter had previously played a King opposite Rathbone the previous year, as King Richard in Warner Brothers' *The Adventures of Robin Hood*, (USA, 1938) alongside Errol Flynn. His only other role in a horror film would be as John Lanyon in M.G.M's remake of *Dr. Jekyll and Mr. Hyde* (USA, 1941), opposite Spencer Tracy, Ingrid Bergman and Lana Turner. Ronald Sinclair, who played the young Prince Edward, who along with his brother is murdered in the tower had his Hollywood breakthrough in *Thoroughbreds Don't Cry* (USA, 1937), starring opposite Judy Garland and Mickey Rooney. He was a child actor originally named Ra Hould, but M.G.M. renamed him. He would go on appearing in films up until 1942 when he joined the US Army. As early as September 1940 he was looking 'outside the box' career wise and looked for a career behind the camera. At the age of sixteen, he produced his first film *It Happened One Day* (USA 1940), and after leaving the forces, he became a film editor and began a long association with Roger Corman, editing his films, starting with Corman's first directorial effort *Five Guns West* (USA, 1955) and finishing with the Jack Nicholson penned *The Trip* (USA, 1967). In an association that lasted over ten years, Sinclair would edit three classic Corman / Poe pictures: *The Premature Burial* (USA, 1962), *The Raven* (USA, 1963) and *The Haunted Palace* (USA, 1963), on which he was also an associate producer. *The Raven* would see him editing his former co-stars Boris Karloff and Vincent Price. The latter actor would also star in Corman's weak remake of *Tower of London* (USA, 1963) and Sinclair would edit. Whether there was a reunion of sorts on any of these productions is unknown. Sinclair would die in 1992.

On January 7th 1940 *Tower of London* opened at the Warfield theatre in San Francisco and to celebrate this event the front of the cinema was transformed into a 'replica of the original Tower of London.'(*Motion Picture Daily*, Jan 1940) The patrons of the Warner Roosevelt Theatre in Philadelphia were treated to a 12-foot lobby display created by manager Artie Cohn, when the film opened there in March. Despite these impressive displays that attracted audiences into the theatres and generated publicity for both the film and theatre, there was one very significant missed opportunity. *Hollywood* magazine columnist Kay Proctor went to interview Basil Rathbone at his home, about his role in the film in January 1940, and instead of the intended interview, she ended up helping Rathbone with his Spring cleaning as the editor wrote: "[ ] and no sooner did Miss Proctor start to bring up the subject of Mr. Rathbone's villainous part in The Tower of London than they had to move… [ ] They had completely forgotten about a discussion of Mr. Rathbone's career and he was expressing pretty heartedly opinions about the theory of spring cleaning." (Hollywood, Jan 1940) An article did appear in March 1940 about this, but there is no mention of *Tower of London* or any of his other roles! Such an interview would have given the reader an insight into how Rathbone saw the character and what he thought of the film.

Although an oddity in the Horror canon of Universal, the film does work. To be fair Lee was no Spielberg or Gibson when it came to directing and his battle scenes may seem poor compared to today's standards, but thanks to the acting abilities of the principal cast, especially Rathbone, Price, Karloff, Hunter and O'Neil, they raise the film out of the 'B' movie mire that many of its contemporaries have fallen into. Rathbone's portrayal of Richard III may not be as grotesquely over- the-top as Olivier's 1955 characterization, but his is the first in a full-length talking film and certainly the better interpretation. Unlike Richard III who (allegedly) skulked in the shadows until the time was right, *Tower of London* deserves to be recognised as the classic it is and treated with the respect it deserves. Long Live the King!

Over the fields and through the Skies, Witches Flying High
I Married a Witch: A Re-Examination (with a brief history of witches in film!)

To fully understand the significance of 'I Married a Witch,' and its lasting influence on the horror genre, you have to know the literature and filmic history that preceded it to understand why it is such a landmark film, and despite being labelled a 'romantic comedy' – at its heart it is a horror film.

Witches, warlocks, and magic have been part of culture since it began. Historically, one of the first recorded accounts comes from The Bible,1 Samuel 28, where Saul visits the Witch of Endor, who raises the spirit of the prophet Samuel; or the line from Exodus 22:18: "Thou Shalt Not Suffer A Witch to Live." During the 16th and 17th centuries there were witchcraft persecutions, where many innocent people were accused of being a witch and either hanged or burnt at the stake, and both in the United Kingdom, which had the witch craze of 1645 – 1647 that seeped across the sea to Puritan America, where the Salem witch craze of 1692 – 1693, these events left a lasting effect on the public consciousness. In literature, Geoffrey of Monmouth's *Vita Merlin* (1150) introduced the world to Morgan Le Fay, through to Shakespeare's *Macbeth*, featuring three witches. A mainstay of the fairy tale was the witch, never more so than in the works of Hans Christian Anderson and the Brothers Grimm in the early 19th century, which were not only broadly read, but turned into theatrical productions for the stage.

Yet from the earliest days of film, the supernatural, ghosts, vampires, haunted houses, and witches have been part and parcel of the horror genre – sometimes overlapping into other genres such as fantasy, through to romantic comedies. Witches in particular have been used as a draw to lure an unsuspecting audience into the theatre – such as *Witches Gold* (6 Reels, Capital Film Company, 1920) about the Texas oil fields, *Sand Witches* (Gayiety- Educational, 1 reel 1921), a comedy; or used to make a story more interesting; such as *The Two Cent Mystery* (Thanhauser, 1 reel, 1915):

> "David, the small boy next door, has been locked in a closet because he has brought home a very villainous report. In the closet he is tormented by witches."[1]

To be clear, between 1896 to 1941 there are an estimated 219 films (many of them now lost) that include witches and / or witchcraft; and within these films the witch is either a minor or secondary character – or as the antagonist and finally the main character. The earliest film being 1896's *The Devil's Castle*. The witch as a character falls into several genres in film. As explained in her book, *Bell, Book and Camera: A Critical History of Witches in American Film and Television*, Heather Greene lists the 'Main Types of American Cinematic Witches' as

1: The Accused Woman
2: Wild Women (e.g. wild child, or teen, vamp, folk witch, the modern clown witch)
3: The Fantasy Witch (e.g. Victorian clown witch, Halloween witch, fantasy crone, child or teen witch, vamp, magical man, good fairy)
4: Other Witches (e.g. the magical man, the magical other)[2]

Emily D. Edwards goes one step further and categorizes the witch into eight separate entities:

1: The Historical Witch
2: The Dubious Witch

3: The Satanic Witch

4: The Fairy Tale Witch

5: The Shamanic Witch

6: The New Age Witch

7: The Ingenue Witch

8: The Enchantress3

The one thing that cinema, and especially early film, was to establish was the witch with dramatic depictions outside of the fairy tale, such as: *The Black Witch* (Pathe Freres, 1908) or *A Daughter of Erin* (Selig, 1908.) Then there are witch hunts / witch trials – for example in 1913 there were no less than seven films about the Salem Witch Trials (the first seemingly to address the American witch trials being *In The Days of Witchcraft* [Edison, 1909] or more specifically, D W Griffith's *Rose O' Salem-Town* [Biograph, 1910]) – this would also fall under the banner of the historical witch (i.e. *Joan the Woman* [Paramount, 1917]. Another genre that Dr. Gary D. Rhodes points to is 'tales of the American West,' citing *The Witch's Cavern* [Selig Polyscope, 1909] and *The Witch of the Range* [American, 1911]. To that I would add *The White Man's First Smoke, Puritan Days in America* [Vitagraph Company of America, 1907]. Then we have the Shakespearean / theatrical witch – *Macbeth* [Cines& Co, 1909] for the former and Faust and Mephistopheles [George Albert Smith Films, 1898] for the latter and also the documentary, which includes *Häxan* [*The Witches / Witchcraft through the Ages* (1920, released 1922)] and *Three Centuries of Massachusetts* – (Salem Witches)' (Bell and Howell Distributers, 1934)[69]. Or as the evil hag, who does malicious deeds in such productions as *A Daughter of the Gods* (Fox, 1916):

> "There are good fairies, cruel witches, gnomes and mermaids to lift the story into the realm of fancy." [*The Witch of Badness* – Ricca Allen.]4

---

69. *Chapters from American History*, prepared and directed by Professor Albert Bushnell Hart of Harvard University. 8 reels – 1 per subject: Salem Witches.

Fairy tales also re-enforced the image of the witch, with *Sleeping Beauty* (1902) being the first filmed. Ever popular *Sleeping Beauty* (Pathe Freres, colored, 1908), remade in 1912 by the Hepworth Manufacturing Co, Ltd. and starred Miss Ivy Close, and remade twice in 1913 by Venus Features[70] and Warners. Not to be out done, *Snow White* hit the screens soon after with 'The Little Old Men of the Woods' (Kalem Films, 1910). Elsie Albert would star in both *Snow White* (Powers' Picture Plays, Inc, 3 reels, 1913) and *Sleeping Beauty* (Powers' Picture Plays, Inc, 1913). Ever popular, *The Legend of Snow White* (Thanhouser, 1914) followed and in 1916 there was a battle of the Snow Whites! Educational Films Corporation and Regent Photo Play Company (starring Aimee Erlich) both released their versions and although successful in their respected right, they were overshadowed by Famous Players-Paramount's version starring Marguerite Clarke in the titular role. Other filmed fairy tales, such as *Hansel and Gretel* (Edison, 1909) followed suit. Shakespeare's *Macbeth* (Cines & Co, 1909), (Reliance Film Corporation, 1916) and (Artclass Pictures Corporation, 1923) all added into the mythos of the witch. The most popular fairy tale appears to be "Cinderella," with many variations, leading to an estimated 41 productions of that tale.

Yet two films stand out as defining the witch as a crone and as the personification of evil, with a pointy hat and broom stick. The former being *Disney's Snow White and the Seven Dwarfs* (Disney, 1937), wherein the cold Queen concocts a potion that changes her physical appearance to that of a bent old woman (loosely based on a previous Disney short *Babes in the Wood* [1932]) and *The Wizard of Oz* (MGM, 1939), where Margaret Hamilton plays the green-skinned, pointy hat, broomstick carrying Wicked Witch of the West, establishing once and for all the traditional image of the witch in the public consciousness. (Though The Mysteries of Myra (1916) had a very similar looking witch!)

---

70. Starring Elsie Albert Producer/Director Harry C. Matthews.

As Heather Greene points out:

> "[ ] it is important to stop and recognize that, by 1940, an evolution was in process for the Hollywood witch. She was slowly becoming a monster unto herself and moving closer to becoming a regular feature of the horror film. The Wizard of Oz was the first film to suggest a biologically-based inhumanity for the witch with the use of green skin, which likened her to the classic horror monster Frankenstein. Similarly, Disney's Wicked Queen, although depicted as a human woman, is visually likened to another popular horror monster – the vampire. While neither film would ever be classified as horror, they contain the first two witch characters that inspired true fear in the same way such a monster might."**5**

What happened next would turn the concept of the witch on its head.

I Married a Witch is based on the incomplete novel "The Passionate Witch" by Thorne Smith, the author of the "Topper" series of books, who has since faded into obscurity. At the time of his death on Thursday June 21st 1934 at the age of 41 /42, Smith had written nine fantasy novels, a mystery, two military themed comedies, a book of poetry, a play, two screenplays, two short stories and the outline for "The Passionate Witch." There is some confusion as to how much work Smith had done on the book as Michael D. Walker states:

> "Based on the research I've done thus far, Thorne never got very far in the actual writing of the book before he died. Norman Matson completed the novel, working from the notes and outline Thorne had created."**6**

Contradicting this, David Langford states:

> "The final novel 'The Passionate Witch' initially drafted by Smith as a film scenario, was completed by Norman Matson after his death. It fails to satisfy. There is something untrue to Smith in the assumption that the beautiful witch who bespells the hero into marriage is necessarily and irremediably evil; in her abrupt death while indulging in sacrile-

gious arson; and in the later, violent death of the semi-comic horse that is possessed by her disembodied spirit. Verbal humour is muted. Even the happy outcome, with the protagonist marrying the 'right' girl at last, includes a sour touch of cynicism which Smith would surely have rejected. This story was heavily reworked for the sunnier, more successful movie adaptation 'I Married a Witch.'"**7**

This confusion over how much was Smith's actual work, and how much of it was Matson's, and what was left behind after Smith's death was originally cleared up in a 1941 review:

> "The nearly complete manuscript of this fantasy was found in Mr. Smith's effects after his death and was finished by Norman Matson."**8**

Therefore, we can deduct from this that Matson completed the nearly completed manuscript from both what was left behind as well as notes and an outline. But going by what was in the book, with Jennifer speaking in tongues, riding a goat through an apple orchard, sacrificing chickens and possessing a horse, there would be no way that the Breen Office would have allowed the film to be released with that content.

After completing *The Flame of New Orleans* (Universal, 1941) Rene Clair was looking for another project to do. His agent Myron Selznick sent him a copy of Smith's book, which he read and thought he could do something with, and talked to Preston Sturges about it, who then agreed to produce it for him at Paramount. As Clair recounts:

> "Paramount had been trying to find something right for Veronica Lake, who had been receiving lots of publicity partly because of her beautiful hair. They didn't want an ordinary role for her, and Preston convinced them that *I Married a Witch* was just what they needed. That's what did it: Veronica Lake got me that job; she was a lot more important to Paramount than I was, believe me."**9**

In her autobiography, Veronica Lake tells this story of how she got the role of Jennifer[71]:

> "Things picked up for me, too. René Clair, a fine director, was casting for *I Married a Witch*. I was in love with the role of Jennifer, the fair witch, and I told René I wanted to play the part.

"No!"

I went to Preston Sturges and asked him to talk to René.

"You know I can play comedy, Preston. Please do what you can do."

Sturges talked with René but René was completely against me for Tonnifer. He referred back to *This Gun for Hire* as an example of the kind of role I did best.

"What about *Sullivan's Travels*?" Preston asked him.

"One good role doesn't mean she's a good comedienne," was René's reply.

"And two good roles does indicate something," I pleaded with René. "I want that part."

Things remained unsettled for a few days. Finally, Preston called me at home with the good news. "I got René to give you the role, Ronni. He's still reluctant and you'll have to do a lot of proving with him, but you're in. And that's the big handle."

"Doesn't *Sullivan's Travels* prove anything to him?" I asked.

"It should, hon. But he hasn't seen it. Doesn't plan on it, either. As far as he's concerned, you're a siren starlet with box-office, but no actress. Prove it to him."

---

71. This story is also reiterated in *Peekaboo: The Story of Veronica Lake*, Jeff Lenberg, Moonwater Press, 2020, Pg.164.

René was terribly nice to me despite his reluctance to use me in the film. And he was certainly a fine director. He had everything – timing, viewpoint, appreciation of the subtle things that made good comedy. And he had a hell of a heart as evidenced during the second week of shooting. He came to me after looking at rushes and said, "I'm here to apologise, Ronni. Preston was right. You are a hell of a good comedienne. I'm sorry."

I loved René for that."[10]

The problem with that, although parts may be true, how Veronica actually got the role is not. On October 8th 1941, *Variety* announced:

> Par's 20G For Post-Mortem Novel
> Paramount paid $20,000 for 'The Passionate Witch,' novel by Thorne Smith which was completed by Norman Matson after Smith's death. Matson is the brother of Harold Matson, Smith's agent. Par. plans the story as a vehicle for Veronica Lake. It will be directed by René Clair. Matson has already begun work on a sequel to be published under his own name.[11]

It is clear from *Variety* (and other news outlets) that Paramount secured the rights especially for Veronica as a vehicle for her. *Film Bulletin* for October 8th followed up the *Variety* piece with:

> "Paramount"
>
> Here's an exciting combination. A novel by the late Thorne Smith, René Clair directing and Preston Sturges producing. Paramount has brought these three very amusing artists together for 'The Passionate Witch' – story of the astonishing transformation in the prosaic life of a millionaire widower following his rescue of a slightly clad woman during a hotel fire. Veronica Lake is the only member of the cast set thus far.[12]

The *New York Post* established these facts for the public the following day:

> "Last Thorne Smith novel, 'The Passionate Witch,' bought by Paramount for Veronica Lake, Rene Clair directing, Preston Sturges producing, B.G. DeSylva supervising, Dalton Trumbo writing, which is a heaping load of talent."**13**

The *Buffalo Courier Express*, October 19th, 1941 (in a syndicated piece) stated: Veronica Lake will be starred in 'I Married a Witch.' Whilst *Variety* for December 24th, 1941 stated:

> Veronica Lake gets the star role in 'I Married a Witch,' currently in the writing mill at Paramount. Rene Clair directs. Play is based on Thorne Smith's unfinished novel, 'The Passionate Witch.' Norman Matson finished the book after Smith's death.**14**

The Exhibitor from January 21st through to February 18th 1942, lists the film as starring Veronica Lake and Joel McCrea, who was her co-star in *Sullivan's Travels* (Paramount, 1941), a comedy drama, written and directed by Preston Sturges. *Boxoffice Barometer* not only backed up the casting, but elaborated slightly on the story:

> Joel McCrea portrays a prosaic small city millionaire whose dull existence is turned topsy-turvy following his marriage to a modern witch (Veronica Lake), whom he has rescued – *sans* clothing – from a hotel fire.**15**

Variety on 21st January announced that Paramount was very busy with 11 films scheduled to roll by the end of the month: Production slate at Paramount calls for 11 starters in the next four weeks, with five scheduled to roll before the end of January. Quintet are 'Black Curtain,' 'The Forest Rangers,' 'My Heart Belongs to Daddy,' 'I Married a Witch,' and 'Wild Cat.'

Somewhere along the way, the script changed from that story to the final, filmed version, with some tweaks, as Hollywood in May 1942 reported that:

> Tops in multiple roles will be achieved by Joel McCrea in Paramount's *I Married a Witch*. He plays an insurance salesman named Wooley and, for a montage sequence, the fellow's ancestors for five generations back. When McCrea accepted the role, Director René Clair wired him: "I'm happy to hear you have agreed to play the whole Wooley Family.**16**

On February 4th, *Motion Picture Daily* announced that: Patricia Morrison will support Joel McCrea and Veronica Lake in Paramount's 'I Married a Witch.' *Variety* announced on February 18th: Robert Benchley is one of the busiest guys on the Paramount lot. Benchley just completed roles in two pics [ ] and now moved into a spot in 'I Married a Witch,' new Sturges Film.

Yet things behind the scenes were not going well with the production. On February 25th, *Variety* reported:

> "McCrea Scrams Witch"
> Joel McCrea caused the postponement of 'I Married a Witch' at Paramount by turning down the co-starring role with Veronica Lake, after first approving the script. Shooting is delayed until studio signs a new male lead. Rene Clair is director and Preston Sturges associate producer. McCrea is under contract to make two pictures for Paramount this year. [ ]**17**

There is no entry for the film in *The Exhibitor* for February 25 and in entries for both March 4th and 18th, lists only Veronica Lake as the star. Why had Joel McCrea gone? According to an article in *Photoplay* in July:

> Joel McCrea was to hold Veronica Lake in his co-starring arms in Paramount's "*I Married a Witch*." The gentleman said no; he'd had an inside hint on Miss Lake.

"I won't take it," firmly said Mr. McCrea.

Paramount had offered the lead to Joel McCrea in *I Married a Witch*, co-starring Veronica Lake. The big idea was to make a really truly starring team of McCrea and Lake, who had co-starred in *Sullivan's Travels*, like Loy and Powell or Turner and Gable. But what Paramount had neglected to find out was how the team of McCrea and Lake felt about each other.

"We will put you on suspension unless you play the role," thundered the Paramount officials, meaning no dough on the line for Joel for a fixed period of weeks.

Mr. McCrea drew himself up to his complete six-feet-three and started walking out. "Money is not that important to me," he said, with deep dignity, but meaning it.**18**

Previously in June, *Photoplay* had given an explanation as to why McCrea left the role:

> Know why Joel McCrea walked out of Paramount's picture "I Married a Witch," a story that pleased him mightily? It was because Joel got one preview glimpse of the billboards that billed Veronica Lake's name all over the place, glorifying the Blonde Bombshell, while down in one insignificant corner was the name Joel McCrea.**19**

It is unclear as to whether McCrea and Lake actually filmed any scenes together before he walked out – we can speculate that some scenes were filmed, due to various reports, but as to what they were appear to be lost to history – but the postponement led Lake into the lead in *The Glass Key*, which was originally slated for Patricia Morrison[72], whom Boxoffice Barometer also listed in the cast for *I Married a Witch*!

---

72. Patricia Morrison having refused to turn up on set for a Gene Autry Western, having been loaned out by Paramount to Republic, Paramount immediately

Paramount looked to find a suitable, versatile actor and had their eyes set on Oscar winning actor Fredric March in early March:

"Par's Dicher For March"

Deal is cooking between Paramount and Fredric March to take over the top male role in 'I Married a Witch,' recently passed up by Joel McCrea after an argument about publicity. Picture is slated to roll as soon as Veronica Lake, femme co-star, has finished her present role in 'The Glass Key.'[20]

The New York Times on 7th March stated:

Fredric March Will Be Seen Opposite Veronica Lake in 'I Married a Witch'

Hollywood, Calif. March 6 – Fredric March will play the lead opposite Veronica Lake in Paramount's 'I Married a Witch,' if the studio's negotiations with the actor are concluded, it was learned today. March has accepted the assignment subject to his approval of the scenario, Paramount disclosed, and production has been scheduled to start in May with Rene Clair directing and Preston Sturges producing.[21]

---

suspended her. As Mank explains: "She had won the part of Janet, sexy heroine of Dashiell Hammett's *The Glass Key*, and was set to co-star with popular Paramount stars Alan Ladd and Brian Donlevy. Patricia had reported for wardrobe fittings when, at the eleventh hour, Paramount's front office yanked her off the picture and replaced her with Veronica Lake [ ] And she was announced to play the second female lead in United Artists' *I Married a Witch* with Fredric March and Veronica Lake – only to be replaced by her ambitious Paramount colleague, Susan Haywood. It was the last straw for Patricia Morrison at Paramount. As she recalled a climactic meeting with Paramount boss, Buddy De Sylva: He said I could stick around and play heavies. I said no! I over-ate my way out of the Paramount contract.

It was announced by *Motion Picture Daily* on 17th that:

> Fredric March was signed today by Paramount to star with Veronica Lake in 'I Married a Witch' taking over the role refused by Joel McCrea.**22**

Production started in April with *The Exhibitor* 1st April noting that Fredric March would star opposite Veronica Lake, and *Variety* later that month:

> "I Married a Witch" Fredric March and Veronica Lake in the first picture to be directed by René Clair for Paramount. Based on the Thorne Smith best seller 'The Passionate Witch.' Started in a blaze this week, as Clair filmed the opening scene – set in a burning hotel.**23**

Yet interestingly, *Variety* for the same date reported that:

> 'I Married a Witch, drama, Asso. Prod. Preston Sturges, dir. Rene Clair; no writing credits; camera John Seltz. Cast: Joel McCrea, Veronica Lake, Patricia Morrison, Robert Benchley, Walter Abel.**24**

Variety again reported on April 8th:

> Eight Pix To Roll in April, Backlog of Twenty on Hand; Five More Already Shooting.
> [ ] Other April starters will include [ ] 'I Married a Witch,' film version of the Thorne Smith novel 'The Passionate Witch,' starring Fredric March and Veronica Lake with Rene Clair directing. [ ] PIX & PEOPLE: Fredric March was to reach Hollywood today to start work in 'I Married a Witch.'**25**

On April 15th Patricia Morrison was off the project as *Motion Picture Daily* reported:

> Susan Hayward will support Fredric March and Veronica Lake in Paramount's 'I Married a Witch.'**26**

According to Hayward's biographer Beverly Linet:

> "Nevertheless, her career still seemed to be stalling, her next two films doing little for her. Rene Clair's *I Married a Witch* with Fredric March and Veronica Lake, in which Susan unhappily played yet another nasty role."**27**

Ben Melford had persuaded the director of *I Wanted Wings* (Paramount, 1941) to screen test Hayward for the lead role as she was 'physically perfect' for the part.

Unfortunately, according to Melford, "Her work was so amateurish the director [Mitchell Leisen] suddenly stopped the cameras, snorted in disgust, and stamped off the set, leaving Susan standing there while the crew squirmed in embarrassment. Shortly afterward, Paramount found that other girl – the one with the hair falling all over her face – and she got the part." The part Melford is referring to was that of Sally Vaughn, the siren in *I Wanted Wings*. It made an overnight star of Veronica Lake, although Lake was dismissed by *The New York Times* as a girl who 'shows little more than a talent for wearing low-cut dresses.' Immediately signed by Paramount, Lake would join Paulette Goddard on Susan's private hate list. She was convinced both women were the cause of her career impasse."**28**

Things were still not going right as somewhere between October 9th 1941 and March 21st 1942, Dalton Trumbo[73] left the writing and Marc Connelly was brought on board as was March:

> "Connelly to Write Play"
>
> Marc Connelly has signed with Paramount to write the screenplay for 'I Married a Witch,' the studio's film version of Thorne Smith's latest Novel, The Passionate Witch.' The picture will co-star Fredric March

---

73. It is unclear just how much input Trumbo had in the final script.

and Veronica Lake under the direction of Rene Clair. It will be Preston Sturges' debut as associate producer."**29**

Behind the scenes, with regards to the script, things were going horribly wrong as Clair would later recall:

"When I first went to work on the film, Buddy de Silva, the producer, assigned me a writer and told me the writer would work on the script and give it to me when he had finished it. As a European director used to writing my own scripts, I couldn't quite believe my ears, so I pretended I didn't understand him. I said 'Well, when can we start?' But he was insistent: 'Let him write it. Are you a writer or a director?' [ ] I started off that picture working with a very fine screenwriter in the naturalistic vein, and it soon became apparent that we shouldn't be working on that particular picture together. One day when we were trying to figure out what to do with the witch's father, he said quite seriously: 'I've got it; we'll have the old witch go to Germany and kill Hitler.' That's all it took to make me realize that no matter how good a writer he was for some subjects, he wasn't my man for this picture."**30**

With regards to Connelly's input to the script, Clair would state:

"I worked more with Bob [Robert] Pirosh than with Marc on that script, Marc collaborated more as an advisor than as an actual writer. [ ] Bob Pirosh and I worked very well together. We got out what we considered to be a reasonable script for *I Married a Witch*. But the front office didn't like everything we'd done, so we changed the script considerably. After a lot of rewriting, we finally got an approval from them and started shooting. Of course, neither of us intended to shoot the approved script exactly as it had been submitted, so we would sometimes sit up late rewriting the script for the next day's shooting."**31**

When describing how he worked, Clair commented:

"For me, after writing, cutting is the most important part of film-making. [ ] There are three important areas in film-making: writing the script, shooting and cutting. If I had to abandon one of them, it would be the shooting. After all, with a bad script and a bad cutter, what can a good director do? But a cutter can often ruin a good film and sometimes even save a bad one. For that reason, I write my scripts so that in a sense I can practically cut with my camera as I am shooting. As a result, the cutting process is very easy and very obvious. [ ] When I was making *I Married a Witch*, Buddy de Silva went to see my cutter, Eda Warren, one day. He had been wondering what had been going on. He was used to seeing several thousands of feet of rushes a day from his directors, and I was only turning in maybe 450 feet a day. He couldn't figure out why I was working so slowly, and he also couldn't imagine how my footage could be cut into coherent sequences, since I didn't make five or six different shots of every scene. So Eda Warren cut a sequence for him to show him that it could indeed be done, and he went away satisfied but surprised, and never mentioned it to me at all. And he was amazed that the picture was shot in five weeks. It wasn't much of a secret. I simply shot exactly what I knew I would need, [ ]."**32**

The *Showman's Trade Review* would announce that:

Rene Clair, the Paramount director, used 200 extras as Pilgrims in the witch-burning scene from 'I Married a Witch.'**33**

Whilst Lake would heap praise on director Clair, for March, it was pure hatred. Not only would Lake share equal billing with him (unlike McCrea), she would have to keep his wandering hands off her! For Fredric March was a womaniser[74], and unless his wife was around, no woman was safe as Teet Carle would recall:

---

74. In an article in *Vanity Fair*, Claudette Colbert would recall: Colbert, in real life, was menaced by a wolf in the person of her co-star Fredric March. "Freddie March was the worst womanizer I ever knew," Colbert told Rex Reed. "His

"Fredric March had worked with many beautiful actresses and found Veronica every bit as breath-taking. Well, she used to rail into him about being a horny old guy, since he tried making advances on her and other women working in the film. He had a reputation for being on the make all the time. March's flirtatious manner didn't set well with Veronica, creating an on-going feud between them on the set."**34**

By all accounts though, Lake could be 'difficult' to work with:

It's no secret to those in the know that when she first skyrocketed to fame, Veronica was extremely hard to get along with ... brutally frank, stubborn, willful, often downright disagreeable. In fact some months ago when she visited New York after her first triumphs, she so annoyed a young man who had taken her to see 'Arsenic and Old Lace' that he excused himself to go out and smoke a cigarette at intermission time, and never came back.**35**

Lake herself would vividly recall one incident:

I had been called in for a portrait sitting with Fredric March for a certain day – and, well, time got away from me. Freddie, however, was

---

hands had 20 fingers, I swear, and they were always on my ass. I finally said, 'If you don't stop I'll walk right out of the scene and tell Mr. DeMille what you're doing.' ... So the camera rolled again. I'm on top of the throne surrounded by four blacks—they called them Nubians then, honey—and all the eunuchs. The blacks and the eunuchs were always shooting craps. Anyway, Mr. DeMille yelled 'Action,' and all of a sudden I felt this hand right around my left cheek and I stopped and walked down to camera and demanded to see Mr. DeMille!" Even when John Engstead was taking publicity shots for the movie, March could not resist fondling her derricre. One photo, "with Freddie's hand wrapped around my rear end," Colbert said, found its way into the *Police Gazette*. "And the caption read, 'Even if the Marines haven't landed, Freddie March seems to have the situation well in hand.'" Affronted, she stormed into the studio boss's office, and as a result, Engstead said, "she was the first star at Paramount to get ... approval of her photographs ... and it was all my fault."

on time. So was the photographer. There they sat and waited on me. Finally, they notified the front office and the front office called me. I tore down to the studio and found Freddie ready to slit my throat, for which I couldn't blame him, but at the moment it made me mad too. The crazy part of the whole affair was that we had to take love scenes, and, when I saw the finished results, I roared with laughter. Such pure loathing you've never seen on two faces, particularly when they were lying so alluringly cheek to jowl. So I went to Freddie and apologized. He agreed to make the sitting over, and that time the results were slick.**36**

Whether Lake's rejection of his advances had anything to do with souring their working relationship, taking into account that March was an Oscar winning, award-winning actor, his comments on her wiped out any chance of being friendly as he labelled her as "a brainless little blonde sexpot, void of any acting ability," which eventually got back to her and she was livid. In fact, that comment would stay with her until she died 31 years later and quoted in her autobiography as to how March thought of her. In her autobiography she would say:

> "I don't believe there is an actor for whom I harbor such deep dislike as Fredric March. It's strictly personal. [ ] But working with him gave me the feeling of being a captive in a Charles Addams tower. He gave me a terrible time *during I Married a Witch*. [ ] He treated me like dirt under his talented feet. [ ]"**37**

She labelled him "a pompous poseur" and swore to get revenge on him. Several magazines at the time labelled her as 'Little Miss Dynamite,' and over the course of making the film, she did indeed get her revenge on him. In one scene, Lake had a 40-pound weight hidden under her costume, and when March had to pick her up for a scene, carrying her off into the distance, he struggled and after doing it three times, he was shattered. In her autobiography, Lake would recount another incident of vengeance:

"One scene had me in a rocking-chair. A picture falls off the wall and strikes me unconscious. I'm supposed to sit in the chair without movement while March desperately attempts to talk to me. The shot was medium, showing only the two of us from the waist high. We were into the scene and he came close to me. He was standing directly in front of the chair. I carefully brought my foot up between his legs. And I moved my foot up and down, each upward movement pushing it ever so slightly into his groin. Pro that he is, he never showed his predicament during the scene. But it wasn't easy for him, and I delighted simply in knowing what was going through his mind. Naturally, when the scene was over, he laced into me. I just smiled."**38**

Reminiscing in 1963, Rene Clair would say this about the differences in the acting styles of March and Lake:

"I think that the great task of a director is to understand actors. Maybe my own experience as a bad actor helped me a lot. Because I discovered a very simple truth. You should never ask an actor to do something you feel he is not able to do. That's all. I think that's the greatest gift a director can have as far as actors are concerned, immediately understanding his reaction. I remember, I directed a picture in Hollywood called, 'I Married A Witch,' with Veronica Lake, and a very good and experimental actor, Fredric March. They were completely opposite because Veronica was a beginner. She was a very gifted girl, but she didn't believe she was gifted. She was good, especially the first take. Second take, she was not as good. Freddie, as an experimental actor, was good at take five, because then he could correct his style and everything. It became very difficult to find an equilibrium between them both. I whispered to Freddie, "We are going to pretend that we rehearse." And during the rehearsal, I was shooting because Veronica didn't know. I give you that as an example. You must understand actors. Some need a lot of work, for other ones you must use their natural gift and not their talent."**39**

Further to that, actress Leslie Caron, who was very close to Rene Clair, in her autobiography says the director spoke of Veronica Lake with affection: "The trouble with her is she didn't have confidence in herself. Nothing could convince her that she was beautiful. It was a fight every morning to get her to face the camera."**40**

Round about the week of May 27th, Frederick C. Othman, *Hollywood* correspondent who witnessed filming had wrote the following:

> We've got some first-class military information today on how to get rid of Germans. You take some mineral oil and put it in a tank and stir in some sulphuric acid and you've got a poison gas that smells like bananas and is tough on Nazis. It also is tough on actors. IT doesn't kill 'em right off, but it sends 'em home feeling dead on their feet. This is a Hollywood invention for the production of white smoke. On stage 14 at Paramount, we watched Miss Veronica Lake and Fredric March through it. Director Rene Clair had before the cameras the picturization of Thorne Smith's last novel, 'The Passionate Witch.' The movies aren't allowed to use titles like that on account of public morals, so they are calling the film 'I Married a Witch.' [ ] It's that kind of movie. Fantastic, like every story Smith ever wrote. Actors, producers and crew were going nuts trying to keep out of the smoke and up with the script. So it was that the red-eyed Othman had a long chat with the red-eyed Kellaway, while the red-eyed Miss Lake and the red-eyed March marched around in the smoke. **41**

Four days previous to Othman's piece, Veronica Lake would tell Paul Harrison:

> "I've had fun being a witch, all except the first day of the picture, anyway. I knew the director (Rene Clair) didn't think I was quite right for the part[75]; so I was extra anxious to get off to a good start. But the first

---

75. As previous established, Paramount bought the rights to 'The Passionate Witch' especially as a Veronica Lake vehicle. It is an established fact that Joel McCrea was originally to co-star and that Rene Clair was happy with this, even sending

scenes he made were where I appear in a lot of smoke in a hotel lobby. I was supposed not to have any clothes on, and because the smoke was so thick they tried putting some wintergreen flavouring in the smoke machine. So there I was trying to impress a strange director, smoke choking me and the sweet smell making me sick. He said I did fine though – What! Oh, sure I had something on – a sort of flesh-colored bathing suit."**42**

The shoot was going well and then Preston Sturges, who was serving as producer, left after artistic differences with Clair and as reported by Erskine Johnson, during filming, Susan Hayward suffers an indignity:

They were shooting a tricky scene [ ] Fredric March and Susan Hayward were about to be joined in holy matrimony. A stringed orchestra in the background strikes up. Veronica Lake suddenly appears in the doorway at the opposite end of the wedding chapel. She's the witch who has come to interrupt the proceedings. With her entrance, they turn on half a dozen big wind machines. Women shriek. Hats and flowers hurtle through the air. The wind gets stronger. Susan faints, sinks to the floor, her veil swirling about her. But something happens that definitely was not planned. Susan's skirt blows right up over her head. "Stop the camera. And don't print that one," was the order. **43**

By Tuesday June 9th 1942[76], filming was completed. March, Lake and Clair all went their separate ways. The film was in the can, until the studio conducted a sneak preview as Rene Clair would later recount to R C Dale:

---

him a welcoming telegram. So I think it is fair to suspect that his walking out on the project because of his not wanting to work with Veronica may have (possibly in her mind) made things awkward with Rene Clair, as he himself said that she was more important to Paramount than he was.

76. There appears to be a discrepancy as to the actual production dates as Jeff Lenburg states that production was between April 15th to May 27th 1942 and is collaborated by IMDb website. It is unclear as to whether any footage was

"But let me tell you about the sneak preview for *I Married a Witch*, which was very instructive. The studio maintained complete secrecy about it. Nobody knew where it would be held; the studio wanted a completely natural audience that wouldn't be affected by the presence of actors or studio people. A half-hour before the preview, a studio limousine came to pick me up to take me to the theatre. The only other studio people there were Buddy de Silva, Eda Warren, and Marc Connelly. After the show, Buddy de Silva was very happy. The audience had enjoyed the picture very much, had laughed and even applauded. He said: 'It's perfect.' But I said, 'No, I have to change something.' 'You're crazy; they loved it.' 'Listen, Buddy, I'll meet you in your office tomorrow morning and show you what I mean.' Then I started looking through the audience reaction cards. I was busy reading them when Buddy said, 'Don't read them; count them.' He was right, in a way. The fact that people were interested enough to fill out a card was more important than their individual reactions. There were about 200 cards, most of them quite enthusiastic. But then there was the inevitable one that said simply, 'It stinks.' I didn't feel bad about that because Preston Sturges had told me beforehand that there was one man in town who went to every preview, apparently with the sole purpose of writing that opinion invariably on every card he filled out. Later Preston asked me if Mr. Stinker had been at the preview, and I replied, 'Yes, and he brought his family along with him.' Another card

---

filmed previous to that with Joel McCrea, though it is possible. *Motion Picture Daily* for Wednesday April 22nd 1942 states that filming had started and this was confirmed by *Motion Picture Herald* for April 25th. *Motion Picture Daily* on June 2nd stated that the film was still shooting, and *Motion Picture Herald* for June 6th confirmed that. *Motion Picture Daily* on June 9th stated that filming had finished and *Motion Picture Herald on* June 13th stated that the film was completed. Then on June 20th *Motion Picture Herald* stated 'Melodramas, Musicals show decrease' [ ] Paramount is at work on 'I Married a Witch' and 'Black Swan.' Finally on June 27th, *Motion Picture Herald* announced that a release date for 'I Married a Witch,' still had not been set.

answered the question, 'Did you think anything was too long?' by saying: 'Yes, Veronica Lake's hair.' As you can see, Buddy de Silva was right; the number of cards did count much more than what was written on them. The next day I went to Buddy's office. He told me again that the picture was perfect, and that I was crazy to change anything. I got out the transcriptions – the records we had made in the theatre the night before during the performance. We put them on his phonograph and started listening. At one point near the end, over the dialogue we could hear someone start to cough, and then somebody else, until for a while it seemed that everybody in the house was coughing. I said, 'Whatever is happening there has to be changed.' It was easy to figure out the location in the film from the dialogue that was also recorded on the transcription. The coughing occurred during the witch's rather poetic dialogue just before she died. Since we had been showing the work-print in the theatre, it was easy to remove that part of the film when we went to cut the negative. Those coughs were just like the cards – better actually, since Mr. Stinker wasn't thinking about what he was doing when he coughed. **44**

Speaking to columnist Hedda Hopper, Preston Sturges had this to say, when she asked him how his three films were 'coming along,' not realizing that he had walked away from one:

> [ ] he said, "What do you mean three?" "Well," I said, "'Palm Beach Story,' 'Great Without Glory' and 'I Married a Witch.'" He replied, "'Palm Beach Story' is in the can, 'Great Without Glory' is waiting for a new title, and as far as 'I Married a Witch' is concerned, the only person who deserves credit on that is Rene Clair. It's going out as a Rene Clair production. And he's done one of the swellest jobs I've ever seen. After all, he was producing and directing pictures when I was taking nickels from my Dad to see them" … That's something new in Hollywood – a producer refusing to take credit on his own picture – and I take off my hat to Preston. **45**

On 16th September, *Variety* announced that United Artists and Paramount had worked out a deal for United Artists to pay Paramount $4,000,000 for product already completed and included in that deal was *I Married a Witch*, and that is how it went from a Paramount Picture to a United Artists production. The National Legion of Decency gave the film a B rating – objection – light treatment of marriage, suggestive in dialogue and costume! The film was initially released on October 30th, 1942 and the Trade reviews were in.

Motion Picture Review had this to say:

> The first shock of surprise in viewing this picture is the realization that the man and woman burned at the stake by Puritan forefathers in 1690 were not innocent victims of Puritan bigotry but actually a sorcerer and his wicked witch daughter. As the film progresses, one is entirely in sympathy with Jonathan Wooley who planted an oak tree over their ashes hoping to imprison them forever. [ ] Some may question the casting of Fredric March in the role of the bewildered, frustrated Wallace Wooley. His talents would seem best expressed in straight drama. Veronica Lake certainly creates a deliciously uninhibited witch, and Cecil Kellaway is excellent as her wicked, bibulous parent. The picture has a number of comical and sophisticated scenes which Rene Clair has directed with complete comprehension of all the gay and whimsical possibilities of bedroom farce. **46**

Motion Picture Daily in their review ignored any critique of March and Lake:

> Herewith United Artists provides another of the Thorne Smith farces of the Topper school which Hal Roach introduced to screen patrons. The formula, under the directorial reins of Rene Clair, is akin to the antecedents. It is based on Smith's novel, 'The Passionate Witch.' [ ] The production and performances are in tune with the story. Robert Benchley as Wooley's best friend contributes to the merriment, and good performances are provided by Cecil Kellaway, as the spirit father,

Robert Warwick as the intended father-in-law of Wooley, and Helen St. Rayner as a vocalist in the wedding scene. **47**

Hollywood gave the film a rating of two and a half stars:

> Witches, sorcerers and spirits wend their fantastic way through this tale of magic and the witches' curse. [ ] The novelty of the plot adds interest to an otherwise entertaining film, abetted by the presence of Cecil Kellaway, a fine actor. **48**

Harrison's Reports had this to say:

> The chief selling point in this fantastic comedy is the marquee value of Veronica Lake and Fredric March. [ ] Trick photography, which allows the witch and her sorcerer father to dematerialize and reappear at will, adds to the amusement. It is a completely nonsensical picture, but it should satisfy those who seek a change from war films. **49**

The film certainly polarized the mainstream press, with Lake's performance dividing critics across the board.

Eileen Credman in her review was scathing:

> "Rene Clair's 'I Married a Witch' does not recapture the magic of the delicious Clair fantasy about a Scottish castle and its ghost, 'The Ghost Goes West.' M. Clair now is a Hollywood director; and that strange little southern California town seems to have flattened the piquancy of his films. [ ] The picture's main fault may lie in the performance of Miss Veronica Lake, who plays the witch. Miss Lake's sulky prettiness permits her to look the part. She has more difficulty in playing it. Her high little voice is far from exotic. She never brings a sparkle to the comedy nor hint of real emotion to the drama. It is a monotonous performance that kills the attempts a light laughter. [ ] Most of the time it is heavy-handed fantasy without either the Rene Clair or the Thorne Smith sparkle." **50**

The *Albany Times Union* seemed to follow suit:

> "Better check up on the time schedule for the Strand Theatre feature, 'I Married a Witch,' or you may think you are having trouble with your eyes – spots in front of them, etc. – if you arrive in the middle of the picture. The plot is goofy enough as it is, harking back to the 'Topper' formula. This is a tale of witchcraft that would put to shame the famous village of Salem, Mass., a few centuries ago. [ ] The story is a reversal of the old saw about the 'spirit is willing, but the flesh is weak.' Even Miss Lake and Mr. March seem to be playing the fantastic tale with their tongues in their cheeks. Don't attempt to find a moral – actually, it borders on the unmoral at times. [ ] Miss Lake, a one-eyed witch, never looked lovelier and proves that she has something above the comedy eyebrows beyond an exotic hair-do [ ] **51**

Both the film and Lake's performance received a better notice via Mildred Martin's review:

> [ ] Dainty, dizzy, rich in sophistication and sprightly humor, Rene Clair's second American – made picture happily proves that the great French director is once more in tip top form. [ ] Tiny Miss Lake's captivating performance as the witch who swallows her own love philtre, thereby becoming considerably more of a problem, will be a revelation to those who never suspected a skilled comedienne was hiding behind all that yellow hair. And March, who plays not only the harassed Wallace Wooley, but flocks of his love-cursed ancestors as well, turns in one of the finest, funniest comedy jobs of the season. **52**

Yet, Hollywood bible *Variety* was less than impressed and followed in the footsteps of Eileen Credman, in their review:

> "'I Married a Witch,' which deals with spirits, is a fantastic type of story that carries some interest on the novelty angles, if nothing else, but on the whole is generally tepid. [ ] Neither March nor Veronica Lake

impresses very importantly, while Robert Benchley has not been well equipped with material designed to effect comic relief." **53**

When the film opened in the United Kingdom on March 19th, 1943, The *Times* had this to say:

"A Rene Clair Film. Continental directors who go to Hollywood normally suffer a sea-change, but this film is proof that M. Rene Clair is beginning to recover from the effects of a voyage which was particularly disastrous for him. Not that I Married a Witch has the sense of style that made the films he directed in France so delightful, but at least the impulse is there, and if the whole seems deliberately dragged down to a lower level of taste and intelligence, its component parts are at any rate intact. [ ] M. Clair is rightly not afraid of repeating his effects and, indeed, gets many of his laughs through simple device repetition – the rehearsals for the wedding become more hilarious with each contretemps – but, amusing as the film often is, it is seldom that his wit amounts to more than a mechanical neatness in ringing the changes on his fantastic theme. Trick photography plays an important part in I Married a Witch and M. Clair's direction has many of its characteristics. The film goes into the London Pavilion programme today." **54**

The film also received a mixed reaction from theatre goers too, and those theatre proprietors that ran the film vented:

"The name drew mostly men as most men feel they all married witches. Patrons well pleased." Bert Axley, New Theatre, England, Ark, small town patronage, May 15th, 1943. **55**

"Possibly the worst picture we ever played. Played Friday, Saturday April 23, 24." Rudolph Covi, Cove Theatre, Herminie, P.A., small town and rural patronage. May 22nd, 1943. **56**

"Good picture – if you like this sort of tommy rot. People around here detest Miss Lake's hairdo. Business below what we expected." Wilson T. Cottrell, Carolina Theatre, Oxford, N.C., June 12th. **57**

"Due to heavy rains business was awful. But those who did see it seemed to enjoy it, although we knew the picture was impossible." Miss Cleo Manry, Buena Vista Theatre, Buena Vista, GA, small town and rural patronage, June 19th, 1943. **58**

Despite the critical division, the film was a huge success, having made $1,100,000 by January 6th 1943[77] and was nominated for an Academy Award for best Music (scoring of a Dramatic or Comedy Picture) for composer Roy Webb, but did little for Lake's career. Between 1941's *I Wanted Wings* through to 1942's *Star Spangled Banner*, Lake made seven films, after which her career was basically over. She made one film in 1943 and then three years later she made *The Blue Dahlia* (Paramount, 1946), which should have re-launched her career, but for whatever reason, did not. 1947's *Variety Girl* saw her playing herself and from 1948 to 1969 she made five films (two in 1948, one in 1949, one in 1952 and one in 1969.) Cecil Kellaway had a long and varied career, working right up until the year before he died in 1973, aged 79 and, like March, would winner an Oscar. Lake's nemesis Fredric March would go on from strength to strength, winning another Oscar for his performance in *The Best Years of Our Lives* and continuing to work up until two years before he died in 1975, aged 77, outliving his former co-star by two years. Robert Benchley would die in 1945 aged 56 from cirrhosis of the liver and Lake herself would die in 1973 of acute hepatitis aged 50 (or 53 depending on source), and outliving everyone, Rene Clair would pass away aged 83 in 1981.

'The Passionate Witch' did, in fact have a sequel, written by Norman Matson and published in 1943 by Doubleday Doran & Co, titled, 'Bats in the Belfry.'

---

77. According to Variety, January 6th 1943, Pg. 58.

To my knowledge, no film rights were ever sold and no film has been made of this novel, though there was a Metro-Goldwyn-Mayer cartoon with this title, released the same year. Nor have I been able to ascertain whether the novel was a huge hit or not and I have only found one review:

> "When Thorne Smith died, Norman Matson finished his 'Passionate Witch,' and now carries on with the further adventures of that fascinating creature. It seems that T. Watson Wooley, safely married to a secretary of comfortable girth, yielded in a weak moment to the pleadings of his old playmate, Jennifer, and disinterred her. What followed must be left to Mr. Matson and Thorne Smith's illustrator, Herman Roese, to make clear. Thorne Smith is sorely missed; and if Mr. Matson is not his equal, he is at least an acceptable substitute." **59**

Following the end of the Second World War, in Amsterdam "nine [ ]theatres reopened June 1, using generators supplied by Allied armies. Public interest in the reopening was enormous, with people lining up before the box office as early as six o' clock in the morning to see such films as 'I Married a Witch'" **60** and "'I Married a Witch,' which was also shown by the British authorities in Berlin."**61** Following its initial release in 1943, the film would be reissued and in 1947 it was announced that "Masterpiece's re-issue combination of 'Woman of the Town' and 'I Married a Witch' will play 12 local houses simultaneously, Albert Dezel, president of Dezel Productions announced. Pictures will open Dec. 7-9." **62** Also announced in December 1947 was the release of the film on 8 reels, 16mm sound for home projectors 'for road shows, clubs, schools and churches.' **63** Despite this it would not be until 1955 that Veronica Lake got around to viewing the film, according to Danton Walker, in his "Hollywood on Broadway" column.

The film's lasting legacy can be found in the comedic sitcom *Bewitched*. Created by Sol Saks and influenced by both *I Married a Witch* and the play (and subsequent film) *Bell, Book and Candle*, the show ran from September 17th, 1964 through to March 25th, 1972. Whilst this was airing, in

1965, Ray Stark produced a musical version of 'I Married a Witch[78],' starring Bert Lahr (of *Wizard of Oz* fame) and Phyllis Newman. It is interesting to note that according to various news outlets, originally Stark had Peter Sellers in mind for the lead, and once he became ill, second choice was Terry-Thomas, then Hans Conried and Larry Blyden. Horror legend Vincent Price even turned down the role! William F. Brown (of *The Wiz* fame) wrote the stage adaptation, with music by Stanley Lebowsky and lyrics by Fred Tobias. Lawrence Kasha was to direct with choreography by Ernest Flat, with a scheduled January 1966 launch date. Initially it was due to be performed on December 22nd, 1965 at the Shubert Theatre, New York.

***

Firstly, by giving us a Puritan setting at the beginning of the film, Clair offers the audience a sense of historical context, one that they can relate to – the Salem Witch trials. He cleverly twists that history, for instead of showing the witches being tried and hanged (as was the custom), he mounts the horror by having had the witches burnt at the stake as the opening shot shows. We see a wood pyre, burning away with smoke rising into the sky as this speech is read out:

---

78. It has been difficult to find out anything about this production. According to Newspapers.com there were 356 mentions of the play in 1964, 329 mentions in 1965 and 243 mentions in 1966 and nothing for 1967 and I can find no trace of it being publicly performed. William F. Brown died in 2019 and Stanley Lebowsky died in 1986. Fortunately, and after a lot of contacting various people across social media, I was able to contact Fred Tobias, (92) the lyricist for the musical. He informed me in an email that the production was on its way to Philadelphia for 'tryouts of the show. Everything was looking very good.' Then Robert Kennedy was shot and 'After that, anything vaguely connected with politics became taboo.' thus killing the production. Fred went on to say, "The script followed very closely the original movie. Bert Lahr was fabulous as was the entire cast. [ ] I believe we stayed very close to the picture with Veronica Lake."

"And may this be the fate of all the witches, warlocks, and sorcerers who attempt to work their evil magic within the township limits of Roxford. The book of exorcism, please. Mayest thou and thy kind be condemned forever to eternal flames, never to return to the neighborhood of Roxford." **64**

This is followed by a comedic element, by having a vendor selling:

"Popped maize, get your fresh Indian popped maize, tuppence a poke. It's buttered, it's hot, it's fresh. An anti-witch charm in every poke. Tuppence please." **65**

The vendor approaches a man, back to the camera, staring intently at the pyre, thus reinforcing that a witch has been burnt at the stake. A woman approaches him, and the camera pans away from the pyre and onto the man.

Mother: What has got into thee? Jonathan?

Jonathan: What?

Mother: Dost doubt she was a witch?

Jonathan: I should never have accused her if I were not sure.

Mother: And her father?

Jonathan: Unquestionably a sorcerer. Mother if thou hadst seen what I saw.

Mother: We both saw our cows turn pink, then blue and our sheep dancing a minuet.

Jonathan: But thou didst not see Jennifer?

Mother: Jennifer?

Jonathan: She told me her name when she chased me into the hayloft. She was young and beautifully fair, fairer than all women that ever were.

Mother: How didst not tell that to the Judges?

Jonathan: Because I could never describe her beauty.

Mother: What happened in the hayloft, Jonathan?

Jonathan: She brought her golden tresses ... close to my face and whispered... "Jonathan Wooley, thou hast denounced me as a witch. For that thou shalt be accused. Thou and thy children and thy children's children all will be under the same curse."

Mother: What was the curse?

Jonathan: I and all my descendants will be unhappy in love. The marriages we make will be disastrous until ...

Mother: Yes...

Jonathan: 'Tis too wicked to tell thee, Mother. **66**

This whole opening scene is reminiscent to those of *Rose O Salem Town*, wherein the heroine was to be burnt at the stake (until rescued), and the true horror of this scene would be seen in a later production, *Horror Hotel* (aka *City of the Dead*, Vulcan Productions, 1960) and to some degree *Black Sunday* (Mario Bava Dir. Galatea Film, 1960), in which a witch casts a curse. Despite the comedy aspect of the speech, Jonathan Wooley's brief description of the witch gives the audience the knowledge that this was a young girl who was burnt at the stake, thus taking away the traditional image of the witch as a hag, mature woman or old woman. This despite the immaturity of what Jennifer's magic had done – "Saw our cows turn pink, then blue ... and our sheep dancing a minuet." They must have done something truly evil (according to what the Puritans thought), because not only were they condemned to be burnt, but their ashes were to be buried within the roots of an oak tree:

Jonathan: Look! The oak tree. 'Twill be planted over their ashes.

Mother: Why?

Jonathan: To hold the evil spirits prisoner in its roots ... thus keeping their wicked powers from surviving." **67**

The audience is never given any more information other than this and they soon learn that the witch's spirits live on in the tree roots. Once the tree is struck by lightning, it releases the spirits of the witches and we learn a bit more about that they have done:

"Where am I? What's happened?"

"A miracle! An infernal miracle! We're free again. Free at last."

"Who speaketh?"

"'Tis I, thy father, Daniel."

"But thou hast no substance."

"Nor hast thou, Jennifer. We are smoke, witches' smoke. But our evil spirits have survived."

"'Twill be sweet to plague the human race again."

"First we'll visit the cornfield and ruin the crop. 'Tis always a good way to limber up."

"Look, Father. The cornfield is no longer there."

"Well, we must expect a few changes in 270 years."

"Were our spirits in the wood that long?"

"Aye. I counted the tree rings."

"See? They've built a new house. It seems all ablaze. Is it on fire?"

"Not yet!" **68**

This adds to what father and daughter did, they liked to set fires, although the justice served upon them seems harsh. Once Jennifer sees how people mingle in the modern age, she decides that she wants a body so as she can torment men:

> "T'would be nice to have lips, lips to whisper lies … lips to kiss a man and make him suffer. Father, why cannot I have lips and eyes and hair?"

Here, Jennifer lays the groundwork to gain what she wants. However, Daniel wants to know more about her curse, which leads Jennifer into manipulating him into getting what she wants:

"Jennifer, what's that curse thou wast chattering about?"

"Each Wooley must marry the wrong woman."

"Ha! What a curse! Every man who marries… marries the wrong woman. True suffering cometh when a man is in love with the woman he cannot marry."

"Father, suppose a man were in love with a witch. With me. I would not marry him."

"Ha! [ ] Let's get out of here. Let's go for a little ride…"

The two streams of smoke fly off on a broom.

"Father, give me a body."

"Oh no (*laughs*) Thou didst get into enough trouble with thy last one."

"Thou canst not give me a body. Thou wouldst not even know how to begin."

"No? I'd merely make a little fire. As thy last body was destroyed by flame… thy new one would be born in flame."

"Prove it. Start that great house on fire."

"A hotel for pilgrims, (*laughs*) 'Twould be a pleasure burning that. All right, I will. **69**

Daniel acquiesces and burns down the Pilgrim Hotel. As the hotel burns down, floor by floor, Wooley hears Jennifer calling out to him. It appears that only he can hear her, and this puts Jennifer firmly in the 'siren' label – she continues to lure him to her, into the burning building.

Fireman: I didn't hear anything.

Wooley: It was so clear. A woman's voice.

Fireman: Aw, there's nobody in there. They've looked everywhere.

Wooley: No! Wait. Wait. There it is again.

Jennifer: Here I am Mr. Wooley … over here.

Wooley (*entering the building*): Where? I … I can't see.

Jennifer: Just walk. You'll find me. Keep walking. This way. This way.

Wooley: Are you all right?

Jennifer: I think so. Two legs, two arms, a face, hair. Yes, I seem to be complete.

Wooley: Why don't you come out?

Jennifer: I've been waiting for you, Mr. Wooley.

Wooley: Where are you?

Jennifer: You're getting warmer. Here's my hand.

Wooley: How can I get you out, I can't see a thing?

Jennifer: I can see you. How do you do?

Wooley (*panicky*): Never mind. Let's get out of here.

Jennifer: Have you a gazing glass?

Wooley: A what?

Jennifer: A mirror. I want to see what I look like.

Wooley: At a time like this?

Jennifer: Oh, I'm cold.

Wooley: Cold? In this furnace?

Jennifer: But I have no clothes.

Wooley: No clothes? (*looks around and finds a fur coat*) Here, put this on. (*coughing*) How did you

get here?

Jennifer: From the top floor (*as she puts the coat on*) Why do you look away? Am I not pretty?

Wooley: Who cares? Come on (*Jennifer coughing*) get up, get up.

Jennifer (*laughing*): I can't.

Wooley: Here, I'll carry you.

Jennifer: Legs are funny when you're not used to them, aren't they? Why are you in such a hurry? **70**

Throughout this whole sequence, Jennifer is in total control. Her life was originally taken by flame and now she has rebirth by the flame, and in doing so, plays a sort of cat and mouse game with Wooley. His fear that they are going to get burned alive if they don't get out of the hotel is matched by her disdain because she knows that they won't, as she knows that her magic will keep them safe.

Wooley: Why? The whole building was on the third floor, and now it's fallen to the second. When this ceiling gives way, we'll be buried alive.

Jennifer: Nothing will happen to us.

Wooley: You don't know what you're talking about.

Jennifer: Yes, I do. **71**

Wooley gets Jennifer out of the hotel safely and to the on-looking spectators, it appears as if he's rescued her. A local reporter rushes up and takes a photograph of them, whilst his enraged fiancée looks on. Jennifer then plagues Wooley, to the point that Wooley thinks that she has been sent by his rivals to taint his name and ruin the election for him. What she is trying to do is break her curse, by making him fall in love with her, but he's already in love with Estelle, so in the end, Jennifer is forced to call on her father for advice.

Jennifer: I wish Father were here.

Daniel: What seems to be the trouble?

Jennifer: Oh, good morning Father. I need some advice. He's tougher than I thought. I can't seem to make him love me.

Daniel: Thou art the veriest bungler. I must have been drunk to give thee a body.

Jennifer: Oh, don't smoke so much, Father.

Daniel: Did something go wrong with thy philter?

Jennifer: My what?

Daniel: Thy love philter. Thou gavest him one, I presume.

Jennifer: No. I thought I could do it barehanded.

Daniel: Art thou a witch or a woman? Prepare a love philter at once. Dost thou recall the incantation? **72**

Between father and daughter, they create a love philter. But things go terribly wrong when Jennifer tries to get Wooley to take the potion, and a falling picture accidentally knocks her out, and Wooley gives her the philter instead. The philter makes Jennifer fall madly in love with Wooley and she plagues Wooley for the rest of the film – until through her own endeavours, she manages to break the curse that she had placed on the Wooley family so long ago. This leads Jennifer into conflict with her father, wherein she not only loses her power, but Daniel implies filicide!

Daniel: I must compliment you on the public confidence you have inspired for Master Wooley.

Jennifer: You're not going to hurt him again?

Daniel: I will attend to him later. I am concerned now with an erring daughter.

Jennifer: I've done nothing except love him.

Daniel: You have informed him that you are a witch. Need I remind you of the punishment that I must perforce administer? At midnight, back to the tree. There to stay until the present race of men is extinguished. A rather light sentence considering the offense.

Jennifer: But if I don't wish to go, there is nothing you can do about it. I'm still a witch.

Daniel: No, my dear. Your heart is so full of human love that I can no longer trust you. Until you have resumed a more spirit-like existence, you shall be a mere mortal.

Jennifer: I've remembered all the spells you've taught me. Out, fire, by Rhadamanthus, out!

Daniel (*chuckling*): You see? Your power is dead[79]. Mine remains.

Jennifer (*repeating the spell*): Out, fire ...

Daniel: Better get ready. Soonest done, soonest mended and midnight approaches.

Jennifer: May I ... say goodbye?

Daniel: Certainly, my dear. I'll be around.

Jennifer races to Wooley, begging him that they have to escape. They leave the house and into a waiting taxi.

Jennifer: I had to get you away. Something might have happened to you.

Wooley: What!

Jennifer: I don't know, but something awful.

Wooley: Can't you tell me about it now?

Jennifer: Wally, I'm afraid.

Wooley: You are afraid! What trouble can you be in that you can't get out of by witchcraft?

---

79. What is clear is that Jennifer believes that her love of Wooley has stripped her of her powers, even Daniel implies this, thus reinforcing her belief, when in fact it is he who has stripped her of her powers. R C Dale confirms this in his *The Films of Rene Clair* (Pg.308) "she has already been purged [ ] of her witchcraft by her father's own vengeful hand."

Jennifer: I've lost my power.

Wooley: What!

Jennifer: I'm not a witch any longer. I'm like any other girl. I wish we could go so fast that no power on earth could overtake us. Is it midnight yet?

Wooley: No. Five minutes to midnight. **73**

Here, not only has Jennifer gone from supernatural entity to a young girl, who is not only afraid for the life of the man that she loves, but also her own from the very person who should be protecting her – her father! (Who, incidentally, tried to turn her into a frog as a punishment for making him revive the body he occupied, until he got Wooley's gun to shoot him, thus framing Wooley for first degree murder.) Whilst this is taking place, the taxi has taken flight into the sky. A flash of lightening exposes the taxi driver's face, revealing it to be Daniel. He crashes the taxi into the oak tree, resulting in a huge explosion. Wooley manages to get Jennifer out of the wreckage, where they are confronted by Daniel in smoke form.

Daniel: Don't worry about me, Master Wooley. I am accustomed to fire. Come Jennifer, I have decided to return with thee to the tree. I am weary of mortals. **74**

Allowing her a brief goodbye, in which she states that she will 'love him through all eternity', Daniel commits filicide in the physical sense by taking back Jennifer's body and returning her to the smoke-like state that she was originally in when released from the tree. Throughout the film, we are led to believe that it is Jennifer who is the main protagonist – we know that it was she who placed the curse on the Wooleys initially, we know that it is she who wanted a body so as to "be nice to have lips, lips to whisper lies ... lips to kiss a man and make him suffer ... Father, give me a body." **75** We also know that she made a 'love potion' for Wooley so as he would fall in love with her (thus negating the curse). Yet, in the final stages of the film, we learn that she is just a puppet for her father's revenge. He not only punishes her by stripping her of her physical form, he also strips her of her emotional state.

Daniel: (*cackling*): He'll remember, that will be his torture.

Jennifer: (*to Wooley*): And I'll remember that I loved you, through all eternity, I'll remember.

Daniel: Thou will remember nothing of this tender feeling. That will be the essence of thy punishment.

Daniel then goes on to gloat as they watch as Wooley carries Jennifer's body towards the house that we see at the beginning of the film.

Daniel: Look at him. Is it not good to see him suffer?

Jennifer: Yes Father.

Daniel: Is this not a perfect revenge on the Wooleys?

Jennifer: Yes, Father. Could we follow him?

Daniel: And why?

Jennifer: To watch him suffer, of course.

Daniel: Well said Jennifer. Thou art a witch again. (*Daniel cackles as he watches Wooley lay Jennifer's still body onto a sofa*) She's dead, Master Wooley. Thy marriage is a mournful memory. Let's be gone, Jennifer.

Here Jennifer cleverly tricks her father into believing that she has returned to form.

Jennifer: Let me tarry but a moment at this window. I wish to see it all.

Daniel: Thou art enjoying it? Eh?

Jennifer: Oh yes. And thou?

Daniel: I cannot remember when I've had a better time.

Daniel slips inside a bottle of whiskey, but still questions his daughter.

Daniel: It's great to be in here. Jennifer! The sound of his voice. (*chuckles*) It no longer thrills?

Jennifer: No, Father.

Daniel: Good. And his worried looks and the warmth of his arms around thee?

Jennifer (*giving the answers her father wants to hear*) These are things that have no meaning for me now.

Daniel (*intoxicated*): And the touch of his lips? **76**

Taking the opportunity, Jennifer re-enters her body, professes her love for Wooley (love is stronger than witchcraft!), and plugs up the bottle that her father is in, trapping him inside.

The final scene is set approximately five to six years in the future and Jennifer and Wooley have a young daughter, who appears to have inherited some of her mother's witchcraft, as she races into the lounge, riding a broomstick! The implication is that far from having her powers stripped from her, as she believed, she regained them and that her daughter has inherited them. In a 2008 interview with *Video Watchdog* editor Tim Lucas, Ann Carter, who played their daughter unwittingly confirmed this while reminiscing:

> "I remember *I Married a Witch*, that one I do have in my head, because it made such an impression. I played Veronica Lake's little daughter and in the last scene, I was supposed to come flying down a staircase on a broomstick. The broom was suspended by a wire from a boom, and it was quite a big deal for them to make a little seat on it for me. Doing it was so exciting that that has stayed in my mind. I got on the broom and I don't recall being afraid, it was just … exciting! I was five then.

I remember being fitted for this thing, and guys making sure the kid wasn't gonna really fly (*laughs*)! But I've never seen the footage, Mom said it ended up on the cutting room floor. And I remember them doing my hair over one eye to make me look like Veronica Lake."

The dark thread of witchcraft, curses, burnings[80], psychological abuse and filicide that give the film the edge of being a horror film at its heart, wrapped up in the guise of a romantic comedy, which it is. Rene Clair's previous 'supernatural' comedy film was *The Ghost Goes West* (United Artists, 1935) and *I Married a Witch* follows in the footsteps of *The Ghost Breakers* (Paramount, 1940) and *Hold That Ghost* (Universal Pictures, 1941), which are comedy horrors.

In 1943, for a cinema audience in London *I Married a Witch* did indeed become a horror film for them, as John Steinbeck wrote:

"London, July 17 – It was late afternoon of the English summer and in one of London's innumerable outlying districts the motion picture house

---

80. In her book, *Bell, Book and Camera A Critical History of Witches in American Film and Television*, Heather Greene points out that the New England opening is irrelevant to the story itself and goes on to say "During production, Paramount executive Luigi Luraschi sent a letter to director Rene Clair and producer Preston Sturges telling them to ensure that the film establishes hangings, not burnings, as the 'method of punishing a witches in New England.'" Noting that "New England is sensitive about this point [ ] This point was handled satisfactorily in the script of February 7th where you stated the fate of witches was – 'first you hang them – Then you burn them – Then you plant an oak tree over their ashes." This phoney formula technically will placate the New Englanders since we mention the hanging." However, the script was never revised, and the film opens on a scene depicting a burning with no mention of hangings." Here, I think that we can safely speculate that this may have been filmed, then edited out as we also know that Clair himself stated that he cut a big speech towards the end of the film, "during the witch's rather poetic dialogue just before she died" and also cut Ann Carter and the broomstick. The hanging and then burning would certainly have taken the film over the line into comedy horror, rather than romantic comedy.

was comfortably filled. There were some soldiers who had been wounded and were on their way to recovery. There were women of the services off duty for a few hours. Some civilian women were there for a quick picture after shopping and there were factory workers off shift. Down in the front were rows of children crowding as close to the screen as they could get. It was just an average afternoon at the pictures. [ ] The picture was I Married a Witch with Veronica Lake. [ ] While Veronica Lake, long blonde hair over one eye, sat in pyjamas on a man's bed and he worried for his good and respectable name and the children crowed with delight – ten German fighter-bombers whirled in over the coast. The spotters picked them up. The Spitfires took the air. The anti-aircraft guns fired [ ] Only one of the raiders got through, twisting and dodging through the defences. He came racing down out of the cloud and right under him was the theater. He was very low when he released his bombs. The top of the theater leaped into the air and then settled back into a rubble. The screen went blank. The raider banked his plane, whipped around, came back and poured his guns into the wreck. Then he [ ] ran for the coast. And he left behind him the most terrifying sound in the world – the screaming of children in pain and fear. [ ] Workmen were digging a great, long common grave for the dead. Veronica Lake had flared up with the quick flash of burning film and only reels she was wound on were left."

Witches and Witchcraft in Film 1896 – 1941

Note: Marie-Georges-Jean Méličs is the first person to incorporate witches into film.

This is far from exhaustive as there are films I may have missed. Due to how film companies made and distributed films, especially in its infancy, there is room for error. For example, 1914's *The Witch Girl* may have been made by Victor Film Co. and distributed by Universal Film Manufacturing or there are two films with the same name made by two different studios. Further, I have not included in this list the following films by Georges-Jean Méličs as advertised in We Put The World Before You by Means of the Bioscope and Urban Films 1903: *The Devil's Castle, The Haunted Castle, The Bewitched Inn, Devilish Magic, The Cave of Demons, The Sorcerer, the Prince and the Good Fairy, The Magic Book, The Bewitched Dungeon, The Gigantic Devil – The Marvellous Growth of Mephistopheles and The Devil's Money Bags*. I am presuming that *The Devil's Castle / The Haunted Castle* are two different productions and not his 1896 film, which went by both titles. Also not included are Lubin titled films from 1903 as I am unsure if they are just copies of other films or Lubin productions: *Cinderella, Joan of Arc, Devil's Castle, Belzebub's Daughter* and the same goes for Edison's *Sleeping Beauty* 1903.

Sources: https://lantern.mediahist.org/?utf8=%E2%9C%93&utf8=%E2%9C%93&q=Edwards, Emily D. *Metaphysical Media: The Occult Experience in Popular Culture*. Southern Illinois University Press / Carbondale. 2005.

Greene, Heather. *Bell, Book and Camera: A Critical History of Witches in American Film and Television*. McFarland & Company, Inc., Publishers, North Carolina. 2018.

Rhodes, Gary D. *The Birth of the American Horror Film*. Edinburgh University Press Ltd, Edinburgh. 2018.

Zipes, Jack. *The Enchanted Screen: The Unknown History of Fairy-Tale Films*. Routledge, New York. 2011.

1896: The Devil's Castle / Le Manoir du diable (aka The Haunted Castle)

1898: Faust and Mephistopheles (George Albert Smith Films. Dir. George Albert Smith)

1902: Sleeping Beauty (La Belle au bois dormant)

1903: Bachelor's Paradise (Chez La Sorciére)

The Enchanted Well (Le Puits Fantastique)

Wonders of the Deep: Kingdom of the Fairies (Bioscope Productions)

The Sorcerer's Revenge

Sleeping Beauty (Edison, 900ft)

Snow White (Lubin)

Dorothy's Dream (Bioscope, 600ft)

Cinderella (Star Films, 400ft. B/w or Coloured. Marie-Georges-Jean Méličs)

Sleeping Beauty (Pathé Frčres. Dir. Lucien Nonguet & Ferdinand Zecca)

1906: The Witch (La fie carabossa on le poignard fatal)

The Witch's Cave (Lántre de la Sorciére) Segundo De Chomó – dir.

Village Witch (Pathé Frčres)

1907: The Witch's Kiss (Le baiser de la Sorciére)

The Witch (Marie-Georges-Jean Méličs)

Babes in the Wood (Miles Bros.)

Waters of Life (Gaumont)

The White Man's First Smoke, Puritan Days in America (Vitagraph Company of America)

Sleeping Beauty (Lux)

Cinderella (Lewis Fitzhanon)

1908: The Black Witch (Pathé Frčres, tint, 328 ft.)

The Witch's Secret (Pathé Frčres)

The Witch's Kiss (Colour, 377ft)

A Sculptor's Witch (Stolen film from Electric Theatre Supply Co.)

A Poor Knight and a Duke's Daughter (Gaumont)

Tricksey, The Clever Princess

A Daughter of Erin

The Witch (Vitagraph)

Pierrette's Talisman (Pathé Frčres, 885ft)

The Leprechaun – The Cloven Foot (Edison)

Sleeping Beauty (Pathé Frčres, 984 ft)

Lord Feathertop (Edison)

A Modern Cinderella (Percy Stowe)

1909: The Witch's Donkey (L'ane de la Sorciére)

In The Days of Witchcraft (Edison) [First film to address witch trials in America]

Hansel and Gretel (Edison)

The Witch's Cavern (Selig Polyscope)

Macbeth (Cines & Co.)

The Evil Philter (Pathé Frčres)

Moon for her Love (Gaumont, Comedy)

The Witch (Le Lions)

A Mother's Heart (Amorosio?)

Tis Now The Very Witching Time of Night (Edison, 500ft, comedy)

Cycle Rider and the Witch/ The Witch and the Cycle (Great Northan)

Hansel and Gretel (J. Searle Dawley)

Faust (Edison Manufacturing. Dir. Edwin S. Porter)

1910: The Little Old Men of the Woods (Karlem Films) [Snow White – This would appear to be the first film adaptation of the Brothers Grimm tale]

Rose O' Salem Town (Biograph)

Witch's Spectacles (Lux, 900 ft.)

The Wonderful Wizard of Oz (Selig Polyscope)

The Witch of Carabose (Urban Eclipse)

Lady Betty's Strategy (Solex Film)

House of the Seven Gables (Edison)

The Witch's Ballad (Ambrosio)

A Modern Cinderella (J. Stuart Blackton)

Sorceress of the Strand (Éclair. Dir. L.T. Meade and Robert Eustace)

1911: The Witch of the Range (America)

The Witch of the Everglades (Selig Polyscope)

A Puritan Courtship (Pathé Frères)

A Modern Cinderella (J. Searle Dawley)

Cinderella (George Nicholy)

1912: A Cowgirl Cinderella (Prod. David Horsely)

Cinderella (Dir. Colin Campbell)

Cinderella (Dir. Arthur Melbourne Cooper)

Cinderella (Dir. Arthur Cooper)

The Wise Witch of Fairyland

The Myth of Jamasha Pass

The Blackened Hills (American Film Co.)

The Trials of Faith (Reliance Studios)

Snow White (Powers California Kids Pictures)

The Magic Sword (Dir. Robert Paul)

The Sleeping Beauty (The Hepworth Manufacturing Co. Ltd. Starring Miss Ivy Close)

1913: A Modern Cinderella (Dir. Eleuterio Rodofi)

Cinderella's Gloves (anonymous)

A Southern Cinderella (Dir. Barton King)

Cinderella and the Boob (Dir. Dell Henderson)

A Reluctant Cinderella (C.J. Williams)

The Evil One (Lubin Manufacturing)

In The Days of Witchcraft (Selig Polyscope)

Condemned for Witchcraft (2 parts. New York Film Co.)

The Mountain Witch (Kalem)

The Sleeping Beauty (Venus)

Witchcraft Continental (3 reels)

Snow White (Powers Picture Players Inc. 3 reels)

The Woman Who Did Not Care (Thanhouser)

The House of Bondage (Kay – Bee)

A Puritan Episode (Eclair American)

The Witch of Salem (Domino)

The Curse (Domino)

Feathertop (Kinemacolor)

The Witch (Éclair American)

Der Student Von Prag (The Student of Prague) (Deutsche Bioscope & L.S.Video. Dir. Stellan Rye and Paul Wegener)

1914: Cinderella (Famous Players Film Co.)

The Story of the Blood Red Rose (Selig Polyscope)

The Legend of Snow White (Thanhouser)

The Witch Girl (Victor Film Co./ Universal Film Manufacturing Dir. Walter Edwin)

His Majesty, The Scarecrow of Oz (Oz Film Manu. Co.)

Neptune's Daughter (Universal)

An Awkward Cinderella (Dir. Otis Turner)

Mr. Cinderella (Dir. Eugene Moore)

Cinderella (Dir. James Kirkwood)

1915: The Witch of Salem Town (Victor Film Co.)

The Witch of the Everglades (Selig Polyscope)

Fanchan the Cricket (Motion Pictures Co.)

The Two Cent Mystery (Thanhouser, 1 reel.)

Lancashire Witches (Big Productions Ltd / Anglo-Italian Films Ltd. 2-4 reels)

The New Wizard of Oz (Possibly His Majesty, The Scarecrow of Oz released under a new title)

The Ever Living Isles

1916: A Daughter of the Gods (William Fox)

Cinderella (Dir. Urban Gad)

Macbeth (Reliance Film Corporation)

Fire of St. John's (V.L.S.E. Inc.)

Snow White (Educational Film Corporation of America. 4 parts)

Snow White (Regent Photoplay Company)

Snow White (Famous Players. Starring Marguerite Clark)

The Witch (Fox)

Witchcraft (Lasky Feature Players Co. [PRMT – Paramount Programme])

The Witching Hour (Frohman Amusement Dir. George Irving)

Little Lady Eileen (Marguerite Clark – Lost)

Mysteries of Myra (Serial Service)

1917: Sirens of the Sea (T.B.M. Film. Starting Louise Lovely)

The Seven Swans (Paramount. Starring Marguerite Clark)

The Witch Woman (Peerless World)

Witchcraft (Paramount Pictures. Starring Fanny Ward)

Joan the Woman (Paramount Pictures)

Babes in the Wood (Fox Film Corp)

The Cinderella Man (Dir. George Sloan Tucker)

A Modern Cinderella (Dir. John Adolfi)

A Kentucky Cinderella (Dir. Rupert Julian)

A Studio Cinderella (Dir. Matt Moore)

Cinderella and the Magic Slipper (Dir. Guy McDonell)

1918: Little Orphan Annie (Selig Production, 6 reels)

Maid of the Storm (W.W. Hodkinson Corp.)

The Star Prince (Little Players Co.)

1919: Snow White (Lea-Bell Company. 4 reels)

Witch's Gulch (Rothacher Outdoor Pictures)

1920: Cinderella (Famous Players. 4 reels)

Cinderella Cinders (Dir. Frederick Ireland)

A Kitchen Cinderella (Dir. Malcolm St. Clair)

The Irish Cinderella (Anonymous circa 1920?)

1921: Witch's Lure (Capital Film Company. 2 reels)

Sand Witches (Gayiety – Education. 1 reel. Comedy)

The Devil Within (Fox Film Corp.)

Cinderella's Twin (Dir. Dallas Fitzgerald)

A Rural Cinderella (Dir. Erle Kenton)

Cinderella of the Hills (Dir. Howard Mitchell)

Connecticut Yankee in King Arthur's Court (Fox Film. Dir. Emmett J. Flynn)

The Witching Hour (Paramount Pictures Dir. William Desmond Taylor)

1922: The Strange Adventures of Prince Courageous (2 reels)

The Witch (9 reels from Denmark)

The Headless Horseman (Starring Will Rogers)

Witch's Lure (Apex Pictures Inc.)

Häxan [Witchcraft Through the Ages] (Dir. Benjamin Christensen)

A Lowland Cinderella (Dir. Sidney Morgan)

Cinderella (Walt Disney)

Cinderella (Dir. Lotte Reininger)

Sleeping Beauty (Dir. Lotte Reininger)

1923: Macbeth (Artclass Pictures Corporation)

Singed Wings (Famous Players / Paramount. 8 reels)

Puritan Passions (W.W. Hodkinson)

Cinderella (Century Film)

Hansel and Gretel (Century / Universal?)

Faust (Butcher Distribution. Dir. Bertram Phillips)

The Hunchback of Notre Dame (Universal. Esmeralda accused of witchcraft)

1924: The Enchanted Cottage

Felix Brings Home the Bacon (Pat Sullivan Cartoons)

Folly of Vanity (Fox Film Corp.)

A Kick for Cinderella (Dir. Bud Fisher)

Cinderella (Dir. Herbert Dawley)

Sleeping Beauty (Dir. Herbert Dawley)

The Wonderful Wizard of Oz (Dir. Larry Semon)

Circe, The Enchantress (M.G.M. Distributing. Dir. Robert Z Leonard)

1925: The Road to Yesterday (Producers Distributing Corporation. Dir. Cecil B. De Mille)

Felix the Cat at Rainbow's End (Pat Sullivan Cartoons)

Cinderella (Dir. Walter Lantz)

A Kiss for Cinderella (Dir. Herbert Brenon)

1926: Mr. Cinderella (Dir. Norman Taurog)

Faust (M.G.M. Dir. F. W. Murnau)

The Sorrows of Satan (Paramount Pictures Dir. D W. Griffiths)

1927: A Bowery Cinderella (Dir. Burton King)

Felix the Cat Switches Witches (Pat Sullivan Cartoons)

The Owl Witch (Produced in Technicolor by J.C. Casler. Written and Dir. William Bertram)

1928: The Bush Cinderella (Dir. Rudall Haywood)

Passion of Joan of Arc (M.J. Gourland. Dir. Carl Theodor Dryer)

1929: Witch's Dance (622 ft)

Love's Witchcraft (UFA Short Stories. 1 Reel. UFA Eastern Dist. Silent)

The Merry Dwarfs (Walt Disney Studios: Laugh-o-Grams / Silly Symphonies)

Seven Footprints to Satan (Warner Brothers. Dir. Benjamin Christenson)

1930: Cinderella (Columbia / Screen Gems Cartoons. Dir. Manny Gould, Ben Harrison)

1931: Lorele (Ruth Sasingle)

Cinderella Blues (Van Beuren Cartoons. Dir. John Foster / Harry Bailey)

Connecticut Yankee (Fox Film. Dir. David Balter)

1932: Babes in the Wood (Walt Disney Studios: Laugh-o-Grams / Silly Symphonies)

Legacy (Dorothy Keppel)

1933: Betty Boop Snow White (Max and Dave Fleischer Studios)

Hansel and Gretel (Terrytoons Dir. Frank Moser)

Betty Boop'sHall'ween Party (Max and Dave Fleischer Studios)

Cinderella (Terry Toons)

1934: Romance in the Rain (Universal)

Three Centuries of Massachusetts

Springtime in Bohemia

The Blue Light (Dir. Leni Riefenstahl)

Betty in Blunderland (Max and Dave Fleischer Studios)

Poor Cinderella (Max and Dave Fleischer Studios)

The Witching Hour (Paramount Pictures. Dir. Henry Hathaway)

She (RKO Radio Pictures Dir. Lansing C. Holden and Irving Pichel)

1935: Betty Boop Baby Be Good (Max and Dave Fleischer Studios)

The Greedy Humpty Dumpty (Paramount Cartoons)

1936: Betty Boop and the Little King. (Max and Dave Fleischer Studios)

1937: Maid of Salem (Paramount Pictures)

Snow White and the Seven Dwarfs (Walt Disney)

1938: Cinderella Meets Fella (Warner Bros. Cartoons. Dir. Tex Avery)

1939: The Wizard of Oz (Metro-Goldwyn-Mayer)

The Bookworm (Metro-Goldwyn-Mayer cartoon)

1941: 3rd Dimensional Murder (Metro-Goldwyn-Mayer. Dir. George Sidney)

1942: Sky Princess (Puppetoon. Dir. George Pal)

I Married a Witch (United Artists. Dir. Rene Clair)

End Notes

1: *Reel Life* Vol.VI, No.15 June 19th, 1915. Pg. 18.
2: Greene, Heather. *Bell, Book and Camera: A Critical History of Witches in American Film and Television*. McFarland & Company Inc. Publishers, 2018.
3: Edwards, Emily D. *Metaphysical Media: The Occult Experience in Popular Culture*. Southern Illinois University Press, 2005.
4: *Motion Picture Mail,* October 28th, 1916. Pg. 9.
5: Greene, Heather. *Bell, Book and Camera: A Critical History of Witches In American Film and Television*. McFarland & Company Inc. Publishers, 2018. Pg. 79.
6: Walker, Michael D. https://www.thornesmith.net/IMarriedAWitch.html. Accessed 09/07/2020
7: Langford, David. https://ansible.uk/writing/dlb-smith-t.html. Accessed 09/07/2020
8: The *New York Sun,* Wednesday August 6th, 1941. Pg. 18 "Thorne Smith's Last – The Passionate Witch Review".
9: Dale, R.C. "Rene Clair in Hollywood: An Interview". *Film Quarterly* Vol. XXIV, No.2 Winter 1970/71. Pg. 34-39.
10: Lake, Veronica. *Veronica: The Autobiography of Veronica Lake*. Dean Street Press. 2020. Pg. 80.
11: *Variety,* October 8th, 1941. Pg. 15.
12: *Film Bulletin,* October 8th, 1941.

13: The *New York Post,* October 9th, 1941. Pg. 9.
14: *Variety,* December 24th, 1941. Pg. 6.
15: *Boxoffice Barometer,* 1942. Pg. 118.
16: *Hollywood* Vol. 31, No. 5. May 1942. Pg. 10.
17: *Variety*, February 25th, 1942. Pg. 6.
18: *Photoplay,* July 1942. "Fearless: The Truth About Co-Stars". Pg. 56.
19: *Photoplay,* June 1942. "Cal York's Inside Stuff". Pg. 16.
20: *Variety,* Wednesday March 11th, 1942. Pg. 6.
21: *The New York Times,* March 7th, 1942. Pg. 13.
22: *Motion Picture Daily,* Tuesday March 17th, 1942. Pg. 2.
23: *The Exhibitor,* April 1st, 1942. Pg. 985(?)
24: *Variety,* Wednesday April 1st, 1942. Pg. 22.
25: *Variety*, Wednesday April 8th, 1942. Pg. 17.
26: *Variety*, Wednesday April 15th, 1942.
27: Linet, Beverly. *Susan Hayward: Portrait of a Survivor.* A Berkley Book published by arrangement with Atheneum Publishers. Dec. 1981. Pg. 65.
28: Ibid. Pg. 55.
29: The *New York Sun,* Saturday March 21st, 1942. Pg. 4.
30: Dale, R.C." Rene Clair in Hollywood: An Interview". *Film Quarterly* Vol. XXIV, No.2 Winter 1970/71. Pg. 34-39.
31: Ibid.
32: Ibid
33: *The Showman's Trade Review*, May 30th, 1942. Pg. 20.
34: Lenberg, Jeff. *Peekaboo: The Story of Veronica Lake.* Revised and Expanded. Moonwater Press. 2020. Pg. 165.
35: *Modern Screen,* January 1943. Pg. 55/80.
36: Lenberg, Jeff. *Peekaboo: The. Revised and Expanded.* Moonwater Press. 2020. Pg. 166-167 Story of Veronica Lake.
37: Lake, Veronica. *Veronica: The Autobiography of Veronica Lake.* Dean Street Press. 2020. Pg. 81.
38: Ibid. Pg. 82.

39: Studs, Terkel Ed. *The Spectator Talk about Movies and Plays with the People who Made Them*. The New Press, New York 1999. (Rene Clair, 1963) Pg. 168-169.
40: Caron, Leslie. *Thank Heaven A Memoir*. Viking / Penguin Publishers, 2009. Pg. 159.
41: *Middlesboro Daily News,* May 27th, 1942. Pg. 6.
42: The *Morning Herald*, Gloversville and Johnstown N.Y., Saturday 23rd May 1942. Pg. 2.
43: *Hollywood* Vol. 31, No. 8. August 1942. Pg. 6.
44: Dale, R.C. "Rene Clair in Hollywood: An Interview". *Film Quarterly* Vol. XXIV, No.2 Winter 1970/71. Pg. 34-39.
45: The *Pittsburgh Press,* Thursday July 23rd, 1942. Pg. 15.
46: *Motion Picture Review*, November 1942. Pg. 7.
47: *Motion Picture Daily*, Monday October 29th, 1942.
48: *Hollywood* Vol. 32, No. 1. January 1943.
49: *Harrison's Reports,* October 24th, 1942. Pg. 171.
50: The *New York Sun*, Friday November 20th, 1942. Pg. 28.
51: *Albany Times Union,* Friday December 4th, 1942. Pg. 18.
52: The *Philadelphia Inquirer,* Thursday Morning. December 10th, 1942 Pg. 16 (?).
53: *Variety,* Wednesday October 21st, 1942. Pg. 8.
54: *The Times,* Friday March 19th, 1943. Pg. 13.
55: *Motion Picture Herald,* May 15th, 1943. Pg. 50.
56: *Motion Picture Herald*, May 22nd, 1943. Pg. 51.
57: *Motion Picture Herald*, June 12th, 1943. Pg. 57.
58: *Motion Picture Herald*, June 19th, 1943. Pg. 67 (?).
59: The *Philadelphia Inquirer,* Sunday Morning. May 9th, 1943. Pg. 4.
60: *Motion Picture Herald*, June 21st, 1945. Pg. 23.
61: *Motion Picture Herald*, November 10th, 1945. Pg. 30.
62: *Film Daily*, Tuesday December 2nd, 1947. Pg. 7.
63: *Home Movies*, December 1947. Pg. 784/785.
64 – 76: Clair, Rene Dir. *I Married a Witch*. Paramount / United Artists, 1942.

77: Weaver, Tom. Ed. *I Talked with A Zombie: Interviews with 23 Veterans of Horror and Sci-Fi Film and Television*. McFarland & Company Inc. Publishers. 2009. Ann Carter Pg. 26-48.

78: Steinbeck, John. "War's Horror Shown in Theater Bombing". *Buffalo Courier Express*. Sunday July 18th, 1943. Pg. 3-A.

NOTE

Note 10: The Passionate Witch: The Musical.
'Witch Musical Is Casting Roles.' *New York Times* July 21st, 1965. Pg. 44.
Email from Fred Tobias dated September 1st, 2020.

FRANKENSTEIN meets THE WOLF MAN

GEORGE WAGGNER
Associate Producer

LON CHANEY
will play the dual role,
portraying the <u>two</u> most terrifying
creatures of all time... in a horror-battle
destined to rock every box-office record of its kind!

THE GREATEST SELLING TITLE IN A CENTURY OF SHOCK SHOWMANSHIP!

<u>A Suicidal Wolf Man and a Cry-baby Monster. What could possibly go wrong? Frankenstein Meets the Wolf Man</u>

"I was afraid you'd run away ..." Bela Lugosi as the Monster in a cut scene.

IN HOLLYWOOD

Universal studio announces horror film to end all horror films "Frankenstein Meets the Wolf Man." Old Doc Frankenstein rolled the words over his tongue with evident relish "Frankenstein Meets the Wolf Man." "How does that sound to you, Wolf?" The Wolf Man started to speak. "Well," he began, then stopped. He had been about to mention that, personally. "The Wolf Man Meets Frankenstein" had its points. Instead he paused uncertainly, for this Doc had begun to rummage among the flasks of chemicals on his work table. The truth was that Wolf didn't quite trust Frankenstein. He had to admit that there was no limit to the Doc's ingenuity and even Wolf's cunning balked at crossing him. Frankenstein elected a flask, turned it up and poured, watching the liquor sizzle and subside in the beaker. He shuddered when Doc turned and extended it. "No thanks, Doc, if you don't mind, I'm sticking to Strychnine." Wolf parried.

...

THE OLD ZING

"Nauseating habit, Wolf. I don't see what you get out of throwing a yardful of convulsions." He shuddered. "On the other hand, straight nitric puts the

*old throat slitting sing in me like nothing else. Tell me Wolf, how do you feel about 'Frankenstein Meets the Wolf Man?' What does it suggest to you?"
"Gee, Doc, We'll lay 'em in the aisles," Wolf yelped with immediate enthusiasm. "What a combination! Pure inspiration!" "Sure, we'll do all that and more, Wolf." Doc interrupted impatiently. "But where do we go from there? Have you ever asked that? What's the sequel going to be to this super-chilling horror epic, "Frankenstein Meets the Wolf Man?" "Gosh, I never thought of that, Doc." Frankenstein shrugged and resumed. "One of the things we've got to guard against, of course, is the attitude of the audience. You scare them half to death and they come back crazy for more. You should read my fan mail. It would make your blood run warm."*

...

AN IDEA

"Say, "said the Wolf Man. "I've got an idea. "Did you see that picture? "Taken of Manhattan?" "Sure," said the Doc, "the picture with all the stars." "Yeah. So you want a sequel. Well, let's give 'em a colossal chiller-killer-diller. An all-star horror film." Frankenstein lighted up with sudden animation. "Wolf," he said, "that's positive genius." "I can see the marquee now," said the Wolf Man. "Frankenstein, the Wolf Man, Dracula, The Gorilla, Dr. Cyclops. Mr. Hyde, The Cat People, King Kong, The Bat and The Phantom of the Opera in – in..." The Wolf Man hesitated.

"I've got it, said the Doc. "Wails of Mad Hattan."
"Positive genius," said the Wolf Man.

(The Morning Herald, Gloverville & Johnstown, pg. 2. Sat Dec 12,1942, Syndicated article)

1

The problem with *Frankenstein Meets the Wolf Man* is not that it is a bad film, but studio interference, harsh critics and time have diminished what is possibly the first major milestone in Horror History – the putting together of two classic monsters in one motion picture. The film follows on directly from its predecessor *The Ghost of Frankenstein* (Universal, 1942) and sees the Frankenstein Monster portrayed by Bela Lugosi. Lon Chaney returned to play his greatest creation, The Wolf Man (Universal, 1941), with a screenplay by Curt Siodmak, based on a joke that he made to producer George Waggner. As Siodmak explained, *"When George [Waggner] (for whom I was writing a screenplay, The Climax, at the time) walked past my table [ ] I wanted to show off my wit and said: 'George, why don't we make a picture Frankenstein Wolfs the Meat Man – I mean, Frankenstein Meets the Wolf Man."* Siodmak goes on to explain that he needed a car and when he went to see Waggner again, in his office, he asked Siodmak if he'd bought a car to which he replied that he had, and so Waggner handed him his assignment: *"Here's your assignment, Frankenstein Meets the Wolf Man."* According to *Motion Picture Herald*, the story was purchased by Universal in March 1942.

Originally intended to be a duel role for Chaney, he was set to play both Frankenstein's Monster and the Wolf Man as *Variety* 6th May 1942 states: *"Universal is playing a double-header in spinal chills. Studio is tossing its Wolf Man and The Ghost of Frankenstein onto one horrendous grapple. Lon Chaney. Jr., ... is slated to clinch with himself in a duplex monstrosity titled Wolf Man meets Frankenstein. General idea is that two monsters are better than one when they work on the same salary, even though there are no priorities on monsters ..."*

It was announced on October 8th that Roy William Neill was set to direct *"The Wolf Man Meets Frankenstein, in which Lon Chaney will play both title roles"* (*Film Daily*, Pg. 9) Neill was well adept for this as he had previously directed Karloff in the dual role of twins in 1935s' *The Black Room*, for Columbia Pictures. Madame Maria Ouspenskaya and Lionel Atwill had also signed.

Although usually professional, when it came to the hours long routine of make-up, Chaney could become erratic and bad tempered, due to his drinking, so it was decided at the last minute that he should just play the Wolf Man. That left the role of the Frankenstein Monster open. Karloff, being the natural choice having created the role, was on a 66-week national tour of *Arsenic and Old Lace*. He had last played the monster in Son of Frankenstein (Universal, 1939), and had vowed never to play the role again. According to *Motion Picture Daily* for October 19th, Bela Lugosi, at 59 and in poor health, having a contract with Universal was given the role. Lugosi had famously rejected the role of the Frankenstein Monster in 1931, stating that *"the monster was a role for a 'scarecrow"* and, in more hostile moods, *"a half-wit extra."* (*Karloff & Lugosi*, Mank, 62) To be fair to Lugosi, his rejection of the Frankenstein Monster in 1931 was based on Robert Florey's script, in which the creature was mute and not the filmed Balderston script. But in doing so, he had created his own 'Frankenstein monster' in the form of Boris Karloff, whose career overshadowed Lugosi's completely. In fact, Amy H. Croughton in her 'Scanning the Screen' column decided to remind her audience of this on March 23rd 1943:

> *Inherits Monster Role*
>
> *Bela Lugosi, who plays the role of the monster in 'Frankenstein Meets the Wolf Man,' at the Century, is said to have refused to play that role in the original film version of 'Frankenstein.' He turned it over to Boris Karloff who staggered about under some 62 pounds of make-up in that film and in subsequent sequels until this last venture. Lugosi created another role, even more horrifying because of its human quality, as the malicious old servant, Ygor in 'Son of Frankenstein' and 'The Ghost of Frankenstein.' In the present film, in which he plays the Frankenstein Monster who is dug out of an ice cave by Lon Chaney, he dons a make-up similar in appearance to that worn by Karloff, but apparently more flexible and lighter. (Rochester Times, 13A)*

Siodmak, who was unimpressed with Lugosi, "[ ]*he was a pest"* stated that the reason Lugosi took the part *"...was glad to get a job again. He was really hard up. He was already under financial pressure in those days, and there were really few jobs about for him. Karloff did much more."*

The Hollywood Reporter of Tuesday 13th October 1942 announced:

> **One Monster Is Enough, So Lugosi Does the Other**
> *Bela Lugosi goes to Universal to portray the Monster in Frankenstein Meets the Wolf Man, which went into production yesterday with Lon Chaney as the Wolf Man. Chaney was originally scheduled to portray both roles, but producer George Waggner decided the idea was not feasible because of the intricate make-ups required for the parts and the terrific physical strain of playing both roles.*

It would be a production full of accidents and twists and decisions that to this day have marred the film. Shooting began on Monday October 12th, 1942, for a 24-day shoot, despite The Breen Office writing to Universal on October 9th, stating that Siodmak's script was unfilmable, due to Larry Talbot's desperate desire to die: *"While the basic story can be approved under the provisions of the Production Code, there is an unacceptable attitude toward 'mercy killings' ... which, even in a fantastic story such as this, could not be approved by us."* (Mank, *The Very Witching Time of Night*. 269)

The beautiful Hungarian bombshell, Ilona Massey, was brought in to play Baroness Elsa Frankenstein. Universal were basically sticking its fingers up at M.G.M. by hiring her. M.G.M had put Massey on a Hollywood blacklist, following a sex scandal at that studio; Lionel Atwill, waiting to receive sentencing for perjury relating to his notorious 'orgy,' was hired to play the Mayor and Lugosi, who turned 60 during production, struggled so much with the costume and heavy make-up that he had to have at least two stand-ins (Eddie Parker, Hollywood stuntman and bit player, and Gil Perkins.) As Ilona Massey would later recall, "Bela Lugosi was a very nice man, but by then he was getting old, and most of his stunts were done by a stunt man and not by him." (Mank, *Karloff & Lugosi*, 452)

The *Syrcuse Herald Journal* announced Lugosi's heavy regime:

> *Bela Lugosi, the original Dracula, makes his debut as the monster [ ]. While working on the picture, the actor arose daily at 2.30am, in order to be on hand in makeup when the rest of the cast appeared at the studio. His early morning preparations included a hot bath, then a rub-down and a half-hour rest. This was followed by the massaging of creams on his face, neck, chest and arms, so that the ingredients used in the monster make-up would not burn or blister. Then came four to five hours' work with Pierce on the makeup proper, during which his head was 'built up' and his legs were weighted to give the effect of mechanical walking...' (date unknown, Pg.18 1943)*

The pressure of this regime and working a 15-16 hour day became too much and on November 5th, he collapsed on set. As *The Hollywood Reporter* stated:

> **Bela Lugosi Collapses Under 'Monster' Make-up**
> *Bela Lugosi collapsed on the set of [ ] at Universal yesterday and was ordered home by his physician. Illness was diagnosed as exhaustion, brought on by Lugosi packing around the 35-pound Monster makeup designed by Jack Pierce, who has handled the chore on the bogey man's previous incarnations when he was played by Boris Karloff and Lon Chaney Jr. Roy Neill, director of the shudder saga will shoot around Lugosi until the actor is well enough to return to the set.*

That same day a horse and cart being used by Maria Ouspenskaya (reprising her role as the Gypsy woman Maleva from *The Wolf Man*) and Lon Chaney overturned. The 67-year-old actress was rushed to Cedars of Lebanon Hospital with a fractured ankle: *"It seems the pair were riding in a heavy iron cart through a wooded path on the set of 'Frankenstein Meets the Wolf Man,' when suddenly the cart overturned, pinning them both underneath. Had the horse bolted, the accident would have had unthinkable consequences. Instead, he had stood still midst the cries and confusion until Lon and Madame could be extracted. Madame's leg was fractured. Lon suffered severe cuts."* (*Photoplay*, Feb 1943) Lugosi was back on set by Saturday November 7th, Ouspenskaya was out of hospital by November 9th, but her absence from the production due to this is possibly why she just disappears from the film, and production wrapped on Wednesday November 11th. Atwill, fearing a jail term; breathed a sigh of relief - when on October 15th, although found guilty of perjury, was given five years' probation. This would be the last film he made at a studio for a year. For Lugosi it had been a bumpy ride, but not without a bit of fun: *"Yes, Hollywood is taking it all with a laugh and a united effort to help each other and Uncle Sam. So far there has been only one mishap and that occurred the day Lon Chaney Jr., on his motorcycle and wearing his make-up of the Wolf Man with Bela Lugosi in his Frankenstein getup in the side car, rode over to see Lon Jr.'s new horse between scenes. The police picked up swooning pedestrians for four blocks. The boys have been studio bound for the duration."* (*Photoplay*, March 1943) The film went into postproduction and editing, and for Lugosi, that is where the fall came.

Universal executives watched a rough edit of the film and enjoyed it up until Lugosi spoke. Forgetting the ending of *The Ghost of Frankenstein* (Universal, 1942), wherein Ygor's brain is transplanted into the monster's head, thus giving him Ygor's voice, the audience laughed at Lugosi's thick Hungarian accent emanating from the Monster. This is suggested in *Showman's Trade Review*, December 5th 1942, under the title 'Comedy Relief in Horror Show;' it details how: *"Lon Chaney, Jr. and Ilona Massey are joined by Director Roy William Neill in enjoying some good laughs as they view rushes for the new Universal picture, "Frankenstein Meets The Wolf Man."* As Siodmak would later recall: *"Lugosi couldn't talk! They had left the dialogue I wrote for the Monster in the picture when they shot it, but with Lugosi it sounded so Hungarian funny that they had to take it out."* (*Universal Horrors*, 340) As now known, Siodmak did not like Lugosi, thought him a 'pest,' and would later state that, *"Bela couldn't act his way out of a paper bag. He could only be Mee – ster Draa-cula, with that accent and those Hungarian movements of his."* It is hard to give a constructive analysis of Lugosi's performance as none of the dialogue or cut scenes have been found and although we have some tantalising stills and the shooting script to go on, that cannot give an accurate picture of how the role was portrayed. Further to that, in an article for *Monsters from the Vault*, Scott Berman points out that the Frankenstein Monster is on screen for 7 minutes, and 30 seconds, Lugosi is 5 minutes and 6 seconds and the stunt doubles 2 minutes and 24 seconds, with about 3 seconds of long shots. The one thing we do know, from Bela Lugosi Jr. is that his father was always prepared for his roles: *"I did watch him prepare for motion picture roles. He would study the script, go over the lines over and over again till he perfected them. By the time he got to the studio and it was time for his scenes, he could do it in one take while the other actors in the same scene would need multiple takes."*

Lugosi's Monster was blind and ill and for the actor a challenge: *"Where are you? I can hardly see [...] Once I had the strength of a hundred men... It's gone...I'm sick."* It is unclear why the problem, if indeed there was one, went unnoticed before post-production. If fault lies anywhere, it is not with Lugosi, but with Siodmak's dialogue for the monster. Such lines as: *"I will live to witness the fruits of my wisdom for all eternity," "I was afraid you'd left me – I thought you'd found that diary – and run away,"* or *"Don't leave me – don't go! I'm weak ... they'll catch me and bury me alive;"* and *"Then I shall see again – and be fit to rule the world,"* are utterly ludicrous and not in keeping with either Ygor or the previous interpretations of the Monster. In fact, no actor could have delivered these lines with any sense of realism. Further to that it is also hard to understand why Universal did not instruct re-shoots for the Monster.

Producer George Waggner, fearing the worst, ordered editor Edward Curtiss to cut all the Monster's dialogue and in doing so cut all references to the Monster being blind and ill, mutilating Lugosi's performance, making it a disastrous mockery of the Monster's previous incarnations. As Mank rightly states, *"Yet it wasn't the actor's fault. For Bela Lugosi hadn't played Frankenstein's Monster – he'd played the ruins of Frankenstein's Monster."* (Mank, *The Very Witching Time of Night.* 287)

The overall product looks slick and Roy William Neill does an outstanding job, directing. The atmosphere, especially at the beginning of the film is just stunning. George Robinson's camerawork gives the opening 'prologue' the edge (and making it the best opening of any Universal film), with an ambitious shot of Llanwelly graveyard, fixing on the sign, before gliding over a high wall, registering the bleak, windswept landscape, cawing birds, before focusing on the approaching grave robbers and following them up to Talbot's Mausoleum as Siodmak's script details:

Fade In:

1 EXT. – The Welsh Mountains – LONG – <u>NIGHT</u> – (miniature)

The pale moon, a diffused halo around its yellow disk, peers

through low hanging clouds at a Welsh valley, imbedded between

dark, barren hills. A howling wind rages over the sloping peaks, whistles through leafless trees, whines through the low brush thickly covering the dark earth.

Crouched in the round saddle of a hill, a graveyard hides its crumbling wall

Behind a thin veil of floating haze …

DISSOLVE TO:

2 EX. – MOUNTAINS – LONG – <u>NIGHT</u>

Two lonely wanderers- one lean, one bulky – grope their way toward the wrought-iron gates of the forlorn burial place. The bulky one carries tools, the other a lantern.

3 EXT. – MOUNTAINS – MED. CLOSE – <u>NIGHT</u>

His face muffled by the high collar of his fluttering cloak, the lean man swings a dark lantern, opening its shutter from time to time to light the narrow pass which winds up to the graveyard. The yellow glare of the lantern shines like the beam of a distant lighthouse through the gray mist.

The bulky man carries some tools.

4   EXT.- THE GRAVEYARD – MED. CLOSE – <u>NIGHT</u>

The two men enter furtively through the creaking wrought-iron gates.

The angry WIND BANGS it behind them, and the rusty HINGES WHINE

Like wandering souls. For a moment the men stop in their tracks, held by a terror which grips their throats and paralyses their movements.

But then the lean one pushes his companion forward, toward a small mausoleum, a round weather-beaten edifice, which stands between the gray tombs, half sunken into the earth.

THE CAMERA FOLLOWS THEM, THEN PANS UP to the top of the mausoleum. Deeply chiselled into the rounded granite over the entrance is the name:

TALBOT

CAMERA PANS DOWN to the door – old oak barred with iron bands, - as if the dead who sleep inside wanted to safeguard their treasures from the greedy world.

The filmed sequence then differs slightly from the script:

9   INT. MAUSOLEUM – CLOSE TO TOMB – <u>NIGHT</u>

It is open now and we see that there is a top layer of dried leaves and shrivelled flowers, covering the body of a man.

The lean one boldly approaches the tomb and picks up a handful of the dried flowers and leaves which fill the coffin. The bulky one holds up the lamp with trembling hands, to light the scene:

LEAN ONE
(puzzled)

<u>Wolf-bane!</u>

As the two men examine the contents of the coffin, the lean one, looks up with a faraway look in his eyes as he recites the 'wolf-man' poem: "Even a man who is pure in heart and says his prayers by night, may become a wolf when the wolfbane blooms and the moon is full and bright," and as he does so, the full moon shines into the mausoleum, lighting up the 'corpse' of Lawrence Talbot. According to the shooting script shots 10 -11 are dropped in the filmed sequence, tightening up an already frightening scene, shots 15 and 16 are cut and shot 20 is cut:

20   EXT. MAUSOLEUM - MED. CLOSE - <u>NIGHT</u>

    The bulky one climbs through the window. Torn pieces from his cloak flutter like mourning flags from the broken window-frame. His face is bleeding, his hands are cut by the glass. Recklessly he jumps to the ground. Then, picking himself up, he limps away as fast as his weak legs can carry him.

    CAMERA PANS UP TO THE WINDOW: The flames of the burning oil blaze away inside the mausoleum, then start to die down slowly.

    AS THE CAMERA HOLDS ON THIS a moment, we HEAR THE VOICE OF THE LEAN ONE.

    His whimpering CRIES are gradually drowned out by the HOWLING OF THE STORM …

SLOW FADE OUT:

In the film the last shot from this prologue is the bulky grave robber running away, leaving the audience to wonder the fate of the other one, and cuts to a police officer finding the unconscious body of Lawrence Talbot. The whole opening scene lasts for 4:53 minutes. This then cuts the film into two distinctive parts: Talbot in the hospital, desperately wanting to die and for people (physician Frank Mannering [Patric Knowles] and Police Inspector Owen [Dennis Hoey]) to believe his story, and the second half is set in Europe. Chaney certainly adds to the angst of his character, brimming over with melancholy and an undeniable desire to die. His performance is utterly electrifying, until Vasaria's Festival of the New Wine, wherein Adia Kuznetzoff sings the faro - La -faro-Li song, and Talbot loses the plot when the line, *"And may they live eternally,"* is sung and goes to attack the gypsy singer: *"Eternally! I don't want to live forever. Why did you say that? Tell me! Why?"* This is the only time where a scene fails, mainly due to the lack of reaction of those around him and briefly weakens Chaney's performance, for he's like a spoilt child, rather than in anguish over his condition. Brunas, Brunas and Weaver would correctly state:

> *"Chaney dominates the film; forlorn but no longer whiny, desperate but not as panic-stricken, he brings some new dimensions to the melancholy Larry Talbot and evokes yet greater sympathy as he searches vainly for the secret of death." (Universal Horrors, .342)*

Chaney, (who may have had a thing for Massey), is truly ignited in every scene with her, as she would later recall: *"I think Lon Chaney is one of the nicest, sweetest people in the world. It was a great deal of fun. You know it took four hours to put on his make-up and when it was on, it was hot under the lights. It was very difficult for him to eat. He mostly had soup which he sipped through a straw, and just for fun, we put hot peppers in it! We had a lot of fun... I never had any difficulty with my co-stars, but Chaney was something special.* (Mank, *It's Alive*, pg.117)

Patric Knowles as Dr Frank Mannering is an interesting character as he starts off as a doctor, then investigator (hunting Talbot down) before morphing into a 'Doctor Frankenstein' character: "*I can't destroy Frankenstein's creation. I've got to see it at its full power.*" Ilona Massey, with her long blonde braided hair and Hungarian accent is bewitching as Baroness Frankenstein, who turned heads towards the end of the film, wearing just a negligee as she is carried away by the monster. Poor Dwight Frye, looking ill as Rudi the Tailor, was not even acknowledged in the opening credits (in what would be his final Universal film; he would die eight months after the film's release of a heart attack – he was only 44.) After failing to be acknowledged in *The Ghost of Frankenstein*, Frye was last on the end credits for players, a sad testament to how Universal credited its actors; after all, twelve years previously, he'd been Renfield to Lugosi's Dracula and Fritz to Karloff's Frankenstein Monster. The *Syrcuse Herald Journal* would remember this when the film opened at The Paramount:

New Horror Film At Paramount

Dwight Frye Again At Castle Frankenstein

The first man to be killed in Castle Frankenstein, came back to the old homestead recently, and found everything changed, even his fellow boarders. He is Dwight Frye, who used to be slaughtered regularly by Boris Karloff as the monster in the early Frankenstein pictures. When Frye returned to the horror film set to play a part [ ] he found that, although he was the first to be killed in the series, he is the sole survivor. Not a single person connected with the direction or acting of the current Frankenstein picture was associated with the first one. The castle set had been changed to a ruin. The monster had a new skull. The only familiar face Frye encountered on the huge sound stage was that of Jack Pierce, makeup man for all the Frankenstein pictures. [ ] Frye now ties Boris Karloff's record, with his third appearance in the Frankenstein series. For a chap destined to win a measure of fame, skulking around the corridors of haunted castle sets and getting himself strangled by living corpses, Frye had a curiously unpromising start of laughter and song. On stage, he was a vaudeville funster and musical comedy star. [ ] Since entering pictures, however, Frye has gone in for the grimmer side of acting. He gets killed, habitually. Lugosi assassinated him in 'Dracula.' Karloff sent him to the morgue in 'Frankenstein' and 'The Bride of Frankenstein.' The grim reaper cut him down in 'The Crime of Dr Crespi,' 'The Vampire,' and 'Doorway to Hell.' [81]*This man who has died so often on the screen was born in Denver, Colo., and went to business school. From business school, he went into the show business, taking a job with a Denver stock company, which moved on to Spokane and there ceased operations. Frye went to New York City and began his vaudeville career. (Date unknown, 1943. 22)*

Released on March 8th 1943, the film was an instant hit: *"DEVOTEES of 'horror,' and they're legion o'er the land – have frequently met Frankenstein's monster as well as the Wolf Man, spine-chilling characters portrayed respectively by Bela Lugosi and Lon Chaney......Currently, John Q.Public is meeting both of these shockers in 'Frankenstein Meets The Wolf Man'...... The picture is doing a land office biz, not only in stands where the demand for horror attractions is consistently high, but in ace houses, too, - many of which don't ordinarily purvey this type of entertainment..."* (Film Daily, March 31 1943, Pg. 4) Some reviews followed suit: *"As if the cavortings of a werewolf were not enough to scare an audience, the company has seen fit to disinter Dr. Frankenstein's monster and blow breath of life back into him. The result is a horror feast in which devotees of the weird and the fantastic will gorge themselves to bursting. The opportunities for screams are offered with unparalleled generosity. Heaven knows what so rich a diet of scariness will do to the kids. The title of the film in itself is an irresistible invitation to those who thrive on horror..."* (Film Daily, March 1st 1943, 8) *"Frankenstein Film has plenty thrills. That shuddery entertainment phenomena, the horror drama, quickens its pace and lengthens its stride in Universal's latest and most pretentious shocker [ ] Ilona Massey, co-starred with Patric Knowles,*

---

81. This piece has some notable errors. Firstly,, it's The Vampire Bat, not The Vampire and secondly, Frye didn't die in either Doorway to Hell or The Crime of Dr, Crespi, where he played a heroic role.

is seen as Baroness Elsa Frankenstein [ ] Bela Lugosi has the role of a giant monster. His difficult portrayal and fantastic makeup highlight many of the film's eerie sequences [ ] skilfully directed by Roy William Neill ...' (The News of the Tonawandas, May 3rd 1943) Other reviews were not as positive: *"On the whole, Universal should be glad it's all over. Both fables have been wrung dry, and the difficulties of catching up past threads of narrative, explaining the bogey men's escape from their last near-annihilation and plunging them into a new catastrophe have long since become too much for the script department. [ ] The cast, for the most part, performs capably, although Mr. Lugosi's monster is more of a clown than a nightmare."* (Syracuse NY Journal, 27 1943 date unknown) or *"The action and the eerie atmosphere conforms to a familiar pattern, but it does not detract from the film's horrendous nature: - [ ] Definitely not for children."* (Harrison's Reports, March 6th 1943.) *"It is less disturbing than the first of the group because it is not so well done, and it is so far outside the normal experience that the average adult will not be adversely affected. For younger people, especially the sensitive, it is not advised."* (Motion Picture Reviews, January/February 1943, 5)

Despite the film being a hit and despite the mixed reviews, Lugosi's career at Universal was over, until 1948s' *Abbott and Costello Meet Frankenstein*, when he returned to the role that brought him fame, Dracula. For Lugosi, the studio always seemed to be contemptuous of him, paid him less than his co-stars, and by stripping him of his performance in *FMTW*, made him look like he could not actually act! Whether Lugosi knew what had happened to his performance is open to debate, but he would have known something was up by the reviews ...

Variety on Wednesday July 26th 1944, had a very interesting article on Universal and its horror films:

> *U Finds Ghouls Pay Off in Gold.*
>
> *It pays to horrify, according to statisticians at Universal where approximately $10,000,000 in profits have been made by the com-*

pany's chiller-dillers in the 13 years since "Frankenstein" started the goose-flesh cycle. Ghoulish films, including "Dracula," "The Wolf Man," "The Invisible Man," and "The Mummy" and others, have been netting around $750,000 annually over a period of years, and the schedule for 1944-45 calls for at least six of the same ghostly brood.

Steady profits have accrued in spite of foreign regulations which have confined horror pictures largely to American continent. They have been barred for the duration in England on the theory that the British public has enough real horror on its hands, but the market will be reopened as soon as the war is settled.

So if *FMTW*'s final cost was $238,071.79 (Mank) and it averaged a profit of $750,000 after costs, then I can see no valid reason as to why there were no re-shoots for Lugosi. In the UK the film was given an 'H' certificate and in 1946, in Glasgow, the police had to be called *"after children stormed a neighbourhood house showing the picture."* The same year, Samuel Brodsky, composer, filed a suit in N.Y. federal court against Universal, claiming that the studio had infringed on his copyright on his unpublished songs in four different films. Part of his suit included an injunction restraining Universal from 'exhibiting the latest, "Frankenstein Meets the Wolf Man." (*Variety*, August 28th 1946) The film would be part of another court case, when screenwriter John L. Balderston filed suit *"for declaratory relief against Universal Pictures Corp., asking 1% of the gross on all Universal films using the 'Frankenstein' character. Writer declares his original contract, signed in 1931, called for that amount. Since the first 'Frankenstein' picture, the studio has made 'The Bride of Frankenstein,' 'Frankenstein Meets Dracula,' 'Frankenstein Meets the Wolf Man,' and 'Abbott and Costello Meet Frankenstein'."* (*Variety*, June 7th 1950) For a film that has garnered such a negative reputation (mainly down to Lugosi's portrayal of the Frankenstein Monster), in 1948 Realart Pictures Inc., chose this and 11 other films to add to its 1948-49 line up of re-issues, (which also included the Lugosi / Karloff classic *The Invisible Ray*) with which it would be double-billed with 1936's *Dracula's Daughter*. In

October 1957, it would be included in Universal's *Shock Theater* package of 52 pre-1948 horror films released for television syndication.

From its opening shots, through to its climatic ending, the film is a joyous ride and it is time to give Lugosi's portrayal as the Frankenstein Monster a new view, knowing that the studio deliberately massacred his performance. Both the Frankenstein Monster and the Wolf Man would return in 1944s' *House of Frankenstein*, with Chaney reprising his Wolf Man role, but Lugosi was nowhere to be seen as John Carradine would take over his role as Dracula.

THE BODY SNATCHER R52-230
SHRIEK AND SHUDDER!
Boris KARLOFF
in ROBERT LOUIS STEVENSON'S
THE BODY SNATCHER
with BELA LUGOSI
HENRY DANIELL · EDITH ATWATER · RUSSELL WADE
SHARYN MOFFETT
PRODUCED BY VAL LEWTON
DIRECTED BY ROBERT WISE
Re-Released by
RKO RADIO PICTURES
R52-230 THE BODY SNATCHER

Where are all the bodies? Karloff and Lugosi's Last haunting collaboration: The Body Snatcher.

"[ ] *The Body Snatcher* (1945), with Boris Karloff, was certainly the superior of all horror films, at least in terms of literacy and mature approach."

Audience Reaction Platters, RKO Idea
St. Louis – In order to catch the audience reaction to the world premiere of 'The Body Snatcher,' Terry Turner, RKO exploitation chief, arranged to have a recording machine placed on the stage apron. The soundtrack and the audience's response were picked up on the platters. The patrons were not aware that the records were being made. Platters have been sent to Hollywood and New York for careful studies by the studio and sales departments. Premiere was held at the Missouri Theater.

What is it that makes RKO's *The Body Snatcher* one of the most enduring and popular horror films of the 1940s? Could it be because Robert Louis Stevenson based his short story on the infamous body snatchers, Burke and Hare in 18th century Scotland? Or is it because director Robert Wise brought out the best performances in his cast, or is it because this is the last teaming of Karloff and Lugosi, their performances reflecting their careers? (Inasmuch as Karloff's career on some level killed Lugosi's)

During the making of *House of Frankenstein* at Universal, Karloff received an invitation from RKO Pictures to discuss making films with Val Lewton.

At this point in his career, Karloff was dissatisfied with continually playing 'horror roles' and longed to break out of that mould as he explained to Victor Gunsox in December 1945, when being interviewed about *Bedlam*, but here he could also be talking about *The Body Snatcher*:

> [ ] Boris Karloff is sick and tired of scaring us poor mortals half out of our wits. So positive is his feeling after years in hideous make-up that he already has spurned a role in a horror picture – the very first time he has ever refused a part. "It was in one of the Universal Frankenstein pictures[82], although he had not been asked to play the Frankenstein Monster in this one.
>
> "It may mean that I'll not do a picture there at all, and I'm supposed to do three," Karloff said. [ ] "I am pursued by a monster," he said. "I created a Frankenstein Monster and so far I haven't escaped from him. May be this picture will do it. Who knows?"
>
> Boris was referring to 'A Tale of Bedlam,' RKO's newest Val Lewton feature. [ ] Director Mark Robson broke in: "It's not a horror picture. Boris is getting away from horror pictures. His last three[83] have been historical suspense films, that is, counting this one."
>
> "Here's what happens," Karloff explained. "They put me in this picture, no more a horror picture than, let us say, 'The Story of Emile Zola.' But originally it was called, 'Chamber of Horrors[84].' Now couple that title with my name on the theatre marquee, and what does the public think?"
>
> "Horror picture," we guessed brightly.

---

82. Probably *House of Dracula* released December 7th 1945, the day before this interview was published.
83. *The Body Snatcher* (RKO, 1945), *Isle of the Dead* (RKO, 1945) and *Bedlam* (RKO, 1946).
84. This would probably be Jack G. Gross, who on some level wanted to turn RKO into the new Universal.

"Of course," replied the screen's No.1 Bogey Man. "And even with the new title, they're liable to think the same thing. But we have here a quality film, based on the stirring events and personages of a remarkable period in English history. So I hope at least it keeps out of those theatres which specializes in chiller-dillers."

It seems that some of the Powers-That-Be fought to retain the 'Chamber of Horrors' label on the picture. They wanted to take the cash and let the credit go – because Karloff's name on what appears to be a horror film means a large, sure-fire audience. But the joint pleas of Karloff and Producer Lewton had their effect. So they changed the title to one more suitable to the story [ ]

It was probably a call from Jack G. Gross, formerly Universal's executive producer of such films as *The Wolf Man* (1941) and *Son of Dracula* (1943), and who had joined RKO in 1944 to oversee Lewton's productions, as studio bosses were unimpressed with the $35,000 profit that *The Curse of the Cat People* netted, despite its troubled production. It would be the beginning of a tense and at times fraught relationship. It was arranged for Karloff to come to the studio to meet with Lewton and directors Mark Robson and Robert Wise. Karloff wrapped up shooting *House of Frankenstein* on Saturday April 29th and the meeting must have happened soon after. Initially, Lewton was reluctant as he saw Karloff as just a horror actor as Robert Wise wrote to author Gregory Mank, *"It was "Mr. Gross" who urged and insisted on bringing Mr. Karloff to RKO for a horror film or a series of them. [ ]Lewton, with nothing personal against Mr. Karloff, found this not really very much to his taste, but searched for story material that would have quality, even though he was using the 'scare' actor who had made his name as Frankenstein's Monster,"* but the meeting would change his mind, as Wise would later recall:

"It was strange – the first meeting. Boris came to the studio for a meeting with Val, Mark and me. I had never seen him except on the screen – and this was before colour film. When he first walked in the door I was *startled by his colouring, the strange bluish cast – but when he turned those eyes on us and that velvet voice said, "Good afternoon, gentlemen," we were his, and never thought about anything else."*

It was a meeting of like-minded people and, during the course of that meeting, Lewton must have pitched two film ideas to Karloff, the first being an adaptation of Sheridan Le Fanu's vampire tale "Carmilla" and Robert Louis Stevenson's" The Body Snatcher." Whatever happened that day, it ended with Karloff signing either a two or three film deal with RKO (depending on sources)

The first film would be "Carmilla[85]" which seems to have got no further than the treatment stage. For the second feature, Lewton looked at Stevenson's 19th Century tale of body snatchers as the following vehicle for Karloff, and wrote a memo on May 10th 1944, to Executive Producer Jack J. Gross, outlining his reasoning for choosing this story:

1: The title seems good to us.

2: There is exploitation value in the use of a famous Robert Louis Stevenson classic.

---

85. As early as October 15th, 1943, it was announced that J. Sheridan Le Fanu's 'Carmilla' had been purchased by RKO for development. *The Exhibitor* for October 27th stated that, "'Carmilla' novel concerning human vampires of the American Colonial era, written several decades ago [ ] will be produced by Val Lewton for RKO." This was reiterated on March 24th 1944. *Film Daily* for May 16th announced that Karloff was attached to this project and *Variety* for May 17th, *Motion Picture Daily* for May 18th and *Showman's Trade Review* for May 27th all reiterated that this would e Karloff's first film for RKO. The *Film Daily* for July 7th 1944 offered a further insight into the production: "RKO is contemplating making 'Carmilla' one of the first horror offerings to be done in Technicolor. It is a costume horror story dealing with the Salem, Mass. witchcraft trials of the 18th century. The Gower Street studio will make two Boris Karloff chillers, with producer Val Lewton assigned to produce six chillers, in all." From this we can speculate that this must have excited Karloff: not only a horror film, but a colour one and not only that but a salary of $6,000 per week!

3: There is a ninety percent chance that this is in the public domain. The legal department is now searching the title.

4: The characters are colourful. The background of London (sic) medical life in the 1830s is extremely interesting. The set are limited in number but effective in type. The costumes are readily procurable and no great difficulties of any sort so far as production is concerned is evident.

5: There is also an excellent part for Bela Lugosi as a resurrection man.3[86]

Jack J. Gross concurred with Lewton and decided to hire Lugosi, to add extra weight at the box-office. Though the role of MacFarlane may have been Gross's choice for Lugosi, it was not to be as Robert Wise had a very definite viewpoint on this: "We never considered giving Lugosi the role of MacFarlane. He didn't have the right quality for it, and he certainly didn't have the acting talent to have provided the acting 'duel' that Henry Daniell had with Boris Karloff ... [ ]"

---

86. Interestingly in *Robert Wise on His Films* (Leeman, Sergio. Silman-*James Press*, Los Angeles, 1995) Wise would recall that "Bela Lugosi was an afterthought. "His character was not in the original script, but the studio felt that it would be great if we had the names Karloff and Lugosi on the marquees. Val didn't like the idea. He tried to talk them out of it but wasn't able to. So, he worked him in by creating the role of the porter." This is contradictory to the memo that Lewton sent out. Further to this, Mank speculates in *Karloff & Lugosi: A Haunting Collaboration* (pg. 495) that when Karloff signed the deal with RKO for *Carmilla* and *The Body Snatcher*, he must have learned of Lewton's plans to add Bela Lugosi and given his blessing. Therefore, this raises the question did Val Lewton add Lugosi to this memo to appease Gross in some way? They (Lewton and Lugosi) do not appear to have had a meeting similar to that with Karloff as we know when Lugosi was signed to the picture, and it would certainly explain why his role was added to the script, rather than having a part all ready for him, and would fit in with Wise's memory. In *Boris Karloff: More Than a Monster* Stephen Jacobs states, 'Lugosi had been added to the picture under the express wish of Jack Gross.' (Pg. 302)

With 'Carmilla' dead in the water, Lewton came up with another film, *Isle of the Dead*, based on a painting by artist Arnold Böcklin. The film went into production on July 13th. Two weeks into shooting, it was evident that Karloff could not continue filming, due to his back troubles and Lewton shut down production. On July 21st Karloff went into hospital to undergo an operation for spinal fusion and Lewton along with writer Philip MacDonald began writing the script – though it is interesting to note that *The Screenwriter* for July 1945 lists Philip MacDonald as sole screenplay writer; under the guise of Carlos Keith, Val Lewton took joint writing credit - and gearing the new production for pre-production. Casting for the role Dr. MacFarlane would prove troublesome with Albert Dekker, John Emery, George Colouris, Alan Napier and Philip Merivale all considered for the role. In a stroke of perfect casting, British character actor Henry Daniell got the role, bringing an extra depth and fear of a man who has secrets to hide. Lugosi was an ill man, his dependency on drugs to ease the pain in his legs was taking its toll, not only on his health, but on his marriage and on August 19th it was announced that his wife Lillian had filed for divorce, describing him as an "inhuman husband."

With a budget of $200,000 and a 20-day shooting schedule, *The Body Snatcher* began pre-production at the RKO ranch in San Fernando Valley on October 13th, utilising sets from other films like the exteriors of 1939's *The Hunchback of Notre Dame* to maximise the budget. Robert Wise was brought in to direct. Wise had come to Hollywood in 1933 and began his career in the cutting department at RKO, working his way up to sound cutter, then assistant editor. In 1939 he became a film editor, being nominated for an Academy Award for his work on *Citizen Kane*. From there he was promoted to director with *Mademoiselle Fifi* (RKO, 1944), following his directorial debut by taking over from Gunther von Fritsch, after von Fritsch had fallen behind on the shooting schedule on *Curse of the Cat People* (RKO, 1944). Lugosi signed on the first day of shooting, on October 25th for $3,000 (half of what Karloff was earning) a week, with a guarantee of at least one week, and second billing under Karloff. He had at least one supporter at RKO and that was Jack G. Gross, who not only brought Lugosi onto the production but issued Lewton on October 20th this RKO memo: I think that it is quite important that you give Bela Lugosi a definite characterization. In one of the Frankenstein pictures he played a hunchback with a muff, which made him a terrifying looking character. This is merely a suggestion. - JG

Lewton's reply was swift: Okay. We'll hump him. - Val

The role of Joseph was especially written for him, but his performance was plagued by ill health as director Robert Wise would later recall:

> "It was a case of having to work very carefully with him. He certainly was willing, but I found getting my thoughts and ideas over to him took more time. He was a little slower grasping what the director wanted than Karloff. Karloff was very quick and very keen ... Lugosi was slower in movement, slower in thought process and slower to grasp everything that was wanted."**4**

Robert Clarke, who played a medical student, would indirectly corroborate Wise's memory as he would recall, "During the time that I was involved on *The Body Snatcher*, he (Lugosi) hardly came out of his dressing room unless the assistant director called him. They had a day bed in there, and he was flat on his back on that couch nearly all the time. He talked very little to anyone and, obviously, he wasn't at all well. It was difficult for him to perform.

Further to that Wise would state:

> "Lugosi ... was not well... It was a small part. It didn't require too much out of him, but I had to kind of nurse him through the whole role, such as it was. He was a little vague. He was not quite on it – which was all right for the role, because he played a not very bright guy ... I think his whole mental and emotional condition maybe helped to contribute to that." **5**

For those hoping for a classic Karloff / Lugosi teaming, they were going to be disappointed. As Rhodes and Kaffenberger state: "Perhaps the larger umbrella of horror as it was being perceived in 1946 could include RKO's film 'Genius at Work', which paired Lugosi with Lionel Atwill. Why the studio did not pair Lugosi with Karloff in another Val Lewton horror film – as they had in 'The Body Snatcher' (1945) – is unknown, as it would have been easy for them to cast Lugosi in either 'Isle of the Dead' (1945) or 'Bedlam' (1946). But that did not happen, which may suggest that Lewton was simply uninterested in working with him again."[87]

This was Karloff's film with Lugosi no more than a cameo, but their one major scene together is tight, intense, and utterly riveting.

Joseph (Lugosi) goes to visit coachman Gray (Karloff) and blackmail him as he knows that he's a body snatcher for MacFarlane (Daniell). Realising that he must do something, Gray gives him the Ŀ16 Joseph demands and plies him with drink and tells him the tale of Burke and Hare, even singing him a little rhyme:

> The ruffian dogs
> The Hellish pair,

---

87. Here we can speculate as to why Lugosi was not used again on two levels. Firstly, we take the fact that Lewton initially did not want to work with Karloff because he saw him as just a horror actor, 'the screen's No.1 Bogey Man,' and it was only once they had had a meeting and discussion that his attitude changed. Therefore, he could have viewed Lugosi in the same light and as there was no similar meeting, that viewpoint would not have changed. Secondly, as Lugosi was so ill during the production of *The Body Snatcher* (as Wise and Clarke both recalled), that it put him off from working with him again. Yet there is a third alternative, Lewton would have been aware that during the 1930s, Karloff and Lugosi were the 'Kings of Horror' at Universal and that he would not want to replicate that. After all Gross brought Lugosi in, and gave him second billing, which would have given the audience the idea that they were watching a Karloff/Lugosi horror film – Something that Gross and the front office would be happy with, and Lewton not wanting his film viewed as such.

> The villain Burke,
> The meagre Hare…
> Nor did they handle axe or knife
> To take away their victim's life…
> No sooner done than in the chest
> They crammed their lately welcomed guest.

Slow-witted Joseph repeats several times that he does not understand and then thinks that they will sell the bodies together. As the tension builds, Gray, maintaining his pose of kindness, says:

> "I'll show you how they did it, Joseph. I'll show you how they 'Burked' them. No, put your hand down – how can I show you man? This is how they did it, Joseph."

Gray then places his hand over Joseph's mouth and nose and suffocates him to death. It is one of the most chilling scenes in any 1930s / 40s horror films, brilliantly executed by Robert Wise's direction and the performances of both Karloff and Lugosi. If there were any truth to the persistent rumour that the actors had a rivalry, then it did not show during production as Robert Wise would state:

> "[ ] I always appreciated Karloff's sensitivity when it came to the scene where they played together in the film - where the Lugosi character came to see the Karloff character. Boris was very, very gentle with him … and was very patient with him … I always respected Karloff for that – for the sensitivity in that situation. I have heard that he [Lugosi] was on drugs at the time but I think it might have been drugs because he was in pain – but he got through it – it was alright – but Karloff was very, very helpful in getting him through the sequence that I had to do with him."

Author William Kaffenberger has stated that: "There are at least one or two existing stills of Lugosi in scenes that were cut from the film. So, his part was somewhat larger before the editor started his work." This is interesting as *The Kinematograph Year Book* 1946 (pg. 102) states that: 'The registered length of the film, 'The Body Snatcher' (F.8725) registered on November 19, 1945 has been amended to 6,549ft.' [from 6,599ft.] Could this edit of fifty feet have trimmed Lugosi's performance?

As Coachman Gray, the script gave Karloff one of the best characters of his career. Here we have the duality of Mord and Richard of Gloucester (*Tower of London*, 1939), Anton and Gregor Berghmann (*The Black Room*, 1935) encapsulated into one riveting performance. Here we have Karloff on the one hand showing absolute kindness to a young girl who cannot walk, talking to her and allowing her to visit his horse, through to manipulating the doctor to operate on her. Gray is MacFarlane's 'Ghost of Christmas Past' – reminding him that he worked with Dr. Knox and was involved with Burke and Hare, and that he used to take the young McFarlane out to meet a lady who would become his future wife. MacFarlane paid for Gray to protect him and his reputation during the trial that followed Burke and Hare's capture and it was he and not MacFarlane who went to prison as Gray states:

> "You'll never get rid of me that way, Toddy. [By dissecting his body] You and I have two bodies – aye, very different sorts of bodies – but we're closer than if we were in the same skin. For I saved that skin of yours once, and you'll not forget it."

Robert Wise would recall:

> What intrigued me about it, and intrigued Boris Karloff particularly, was the relationship between the cab driver and the doctor, because there's some marvellous antagonism from [them] ... the duel that went on – marvellous scenes between the two. And Karloff realized, or felt, that this was a chance for him to show that he ... was an actor, and not just some kind of monster to be in films – that he could really hold his own with top actors in town. And he had to prove that with a man named Henry Daniell, who was one of the top English character actors

in Hollywood at the time … And so Karloff saw this as a chance; in those scenes, the kind of duels between the two – duels of personality and viewpoint and dialogue – that he could hold his own with Daniell, and he did. Some of the best parts of the film, for me, are those two or three sequences where they're kind of … duelling with each other, in terms of the philosophies. So that's one of the things that intrigued me very much about the thing.

Both men are equally intelligent, but whereas MacFarlane is emotionally stunted – Fettes, his student states, "He taught me the mathematics of anatomy, but he couldn't teach me the poetry of medicine." And Mrs. MacFarlane states when talking about her husband and the trial, [he] "couldn't swallow the shame of it." Gray is fully aware of people, understands the human condition and is a master manipulator. He understands MacFarlane better than the man himself does as the following emphasizes:

MacFarlane: Gray! You know something about the human body.

Gray: I've had some experience.

MacFarlane: Then you can understand this: the backbone is a lot of little blocks, and those blocks are all held together so that it works, works like that whip of yours. You know that, don't you?

Gray: Never had it all explained by so learned a man.

MacFarlane: I set those blocks together, patch the muscles, put the nerves where they should be. I did it and I did it right. (*pause*) She won't walk –

Gray: You can't build life the way you put blocks together, Toddy.

MacFarlane: What the devil are you talking about? I'm an anatomist. I know the body; I know how it works.

Gray: You're a fool, Toddy, and no doctor. It's only the dead ones you know.

MacFarlane: I am a doctor, I teach medicine.

Gray: Like Knox taught you? Like I taught you? In cellars, in graveyards? Did Knox teach you what makes the blood flow?

MacFarlane: The heart pumps it.

Gray: Did he tell you how thoughts come and how they go and why things are remembered – and forgot?

MacFarlane: The nerve centres of the brain.

Gray: What makes a thought start?

MacFarlane: The brain, I tell you. I know!

Gray: You don't know, you'll never know or understand, Toddy. Not from Knox or me would you learn those things. Look, look at yourself. Could you be a doctor, a healing man, with the things those eyes have seen? There's a lot of knowledge in those eyes – but no understanding. (*pause*) You'll not get that from me.

One of the most chilling scenes in the film comes with the murder of the blind street singer. As Fettes, who has gone to Gray looking for a new 'subject,' leaves, we hear her voice. Gray watches Fettes leave from the doorway, and using the camera as Gray's vision, we see Fettes walk directly away, and the blind singer crosses his eyesight from right to left. Cut to Gray's face; his expression changes as he acknowledges where the said subject would come from. Here, Karloff is brilliant as his look changes ever so slightly, that you are not too sure of his thoughts. Cut to a dark, deserted side street, the girl, still singing comes into vision, walks down the street and into the darkness. Gray's cab comes into focus and follows slowly (the girl can still be heard singing) before it disappears into the darkness ... then the girl's singing is cut off sharply mid-verse and the camera lingers on the dark street, giving the audience a chance to realise what has just happened before fading out.

The film was released in February 1945. The National Legion of Decency rated the film B, their objection: Excessive gruesomeness. On May 2nd 1945, *Film Daily* announced:

Sergt. L S White has been named acting director of the Chicago Police Censor Board [ ] April inspections by the board included 82 films [ ] RKO's The Body Snatcher was rejected.

On June 7th, *Motion Picture Daily* made a follow-on announcement:

The Body Snatcher originally rejected was given an adult permit.

As the film stormed the box-office, the reviews, mostly positive came in:

Harrison's Reports for February 24th states that:

"Skilfully produced and directed, this horror melodrama should more than satisfy those who like their screen entertainment weird and spine-chilling; it is far superior to most pictures of this type. [ ] Boris Karloff, as the blackmailing grave-robber, gives one of the best performances of his career, while Henry Daniell is not far behind him as head of the medical school; their ghoulish, maniacal doings keep one on the edge of his seat. Unlike most horror pictures, this one does not resort to the fantastic for its chills and shudders; it makes sense []

"Vastly different from the usual far-fetched themes starring the Karloff-Lugosi combination, "The Body Snatcher," film version of an excellent short story by Robert Louis Stevenson, comes as a special treat for those who seek entertainment of the hair-raising variety. With all due recognition to Karloff's fine characterization, Henry Daniell's impressive performance is outstanding. Aimed at better-than-average audience appeal, a better-than-average budget for this type of film is evident; and the direction is noteworthy for its lip-biting suspense." (*Film Daily*, February 20th 1945 pg. 8)

"It is not often that a 'horror film' transcends its class but *The Body Snatcher* does it hands down. Its serious theme and historical background give it a dignity that is not found in movies conceived to scare you out of your seat. And the skill with which the movie is made places it in the list of those none too frequent products that may be viewed as examples of cinematic art. Val Lewton has been making quite a name for himself ever since he produced *The Cat People* in 1942. Characteristic of his films are themes that deal with the psychic aberrations of the human mind, that are mounted with imaginative settings and recorded with a knowing camera, that are intensified with a compelling usage of music and sound. [ ] The cast includes Boris Karloff as the cabman portraying his part with a wickedness devoid of burlesque, Bela Lugosi who, freed of his Draculesque idiom, enacts a stupid and voracious Portuguese, and Henry Daniell who brings McFarlane a wealth of strength and even warmth. [ ] as handsome a film production as any top writer could wish. (A.B. 'New Movies,' The *National Board of Review Magazine*, June 1945 pg. 7)

The *New York Post* gave Karloff a rather good review: " [ ] As our story opens Dr. Henry Daniell of Edinburgh, Scotland gets his cadavers from cabdriver Boris Karloff. This wouldn't be so bad if it weren't for the fact that when Karloff can't dig up an unprotected corpse, he's likely as not to manufacture one out of a living person. Karloff is a very evil person, though it must be admitted that in the course of his evil doings turns in one of his very best performances."

As if reality were mimicking art, on 20th June, *Film Daily* announced that 'as the United Detroit Circuit was building up its publicity campaign for RKO's "The Body Snatcher," an old Detroit cemetery was the scene of a grave robbery!'

In 1946, the film was nominated for a Hugo Award for Best Dramatic Presentation but lost out to *The Picture of Dorian Gray* (M.G.M., 1945). After its initial theatrical release, *The Body Snatcher* refused to die, as the *Independent Exhibitors Film Bulletin* for May 27th 1946, hailed Karloff as the King of Horror:

Still another Universal picture, 'The Cat Creeps,' is now at the Rialto following four strong weeks of 'Bedlam.' This Karloff was the only film to play this long at the Rialto this season and the only pictures to play three were RKO's 'The Body Snatcher,' and 'Isle of the Dead,' making Karloff the King of this horror house.

However, for A.J. Sindt at the Rankin Theatre, Rankin, Ill. things were a lot different:

"Body snatcher, The: Boris Karloff, Bela Lugosi – Man, what this picture did for me! I stood in the lobby all evening and watched the patrons walking past the theatre. Doubled with 'Pan Americana,' and thought I had a real program. Could have done worse if I played 'Pan Americana' single on Sunday. No more horror pictures for me. Enough is enough." (*Motion Picture Herald*, May 18 1946. Pg. 50)

On October 25th 1947 it was announced that:

Norman Willis, who gets better-than-average results with less-than-average expenditure for advertising at the Corbett Theatre, Wildwood, Florida, planning a spooky midnight show of 'Body Snatcher,' for Halloween. (*Motion Picture Herald*, pg. 41)

All was quiet until 1949, four years after its initial release, when *Variety* announced on August 17th 1949 that, 'Bandbox Rialto is doing all right with horror combo of 'Body Snatcher,' and 'Bride of Death' at $10,000.' *Variety* followed this up the following week with, 'Body Snatcher & Bride of Death (2nd - final week). Down to $7,500 after solid $10,000 opener.' [It was $7,000 in the end] Three years later, *Variety (Wednesday May 4th 1952, Pg.10)* announced under the title that:

RKO Still Eyes Indie Releases, Offbeat, Foreign.

In addition to its search for indie product, company has also been combing its film vaults for suitable re-releases. It has chalked up a degree of success with chiller combinations, presently readying its third horror package. Based on results achieved with 'The Hunchback of Notre Dame,' and 'The Cat People,' it is currently bringing out 'King Kong,' and 'The Leopard Man.' For latter combination it has set up an area preem in Ohio, Michigan and Indiana, with 200 playdates set. Third combination will be 'Body Snatcher' and 'I Walked with a Zombie.'

It was a combination that was set to let RKO down as *Variety* announced on July 2nd that: 'San Francisco – Golden Gate – Body Snatcher and I Walked with a Zombie reissues – Poor. $5,000 in four days.' That averages out at $1,250 a day. In comparison to the Palace Theatre, Cincinnati, for the same time period: 'Last week King Kong & Leopard Man atomic $20,000 and town's top for some time.' By December 1952 *The Body Snatcher* and I Walked with a Zombie combination was failing at the box-office: 'St. Louis (F & M): Last week: Body Snatcher and Zombie (RKO) (reissues) $6,00,' and in Indianapolis at the Lyric Theatre for December 24th: 'Body Snatcher (RKO) and I Walked with a Zombie (RKO) (reissues). NSG $4,500.' The previous week had seen *Untamed Woman* and *The Ring* bring in $5,500! By January 1953, RKO decided to add *The Body Snatcher* to *King Kong* and *The Leopard Man* combination, but it appears not to have circulated. In 1955 RKO was sold to General Teleradio for $25,000,000, with GT's six TV stations showing films from RKO's 700 film back catalogue the following year. It was also announced that: 'A score of other stations have been approached with RKO Picture Package in recent weeks [ ]' (*Television Digest with Electronics Reports*, November 12 1955, pg. 4) The following August, on the New York City & Suburbs and New Haven area, Channel 8 broadcasted *The Body Snatcher* from Monday to Friday at 9pm every night for a week. Interestingly, they gave Bela Lugosi top billing over Karloff! Over in the UK scenes from the film were featured in *Film Review* 5th December 1967, when the programme showcased an interview with director Robert Wise on location in the South of France and on December 19 1967, the same programme showed clips in the 'World of Cinema Observed by Philip Jenkinson.' It made its television debut as part of a horror double bill on August 22 1981. It was shown again as part of a Val Lewton season in 1988. Following that it was shown again in 1995, 1999, 2003 and lastly 2005. It was released on Region 1 DVD in 2005 and 2011 for the UK.

The film still stands out as one of the best horror films of the 1940s. Karloff gives one of his most chilling portrayals, f or which he should have been Oscar nominated, and director Robert Wise showed that he knew how to make a good riveting film, his next foray into the horror / supernatural would be 1963's *The Haunting*.

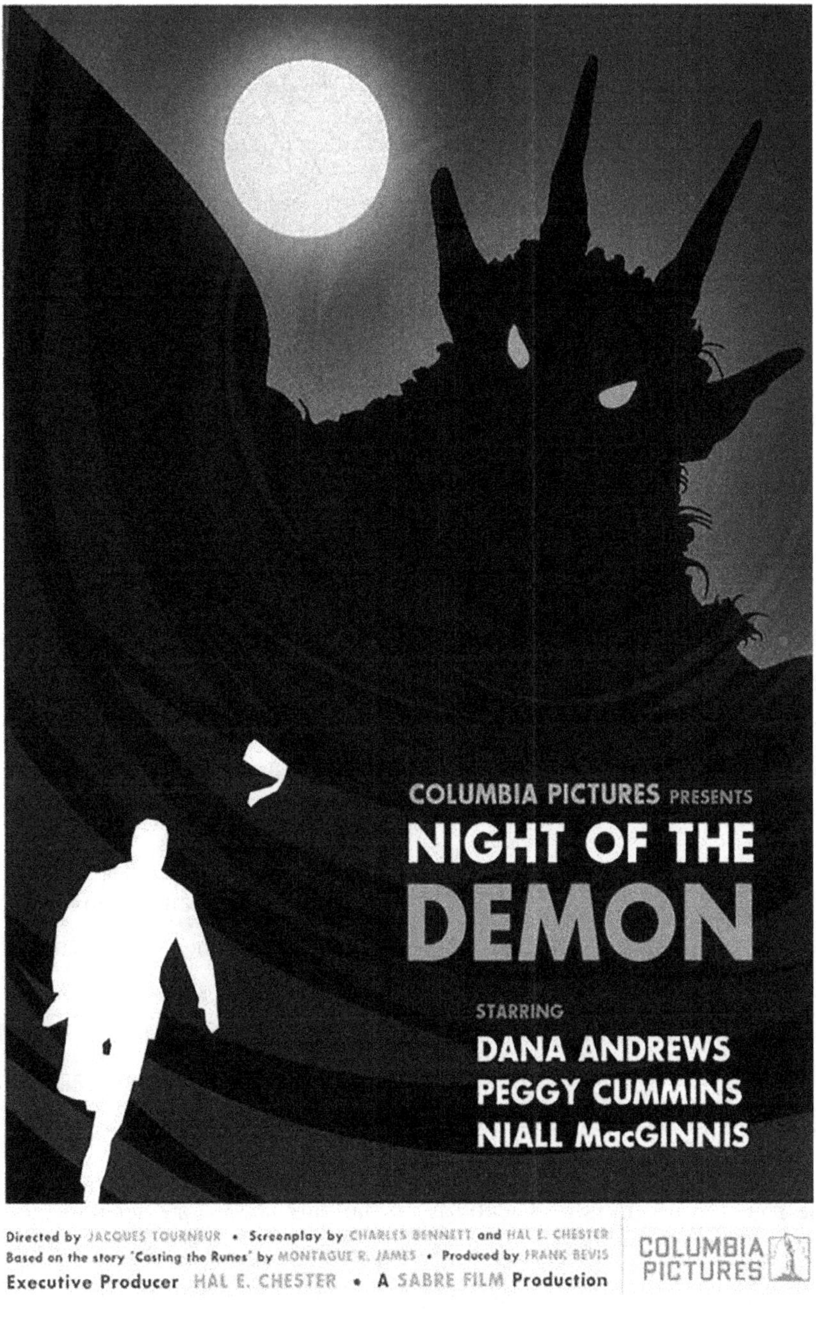
COLUMBIA PICTURES PRESENTS
NIGHT OF THE
DEMON
STARRING
DANA ANDREWS
PEGGY CUMMINS
NIALL MacGINNIS
Directed by JACQUES TOURNEUR • Screenplay by CHARLES BENNETT and HAL E. CHESTER
Based on the story 'Casting the Runes' by MONTAGUE R. JAMES • Produced by FRANK BEVIS
Executive Producer HAL E. CHESTER • A SABRE FILM Production
COLUMBIA PICTURES

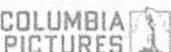

"Where does imagination end and reality begin?"
Night of the Demon / Casting the Runes – A Comparison

M. R. James (Montague Rhodes James) was arguably given the best epitaph for his ghostly writings with the cinematic release of the Sabre / Columbia film *Night of the Demon*, loosely based on his short story 'Casting the Runes.' This is the only cinematic translation of one of James' short stories, although there have been numerous television and radio adaptations.

The film tells of Doctor Holden (Dana Andrews), an American psychologist, who is coming to England to join an investigation into a Satanic cult led by Karswell (Niall MacGinnis). He is asked by Joanna (Peggy Cummins) to look into the mysterious death of her uncle Professor Harrington (Maurice Denham) who was leading the investigation.

The mysterious Karswell passed the runes to Harrington; and when failing to get Holden to drop the investigation he passes him the runes and tells him that he has three days left to live. It emerges that whoever possesses a small piece of parchment meets with a terrible fate. When the sceptical Holden is finally convinced that he is in danger, he manages to pass the parchment back to the warlock in a train and the occultist becomes victim to a demon.

The film script differs drastically from the published story yet manages to capture brilliantly the essence of the published work. In the story Holden is Henry Dunning, who has dismissed an essay by Karswell and as a result is passed the runes, just as Harrington was after giving a scathing review of a book written by the occultist eleven years previously. By sheer chance Dunning meets with Harrington's brother with whose help he manages to pass the runes back to Karswell.

In the film, John Harrington (the first victim) becomes Professor Henry Harrington (Maurice Denham), George Dunning becomes Dr. John Holden (Dana Andrews) and Henry Harrington becomes Joanna Harrington (Peggy Cummings). Having Henry Harrington's brother become his niece in the film not only adds a romantic dynamic to the plot, but it can also be seen to be a precursor to *The X-Files*. This is evident in the relationship's structure. Holden's scepticism coupled with Harrington's willingness to believe in the supernatural is similar to that of Mulder and Scully. Each character relies upon the other to question, inform and – ultimately – justify their own motives and beliefs. In the screenplay Charles Bennett makes a masterstroke of genius. He gives Karswell a Christian name: Julian. The significance of this is that it makes him more of a realistic figure. In 'Casting the Runes,' James gives us, the reader, very little to go on:

> "There was really nothing to be said for Mr. Karswell. Nobody knew what he did with himself: his servants were a horrible set of people; he had invented a new religion for himself, and practised no one could tell what appalling rites; he was easily offended, and never forgave anybody; he had a dreadful face; he never did a kind action, and whatever influence he did exert was mischievous."[1]

In the film Karswell is portrayed as a sympathetic villain despite having already dispatched Harrington by passing the runes (he'd given Harrington the chance to call off the investigation and thus save himself, but it was too late as the parchment of runic symbols has been destroyed). He gives Holden the same opportunity, but his stubborn attitude not to believe in the supernatural and the warlock's power lead him to almost the same fate as Harrington.

Holden could be seen as a mirror image of Karswell - Karswell's belief in the powers of evil and supernatural are as strong as Holden's disbelief and scepticism. In fact, Holden's disbelief causes more harm than good, resulting in a kidnapping, the death of a psychiatric patient, Rand Hobart (Brian Wilde), the near mental collapse of a medium called Mr. Meeks (Reginald Beckwith), and his own close call with a demon. All this damage is caused by his utter refusal to believe in the supernatural despite some pretty unnerving proof. As he tries to explain to Joanna Harrington:

Holden: Joanna, let me tell you something about myself. When I was a kid, I used to walk down the street with the other kids and when we came to a ladder they'd all walk around it. I'd walk under it, just to see if anything would happen. Nothing ever did. When they'd see a black cat they'd run the other way to keep it from crossing their path. But I didn't. And all this ever did for me is make me wonder why, why people get so panicky about absolutely nothing at all. I've made a career studying it. Maybe just to prove one thing. That I'm not a superstitious sucker like ninety percent of humanity."[2]

On being invited to Lufford Hall (Lufford Abbey in the story) by Karswell, Holden mocks the occultist despite being shown some of his power. Karswell is in the midst of throwing a children's party, again showing a more humane side to him as he is dressed as Doctor BoBo the Magnificent - a children's magician. To show Holden the scope of his power, Karswell conjures up a tempest on a previously calm day and then gleefully informs Holden that it was a typical work of medieval witchcraft:

Holden: I see you practice white magic as well as black.

Karswell: Oh yes, I don't think it would be too amusing for the youngsters if I conjured up a demon from Hell for them.[3]

In the film Karswell's malevolence comes not only from trying to protect his cult, but mainly from trying to protect himself, which is the opposite of his literary namesake. Karswell in the story is undeniably evil and vindictive. There is no redeeming characteristic to him at all. In contrast to the children's party from the film, in the story events take on a more sinister turn:

> "...*The first winter he* [Karswell] *was at Lufford this delightful neighbour of ours wrote to the clergyman of his parish ...and offered to show the school children some magic lantern slides.* (sic) *Mr. Karswell had evidently set out with the intention of frightening these poor village children out of their wits...And then, if you please, he switched on another slide, which showed a great mass of snakes, centipedes, and disgusting creatures with wings, and somehow or other made it seem as if they were climbing out of the picture and getting in amongst the audience; and this was accompanied by a sort of dry rustling noise which sent the children nearly mad, and of course they stampeded. A good many of them were rather hurt in getting out of the room, and I don't suppose one of them closed an eye that night."*4

Later, after being provoked by Joanna into breaking into Lufford Hall, Holden is attacked by Karswell's familiar - a cat that transforms into a leopard. Karswell enters the room just as Holden is about to hit the leopard with a fire poker and as Karswell turns on the light, not only does Holden drop the poker for being 'too hot', when it is cold, the leopard changes back into a cat. Despite being warned by Karswell not to go back through the woods, Holden ignores this advice and leaves the Hall by the way he came, and it proves almost fatal for him. As he makes his way back through the woods he is chased by an un-seen demon, making it one of the most intense and gripping scenes in the film. In fact, it could almost be seen as a reiteration of the opening scene where Professor Harrington dies. These two scenes are the closest to a visualization of the death of John Harrington from the story. Furthermore, the scene is an inversion of the slide scene in 'Casting the Runes' where Karswell: '...produced a series [of slides] which represented a little boy passing through his own park ... in the evening... this poor boy was followed, and at last pursued and overtaken and either torn to pieces or somehow made away with by a horrible hopping creature in white, which you saw first dodging about among the trees and gradually it appeared more and more plainly.'5

Every step of the way, Karswell is made out to be sympathetic and his personality and motivations are very carefully revealed. He wants to be left alone with his cult and for the investigation to be stopped, despite the fact that his actions and those of his cult are obviously evil. In fact the film shows us that Karswell is just as trapped by the evil that he dabbles in, just as much as Holden who he's passed the runes to is. He understands perfectly what he has done and what will befall him if he tries to give up the power that he has been granted, hence the scene in the train where Holden finally manages to pass back the runes. The sheer fear and panic that Karswell feels in knowing what his fate is going to be says more than the suggestiveness of James' story. It has already been foreshadowed in the conversation with his mother in the scene in the film where Karswell says to her:

Karswell: (sic) *How can you give back life? I can't stop it, I can't give it back! I can't let anyone destroy this thing, I must protect myself, 'cause if it's not someone else's life, it'll be mine, you understand Mother, it'll be mine.*6

Why then such a difference in the personification of evil? As I have previously stated the celluloid Karswell wants only to protect himself and his cult from investigation. The literary Karswell is sociopathic with underlying psychopathic tendencies, as the children's party and the reasons for passing the runes indicate. In fact, James gives us little to go on other than hearsay and rumour as to the character of Karswell. He is not given a Christian name; a brief description, "A stout gentleman"7 and "a stout, clean-shaven man"8 and just three lines of dialogue. But two of those lines are central to the telling of the story. The first being when he passes the runes to Dunning at the British Museum and the second being when he inadvertently accepts the runes from Dunning towards the end of the story. Instead of confronting what he would see as his 'persecutors' he passes them the runes and doesn't give them a second chance. This is where the film differs: though Karswell is undeniably evil - he is not vindictive. Nor is he two-dimensional like many horror film villains and this I would suggest is one of the scripts' successes as it makes Karswell a realistic figure. The literary Karswell hides behind the walls of Lufford Abbey and doesn't know his victims personally. The celluloid Karswell, however, personally knows his victims, has conversed with them and has tried his best to put a stop to their investigation, and only after failing in that has he passed the runes. He even shows remorse at the death of Harrington, who has come to him for help:

Harrington: Call it off Karswell, stop this thing you've started and I'll admit publicly that I was totally wrong and you were totally right.

Karswell: It's gratifying to hear that, but some things are more easily started than stopped.

Harrington: But I've heard it, I've seen it, I know it's real ...

Karswell: You involve me in a public scandal - I protested. You said do your worst, and that's precisely what I did.

Harrington: Please Karswell, I'll stop this investigation. When Holden arrives I'll tell him I made a mistake. I'll send a statement to the newspapers.

Karswell: Oh, no, no, no, no-more newspapers. All I ask is privacy for myself and my followers.

Harrington: Well, I promise.

Karswell: All right, that's good enough.

Harrington: Then you'll stop this?

Karswell: You've still got that parchment I gave you?

Harrington: The Runic symbols! No, they burned. I couldn't stop it.

Karswell: Oh, I see. Er, well I think perhaps you'd better go home.

Harrington: Then you will help me?

Karswell: I'll do what I can.

Harrington: Karswell, if you only knew.

Karswell: I do know.**9**

Harrington leaves only to be killed by the demon after crashing his car into a telegraph pole. Karswell is then seen looking forlorn as he throws some newspaper cuttings about himself into the fire. Had the runes not burnt then Karswell would have saved Harrington's life. In both versions, Harrington – literary and celluloid - is passed the runes at a music concert in a concert programme. The death of the literary Harrington - I would suggest - is more gripping:

> "...Why, what happened was that he fell out of a tree and broke his neck. But the puzzle was, what could have induced him to get up there. It was a mysterious business, I must say. Here was this man - not an athletic fellow, was he? And with no eccentric twist about him that was ever noticed - walking home along a country road late in the evening - no tramps about - well known and liked in the place - and he suddenly begins to run like mad, loses his stick, and finally shins up a tree - quite a difficult tree - growing in the hedgerow : a dead branch gives way, and he comes down with it and breaks his neck, and there he's found next morning with the most dreadful face of fear on him that could be imagined."**10**

Harrington - like Dunning - has no chance of a reprieve. In fact, Karswell seems to relish disposing of his enemies and whereas the celluloid Karswell takes every opportunity to give his victim a chance to redeem themselves, the literary Karswell does not. In fact, the literary Karswell is not only 'An astute man'**11** he is a devious one. After being refused the name of the man who rejected his paper, he simply enquires to a member of staff at the British Museum as to the identity of the academics who have researched the same subjects, and from there deduces who rejected his paper. In comparing the British Museum reading room scenes again one can see the pleasant side to Karswell via the film compared to the devious side shown in the story:

After eavesdropping on Holden, at the British Museum, Karswell introduces himself:

Karswell: Apparently not, Doctor Holden. I have what is perhaps the finest library in the world on Witchcraft and the Black Arts.

Holden: You know my name?

Karswell: Oh yes, and you know mine! I'm Julian Karswell.

Holden: How did you know I was here?

Karswell: Oh, isn't it the scientist to always call what he can't explain otherwise by the word coincidence. Let's call this coincidence.

Holden : I wouldn't like to think that I'd been followed from my hotel this morning.

Karswell: Oh, I assure you, you weren't followed. I just thought it might be profitable for both of us to meet you see. (*he laughs*)

Holden : Shh!

Karswell: It's rather difficult to talk here, why not come out to my place in the country, the books there.

Holden : If I don't find what I want I might take you up on that.

Karswell: Delighted!

Holden: Just one thing. Let's understand each other, Mr. Karswell; my investigation of you and your cult won't be stopped.

Karswell: Oh, but, er, if I could make my point, I could persuade you?

Holden: I'm not open to persuasion.

Karswell: But a scientist should have an open mind.

Holden: That's what investigations are for.

Karswell: Oh! In any event here's my card. Lufford Hall, near Wargreave. I'll be seeing you soon, I'm sure. (*Karswell knocks some of Holden's papers onto the floor*) Oh, excuse me, how clumsy. (*As he picks up the papers, he passes the runes.*) So, so sorry. Here are your papers, sir.

(*Holden takes the folio, and unknowingly accepts the runes*).

Holden: Thank You.

Karswell: Goodbye. Don't leave it too long. **12**

> "... *It was in a pensive frame of mind that Mr. Dunning passed on the following day into the Select Manuscript Room of the British Museum; and filled up the tickets for Harley 3586, and some other volumes. After a few minutes they were brought to him, and he was settling the one he wanted first upon the desk, when he thought he heard his own name whispered behind him. He turned round hastily, and in doing so, brushed his little portfolio of papers on to the floor. He saw no-one he recognised except one of the staff in charge of the room, who nodded to him, and he proceeded to pick up his papers. He thought he had them all, and was turning to begin work, when a stout gentleman at the table behind him, who was just rising to leave, and had collected his own belongings, touched him on the shoulder, saying, 'May I give you this? I think it should be yours,' and handed him a missing quire. 'It is mine, thank you,' said Mr. Dunning. In another moment the man had left the room. Upon finishing his work for the afternoon, Mr. Dunning had some conversation with the assistant in charge, and took occasion to ask who the stout gentleman was. 'Oh, he's a man named Karswell,' said the assistant; 'He was asking me a week ago who were the great authorities on alchemy, and of course I told him you were the only one in the country. I'll see if I can't catch him: he'd like to meet you, I'm sure.'*

*'For Heaven's sake don't dream of it!' said Mr. Dunning, 'I'm particularly anxious to avoid him.'***13**

The dark brooding intensity of the story flows though the film, but the tense melancholic atmosphere of the film owes more to *The Seventh Victim* (RKO 1943) which is an earlier film about witchcraft. The driving force behind 'Casting the Runes' is a passage from S. T. Coleridge's 'The Rime of the Ancient Mariner':

'Like one who having once looked round, walks on

And turns no-more his head;

Because he knows, a frightful fiend

*Doth close behind him tread.***14**

Night Of The Demon is classed a classic is because the director Jacques Tourneur brought all of the best elements of his earlier film career and placed it all into one film package. Here, his extraordinary use of the camera imbues seemingly ordinary surroundings with a deep brooding sense of menace. The trees, objects or simply unlit areas darkly obtruding in the foreground, give the suggestion of the presence of implacable forces waiting to pounce on vulnerable, isolated figures, (something M.R. James did in all his writings): Dana Andrews walking down a long dark corridor, and only he can hear the odd pagan chant. Suddenly as a door opens, the chant ceases as light shines into the corridor. The darkness overpowers the light, suggesting a menace closing in – but aligning the demon's presence within the darkness – this is amplified by the strange chanting. The scene is reminiscent to a scene in Tourneur's earlier film *The Cat People* (1941), where Alice Moore is walking down a darkened street and is convinced that she is being followed by 'something.' Similarly the scene in the woods, where Andrews is convinced he's being followed, until suddenly we see a smoky cloud chasing him and something invisible making footprints in the earth.

The construction of the film and the scenes where the demon's presence is felt, even when not seen, leave no doubt to the creature's existence. Tourneur himself said that he was not happy with showing the demon so early on in the film. Tony Earnshaw's in-depth book *Beating the Devil: The Making of Night of the Demon* (pg. 54) suggests that it is the close-ups of the demon that Tourneur objected to. Yet by showing the demon so early on in the film, the viewer is left in no doubt to the power that Karswell has at his disposal. According to the production designer, Ken Adams, the demon featured in the film was based on a sixteenth century woodcut. Perhaps M. R. James as an antiquarian had viewed the same wood cut? Furthermore, the scenes depicting the demon would suggest that the script writer Charles Bennett may have read the edited / cancelled ending of the original story, as James actually makes mention of the demon:

> 'between Abbeville and St Riquier', a large bird 'of the vulture type' was sighted heading north-ward by a local naturalist: 'The failing light prevented the man from making an accurate observation; but he states his conviction that the creature was not a vulture.' **15**

With regards to this possibility, in a private email Tony Earnshaw states that: '...Bennett was an assiduous researcher so one could safely assume that he was aware of the deleted passage. On that basis making the link between the giant winged thing and the demon may be a logical one.' **16**

Nevertheless, the rest of the film is an object lesson in atmospheric horror. The film is intelligently scripted and goes to show that it is not that horrors can be created within the mind, but that some horrors are so inconceivable that the mind must deny them in order to retain its sanity - which is probably why Holden is so sceptical. As he states to Joanna, after talking to Scotland Yard:

Holden: Well, what do you expect me to do? Nobody's free from fear. I have an imagination like anyone else. It's easy to see a demon in every dark corner. But I refuse to let this thing take possession of my good senses. If this world is ruled by demons and monsters we may as well give up right now.**17**

The final train sequence is another inversion. In the story, Harrington informs Dunning that Karswell is catching the train. Dunning, who has shaved off his beard, meets up with Harrington in the same carriage as Karswell. They pretend not to know each other, and Karswell falls for the ruse. The tension builds as Dunning looks for an opportunity to pass the runes whilst remaining unrecognised. It is by sheer chance that Karswell's cook's ticket case, with tickets in it **18** falls to the floor and Dunning is finally able to pass the runes by placing them into the side pocket of the case. He gives Karswell his ticket holder back and he accepts both the ticket case and (unwittingly), the runes; Karswell is oblivious as to what has happened. Perhaps he wasn't such 'an astute man'**19** after all.

Bennett cleverly inverts this in the script, by having Karswell's mother betray him, and so the ensuing chase begins. Holden catches up with the warlock on the train, only to find the hypnotised Joanna (whom Karswell has kidnapped) with him. Karswell wakes her from her trance and she excitedly informs Holden that Karswell is afraid of him. Karswell dismisses this and as he tries to leave, Holden astounds him with the extent of the effect that he has had on him:

Holden: Sit down. Your generosity is becoming overwhelming as it gets closer to ten o'clock. You're staying with me, Karswell. You've sold your bill of goods too well, because I believe you now. I believe that in five minutes something monstrous and horrible is going to happen. And when it does, you're going to be here so that whatever happens to me will happen to you. **20**

In Bennett's script, Holden cleverly uses reverse psychology on Karswell as nothing had moved Holden from his position of scientific fact. In fact the only time that Holden seems to waver is at Scotland Yard and even then he admonishes himself and walks out. It is only with the intervention of Scotland Yard, to whom Holden had originally gone for help that Karswell believes he can make his escape. In his haste Karswell leaves his coat on the carriage seat and Holden is able to pass the runes by slipping them into a pocket as he gives Karswell his coat. Upon realising what has happened Karswell has to chase the runes as they take flight from his grasp and his fate is sealed. The ending of the film could be seen as being ambiguous as when Holden and Joanna walk away along the platform, a train drives past them and once its passed they are nowhere to be seen – this could be seen as that they just walk away or it could be that the demon got them in the end as well. It is left open to interpretation.

The script certainly captures the essence of the story on which it is based. There has been much debate as to whether James based the character of Karswell on the 'Great Beast' Aleister Crowley. By the time James wrote 'Casting the Runes,' Crowley had already been featured as a villain in W. Somerset Maugham's 1908 novel 'The Magician.' It features a sinister character, Oliver Haddo, whom Maugham admitted was based on Crowley. However, it was not until the 1920s that Crowley had become perceived to be 'The Wickedest Man in the World'. This does not mean that he was not also the inspiration for James. Further to this, in her 1934 critical essay on James, the author Mary Butts states this about the story 'Casting the Runes': 'We have seen how the first Harrington died, and how near death came the next person who happened across Mr. Karswell and his receipts. (The writer has an idea, from wholly different sources, that one part of this story is "founded on fact.")'[21]. With this throwaway comment Butts implies more than what the average reader may have taken in, for I believe that the 'sources' mentioned implicate none other than Aleister Crowley, with whom she was at one point on friendly terms.

Jacques Tourneur died in 1977 - and had he had the chance to direct - say – 'Oh Whistle and I'll Come to You, My Lad' or 'Count Magnus' - I believe he would have given us the most frightening horror film of all time. *Night of the Demon* comes very close to this.

Both the short story and the film have been influential across modern popular culture and the evidence is demonstrated in the following: In 1928, in his ghost story anthology 'They Return at Evening,' the author H. R. Wakefield features story, 'He Cometh and He Passeth By,' which is clearly an interpretation of 'Casting the Runes.' The central villain, Oscar Clinton, is undoubtedly based on Crowley. In 1985, the singer Kate Bush sampled a couple of lines from the film for her hit album and single, *The Hounds of Love*. The lines sampled are from the séance scene where Holden is hood-winked in to seeing a medium, Mr. Meeks:

"... It's In the Trees ...It's Coming!!"[22]

Other than this there are three films that have 'borrowed heavily from James' short story. Hideo Nakata's *Ringu* (1998) and its subsequent American remake *The Ring* (2002), where a video tape is passed from person to person to view and if not passed within seven days then the viewer will die. *Shriek* (1997), which owes more to H. R. Wakefield's 'He Cometh and He Passeth By,' and *Drag Me to Hell* (2009), which 'borrows several scenes from *Night of the Demon*. Tony Earnshaw's *Beating the Devil: The Making of Night of the Demon* (The National Museum of Photography, Film and Television and *Tomahawk Press*, 2005) is an informative book on the making of the film and some of the controversies surrounding it.

So next time you give someone a scathing review or slate them in any way beware that they do not pass you anything. *If* you find they have, give it back. But whatever you do, do not let it burn.

End Notes

1: Cox, M ed. M. R. James. *Casting the Runes and other Ghost Stories.* Oxford World Classics, Oxford University Press, 1987. Pg. 137.
2: *Night of the Demon (US. Curse of the Demon),* Dir. Jacques Tourneur, Perf. Dana Andrews, Niall MacGinnis, et all. Columbia Pictures, 1957.
3: *Night of the Demon (US. Curse of the Demon),* Dir. Jacques Tourneur, Perf. Dana Andrews, Niall MacGinnis, et all. Columbia Pictures, 1957.
4: Cox, M ed. M. R. James. *Casting the Runes and other Ghost Stories.* Oxford World Classics, Oxford University Press, 1987. Pg. 137.
5: Ibid. Pg. 137.
6: *Night of the Demon (US. Curse of the Demon),* Dir. Jacques Tourneur, Perf. Dana Andrews, Niall MacGinnis, et all. Columbia Pictures, 1957
7: Cox, M ed. M. R. James. *Casting the Runes and other Ghost Stories.* Oxford World Classics, Oxford University Press, 1987. Pg. 144.
8: Ibid. Pg. 149.
9: *Night of the Demon (US. Curse of the Demon),* Dir. Jacques Tourneur, Perf. Dana Andrews, Niall MacGinnis, et all. Columbia Pictures, 1957.
10: Cox, M ed. M. R. James. *Casting the Runes and other Ghost Stories.* Oxford World Classics, Oxford University Press, 1987 Pg. 139
11: Ibid. Pg. 140.
12: *Night of the Demon (US. Curse of the Demon),* Dir. Jacques Tourneur, Perf. Dana Andrews, Niall MacGinnis, et all. Columbia Pictures, 1957.
13: Cox, M ed. M. R. James. *Casting the Runes and other Ghost Stories.* Oxford World Classics, Oxford University Press, 1987. Pg. 144/145.
14: *The Rime of the Ancient Mariner.* S. T. Coleridge - Lyrical Ballads 1798.
15: Cox, M ed. M.R. James. *Casting the Runes and other Ghost Stories.* Oxford World Classics, Oxford University Press, 1987. Pg. 332.
16: Earnshaw, T. *Beating the Devil: The Making of Night of the Demon.* [email] Message to Banks, M.E. 28th June 2011.
17: Night of the Demon (US. Curse of the Demon), Dir. Jacques Tourneur, Perf. Dana Andrews, Niall MacGinnis, et all. Columbia Pictures, 1957.

18: Cox, M ed. M. R. James. *Casting the Runes and other Ghost Stories.* Oxford World Classics, Oxford University Press, 1987. Pg. 154.

19: Ibid. Pg. 140.

20: *Night of the Demon (US. Curse of the Demon),* Dir. Jacques Tourneur, Perf. Dana Andrews, Niall MacGinnis, et al. Columbia Pictures, 1957.

21: Butts, M. *The Art of Montagu [sic] James,* London Mercury 29 (February 1934): Pg. 306-17.

22: *Night of the Demon (US. Curse of the Demon),* Dir. Jacques Tourneur, Perf. Dana Andrews, Niall MacGinnis, et all. Columbia Pictures, 1957.

www.ingramcontent.com/pod-product-compliance
Lightning Source LLC
Chambersburg PA
CBHW060117170426
43198CB00010B/931